'At the time of writing my endorsement of this fascinating book, the 2020 global Covid-19 pandemic is creating profound uncertainty about which universities will survive and new questions about who they are for and what, and how, to teach in them. The timely publication of this thought-provoking and wide-ranging book will enable readers to locate the fallout from the pandemic in a longer history of constant change, growing government regulation, risk, precariousness and fluctuating educational and social tensions around diversity, well-being and participation in the British higher education system.'

Kathryn Ecclestone, retired professor of education and co-author of *The Dangerous Rise of Therapeutic Education*, published in 2008 and reissued in 2018 as part of Routledge's Classics in Education series

'This book provides a thorough overview and analysis of contemporary trends and issues in higher education, focusing on many of the tensions and contradictions that are embedded in universities today. It will inspire and motivate further discussion and debate on key issues in the field. As higher education continues to adapt to new challenges and opportunities, *Understanding Contemporary Issues in Higher Education* is essential reading for students and researchers alike.'

Professor Robin Shields, School of Education, University of Bristol, UK

UNDERSTANDING CONTEMPORARY ISSUES IN HIGHER EDUCATION

This insightful book offers a wide-ranging collection of lively discussions on contemporary issues, policies and practices in higher education. Bartram integrates contributions from experienced academics, teachers and students in a unique approach and structure, designed to enable students with both specific and wide-ranging interests in higher education to extend their understanding.

Including discussion points, research tasks and suggestions on further reading in each chapter, *Understanding Contemporary Issues in Higher Education* discusses a range of topics, such as:

*   universities and the mental health 'crisis';
*   knowledge, the state and the market;
*   the role of technology in teaching and academic celebrification;
*   disability, diversity and inclusive placement learning.

Written specifically for Education Studies students, this book constitutes a timely addition to student-focused themed studies looking at aspects of higher education.

Brendan Bartram is Reader in Education at the University of Wolverhampton, UK.

The Routledge Education Studies Series

Series Editor: Stephen Ward, Bath Spa University, UK

The Routledge Education Studies Series aims to support advanced level study on Education Studies and related degrees by offering in-depth introductions from which students can begin to extend their research and writing in years 2 and 3 of their course. Titles in the series cover a range of classic and up-and-coming topics, developing understanding of key issues through detailed discussion and consideration of conflicting ideas and supporting evidence. With an emphasis on developing critical thinking, allowing students to think for themselves and beyond their own experiences, the titles in the series offer historical, global and comparative perspectives on core issues in education.

Inclusive Education
Perspectives on Pedagogy, Policy and Practice
Edited by Zeta Brown

Gender, Education and Work
Inequalities and Intersectionality
Christine Eden

Contemporary Issues in Childhood
A Bio-ecological Approach
Zeta Brown and Stephen Ward

International and Comparative Education
Contemporary Issues and Debates
Brendan Bartram

Psychology and the Study of Education
Critical Perspectives on Developing Theories
Edited by Cathal O'Siochru

Philosophy and the Study of Education
New Perspectives on a Complex Relationship
Edited by Tom Feldges

Sociology for Education Studies
Connecting Theory, Settings and Everyday
Experiences
*Edited by Catherine A. Simon and Graham
Downes*

Understanding Education and Economics
Key Debates and Critical Perspectives
*Edited by Jessie A. Bustillos Morales and
Sandra Abegglen*

**Understanding Contemporary Issues in
Higher Education**
Contradictions, Complexities and Challenges
Edited by Brendan Bartram

For more information about this series, please visit: www.routledge.com/The-Routledge-Education-Studies-Series/book-series/RESS

UNDERSTANDING CONTEMPORARY ISSUES IN HIGHER EDUCATION

Contradictions, Complexities and Challenges

Edited by
Brendan Bartram

Routledge
Taylor & Francis Group

LONDON AND NEW YORK

First edition published 2021
by Routledge
2 Park Square, Milton Park, Abingdon, Oxon, OX14 4RN

and by Routledge
52 Vanderbilt Avenue, New York, NY 10017

Routledge is an imprint of the Taylor & Francis Group, an informa business

British Library Cataloguing-in-Publication Data
A catalogue record for this book is available from the British Library

Library of Congress Cataloging-in-Publication Data
A catalog record has been requested for this book

ISBN: 978-0-367-37413-6 (hbk)
ISBN: 978-0-367-37415-0 (pbk)
ISBN: 978-0-429-35427-4 (ebk)

Typeset in News Gothic
by Deanta Global Publishing Services, Chennai, India

Contents

List of illustrations

Figures

Tables

Contributors

Carol Bailey is a senior lecturer in English for Academic Purposes at the University of Wolverhampton and has taught in Morocco, China and Britain. As a language teacher, she aims to help people understand each other. In teaching, this includes helping students in transition understand and maximise their success in the UK higher education context, particularly with regard to academic writing and academic integrity. In academic management, it involves helping colleagues understand the challenges faced by students from non-UK academic backgrounds. She has published on the international student experience, comparative education, writing software and paraphrase. Her main research interest is student academic writing, with particular reference to writing from sources.

Brendan Bartram is Reader in Education at the University of Wolverhampton. He was awarded a National Teaching Fellowship by the Higher Education Academy in 2012. His research and publications cover a wide range of issues which reflect the eclectic nature of Education Studies. Focusing primarily on comparative issues in secondary education and the student experience in higher education, Brendan's research has explored staff–student interactions and university student mobility, support and motivation. His book *Attitudes to Modern Language Learning – Insights from Comparative Education*, examining language learning in the UK, USA, Australia, Germany and the Netherlands, was re-issued in paperback in May 2012. He has presented on the above themes at a number of national and international conferences. Brendan is a member of the British Education Studies Association (BESA) and was an honorary secretary of the British Association of International and Comparative Education (BAICE).

Hazel Bowley is an academic skills tutor at Arden University, having previously worked at the University of Wolverhampton as a learning and skills librarian. As a War Studies graduate, she has taught History and War Studies at the undergraduate level whilst completing her Masters and Postgraduate Certificate in Education (PGCE), before moving onto academic skills support. Her research interests include how students employ academic skills and how processes can become more easily accessible.

Stephanie Brewster's background is in Speech and Language Therapy, in which she qualified in 1989 at the University of Sheffield. For 14 years, she worked in a broad range of Speech and Language Therapy posts in the New Zealand and UK health services, in clinical practice, management, research and teaching. Her doctorate in Education at the University of Birmingham (completed 2007) investigated the communication of adults with learning disabilities and little or no speech. Subsequent teaching, research and consultancy work has centred on the participation of disabled people in society, especially in relation to speech, language and communication. She currently works at the University of Wolverhampton, where she teaches and conducts research focusing on inclusive practice and disabled students in higher education.

Rowan Campbell is a PhD student in sociolinguistics at Cardiff University and a vice-president of the Cardiff UCU branch. After completing an undergraduate and a masters degree at Cardiff University, she worked at a circus for two years before receiving ESRC funding to work on a PhD project about changes in the Cardiff accent and dialect. While on a placement at the British Library, the USS Pension Strike struck, and she avidly followed the resultant memes on Twitter. She met a group of active and like-minded colleagues when she moved back to Cardiff, started making zines, co-founded Anti-Precarity Cymru and joined her local UCU branch as an Anti-Casualisation Officer. Since 2018 she has worked to improve the rights of casualised staff at Cardiff, including PhD students who teach, and has taken her 'zine suitcase' across the border to deliver workshops in far-flung England.

Clare Dickens is a senior lecturer in Mental Health Nursing at the University of Wolverhampton. She is also an independent chair of Wolverhampton's Suicide Prevention Stakeholder's forum. Originally from a mental health nursing background, Clare has been passionate about suicide prevention throughout her career and became a licenced trainer for the Connecting with People approach in 2013. She is currently working on her professional doctorate and has a growing interest in pedagogical curriculum design. She was shortlisted in 2017 for the Nursing Times nurse of the year award for her efforts in suicide prevention in her home city. Prior to this, in 2016, Clare's work won the *Times Higher Education* Award in the category of outstanding student support for her innovation and commitment to address suicide mitigation across the higher education sector.

Sinead D'Silva is a research fellow at Instituto de Ciências Sociais – Universidade de Lisboa (ICS-ULisboa). Her current research on youth employed in tourism in Goa (India) and Lisbon (Portugal) has received funding from the European Union's Horizon 2020 research and innovation programme. Her PhD at the University of Leeds focused on young people's decision-making as they transitioned from their STEM (science, technology, engineering and mathematics) degree to their graduate lives. At Leeds, Sinead also evaluated higher education policy and provision implementation relating to employability and widening participation, with reports informing policy and practice changes, and she was a member of the steering group for the Inequalities Research Network. Her work broadly intersects with three key themes: youth; work and employment; and spaces of becoming and being.

Mark Elliot is a PhD student at the Institute of Education at the University of Wolverhampton. He has worked in higher education (HE) for over 15 years as a lecturer/senior lecturer in the Sociology of Sport, Sport Development and Sport Management, and has also held leadership and pastoral care roles. His current research interests include, but are not restricted to, the consumerisation of HE and its effect on student behaviours, the impact of neo-liberalism on HE and the use of metrics to measure performance in HE. Mark retains an interest in teaching and learning in HE and is a Fellow of the Higher Education Academy.

Tanya Hathaway is a lecturer in Geography at Coleg Llandrillo-Menai in North Wales and a freelance academic in the online higher education scene. She is a senior fellow of the Higher Education Academy. She has a PhD in Higher Education from Bangor University and has taught a wide range of undergraduate and postgraduate courses in the areas of teacher learning and professional development, teaching and learning, research methods, values and beliefs in education and early childhood education. Her research interests include personal epistemologies, teaching and learning in higher education, comparative education and, more recently, young children's play.

Anesa Hosein is a senior lecturer in Higher Education at the University of Surrey. She has worked in the higher education systems of the Caribbean and the UK. She has an eclectic collection of qualifications in the areas of physics, engineering and education. Her career aim is to help people (students, lecturers, etc.) to achieve their intrinsic needs, namely self-growth, which she has accomplished in a variety of research areas including academic practice, mathematics education, research methods, educational technology and academic mobility.

Grace Krause works for Learning Disability Wales. Prior to this, she worked as a researcher and is currently finishing her PhD in social sciences at Cardiff University. She has previously worked as a support worker for people with learning disabilities and as a project worker for Newport People First and Cardiff People First. She is an active trade union member in the University and College Union (UCU), where she campaigns for secure working conditions.

Ruth Mieschbuehler is a senior lecturer in Education Studies at the University of Derby and an executive committee member of the British Education Studies Association (BESA). Previously Ruth worked as an education researcher at the International Centre for Guidance Studies (iCeGS) at the University of Derby and at the Centre for Diversity Policy Research and Practice (CDPRP) at Oxford Brookes University. Among her many publications are an important report on *World-Class Apprenticeships Standards: Report and Recommendations* (2016) and a controversial book, *The Minoritisation of Higher Education Students: An Examination of Contemporary Policies and Practice*, Routledge 2018.

Esther Muddiman is a postdoctoral researcher at the Wales Institute for Social and Economic Research, Data, and Methods (WISERD) in the School of Social Sciences at Cardiff University, and vice-president elect of the Cardiff University branch of the University and College Union (UCU). She graduated from an ESRC-funded PhD in Cardiff in 2015, and has since held a number of fixed-term research contracts. Her doctoral work considered different ideas about the purpose of higher education to explore student experiences and perceptions of civic responsibility. Her current research explores the intersections between education, civil society and youth engagement. After meeting like-minded colleagues and activists in 2018, she began creating zines and co-founded Anti-Precarity Cymru, later becoming involved with the local UCU branch as a member of the Anti-Casualisation committee and executive branch committee.

Samantha Pugh is an associate professor in STEM Education and Faculty Lead for Teaching Enhancement at the University of Leeds. She is currently the director of Student Education for the School of Physics and Astronomy. She is known for developing context-based learning and working in partnership with students in the Physical Sciences. Her contribution to the sector was recognised with the award of University Student Education Fellowships in 2012 and 2014. She was also a finalist for the National Centre for Entrepreneurship in Education (NCEE) Enterprise Educator in higher education in 2014. She was made a National Teaching Fellow in 2017. Her research interests are in employability, curriculum development and the impact of outreach in the STEM disciplines.

Namrata Rao is a principal lecturer in Education at Liverpool Hope University, where she is based in the Centre of Education and Policy Analysis. She is a senior fellow of the Higher Education Academy, executive member of the British Association of International and Comparative Education (BAICE), member of the Research and Development working group of the Association for Learning Development in Higher Education (ALDinHE) and co-convenor of the Learning, Teaching and Assessment Special Interest Group (SIG) of the Society for Research in Higher Education (SRHE). Her key areas of research and publication include (but are not restricted to) various facets of learning and teaching in higher education and factors that influence academic identity and academic practice.

Bethany Sumner is a lecturer in Education and Inclusion Studies at the University of Wolverhampton. Her research interests include non-privileged student experiences at university and the way in which inequality operates within the higher education system. She is currently in the process of writing up her doctoral study which is titled 'University as a pathway to "the good life": Hope, risk and regret in the post-92 university'. This sociological research utilised a biographical methodology to examine first-generation student transitions into, through and out of a post-92 university.

David Thompson studied History for his first degree and has worked in higher education in the United Kingdom since 1998. This has been in a variety of roles and areas including research, lecturing, lifelong learning, international education and widening participation projects. The latter led to him completing his doctorate in Education at the University of Birmingham (2007). His thesis considered how universities encourage a greater diversity of students to experience and benefit from university study. Currently his teaching and research at the University of Wolverhampton is focused on inclusion, social justice in education, lifelong learning and work-based learning. More recently, David has written on the themes of placement provision, work-based learning opportunities and higher education policy and practice.

Stephen Ward is emeritus professor of Education, Bath Spa University, formerly dean of the School of Education and subject leader for Education Studies. A founder member of the British Education Studies Association, he continues to be a member of its Executive Committee and edits the reviews section of the Association's journal. He has published on the primary curriculum, primary music teaching and Education Studies. His research interests are education policy and university knowledge. He edited an introductory text on Education Studies first published by Routledge in 2004: *A Student's Guide to Education Studies*. A fourth and revised edition has been recently published. He is editor of the Routledge Education Studies Series, of which this book is part.

Jodi Withers is senior lecturer in Academic Skills at the University of Wolverhampton and co-ordinates the foundation year programme for the Faculty of Arts, Business and Social Sciences. Prior to working in higher education (HE), she worked in further education as an adult literacy specialist, and taught on Access to HE programmes. Her research interests include the foundation-year student experience, and in 2019 she was co-author of a student guide to successfully navigating the first year of a degree, *Making it at Uni*. She has also published research on student writing and has a keen interest in student reading practices. A Psychology graduate, she is currently completing a PhD at the University of Leicester.

Series editor's preface

Education Studies has become a popular and exciting undergraduate subject in some 50 universities in the UK. It began in the early 2000s, mainly in the post-1992 universities which had been centres of teacher training. Gaining academic credibility, the subject is now being taken up by post-1992 and Russell Group institutions. In 2004, Routledge published one of the first texts for undergraduates, *Education Studies: A Student's Guide* (Ward, 2004), now in its fourth edition (Simon and Ward, 2020). It comprises a series of chapters introducing key topics in Education Studies and has contributed to the development of the subject. Targeted at students and academic staff at levels 5, 6 and 7, the Routledge Education Studies Series offers a sequence of volumes which explore such topics in depth.

It is important to understand that Education Studies is not teacher training or teacher education, although graduates in the subject may well go on to become teachers after a Postgraduate Certificate in Education (PGCE) or school-based training. Education Studies should be regarded as a subject with a variety of career outcomes, or indeed, none; it can be taken as the academic and critical study of education in itself. At the same time, while the theoretical elements of teacher training are continually reduced in PGCE courses and school-based training, undergraduate Education Studies provides a critical analysis for future teachers who, in a rapidly changing world, need so much more than simply the training to deliver a government-defined school curriculum.

Education Studies is concerned with understanding how people develop and learn throughout their lives, the nature of knowledge and critical engagement with ways of knowing. It demands an intellectually rigorous analysis of educational processes and their cultural, social, political and historical contexts. In a time of rapid change across the planet, education is about how we both make and manage such change. Education Studies, therefore, includes perspectives on international education, economic relationships, globalisation, ecological issues and human rights. It deals with beliefs, values and principles in education and the way that they change over time.

Since its early developments at the beginning of the century, the subject has grown in academic strength, drawing on explicitly on the disciplines of Psychology, Sociology, Philosophy, History and Economics. But it has also broadened in scope to address the many social and political questions of globalisation, international education and perceptions of childhood. A glance through the list of book titles in the series on page xvi reveals the ever-growing range of topics which Education Studies embraces. The Coronavirus pandemic prevalent at the time of writing (April 2020) highlighted the role of schools not simply as a childminding service, but also in terms of how education can help to manage the crisis. Health Education, then, becomes the next topic to address with a book in the series.

Given the creative and imaginative developments in the Education Studies curriculum, it is surprising that there has been relatively little research on the topic of higher education. In the past, universities were perhaps taken for granted as a fixed entity in the education system. However, recent years have seen higher education become a highly politicised topic with the introduction of government policies on student fees, the marketisation of universities and debates about the university curriculum and graduate employment. This book is the first in addressing these questions thoroughly and systematically for Education Studies. Its readers are likely to be learning or teaching in a higher education institution, and it will provide an academic basis for their analysis and discussion.

Stephen Ward

Series Editor, Bath Spa University

References

Committee on Higher Education (Robbins) (1963) *Report*. London: HMSO.

D. Crook (2002) Education studies and teacher education. *British Journal of Education Studies*, **50**(1), pp 55–75.

S. Ward (Ed.) (2004) *Education Studies: A Student's Guide*. Abingdon: Routledge.

Books available to date in the series

Brendan Bartram (Ed.) (2017) *International and Comparative Education: Contemporary Issues and Debates*. Abingdon: Routledge.

Zeta Brown (Ed.) (2016) *Inclusive Education: Perspectives on Pedagogy, Policy and Practice*. Abingdon: Routledge.

Zeta Brown and Stephen Ward (Eds) (2018) *Contemporary Issues in Childhood: A Bio-Ecological Approach*. Abingdon: Routledge.

Christine Eden (2017) *Gender: Education and Work: Inequalities and Intersectionality*. Abingdon: Routledge.

Tom Feldges (Ed.) (2019) *Philosophy and the Study of Education: New Perspectives on a Complex Relationship*. Abingdon: Routledge.

Nicholas Joseph (Ed.) (2020) *History of Education*. Abingdon: Routledge.

Jessie Bustillos Morales and Sandra Abegglen (Eds) (2020) *The Study of Education and Economics: Debates and Critical Theoretical Perspectives*. Abingdon: Routledge.

Catherine A. Simon and Graham Downes (Eds) (2020) *Sociology for Education Studies*. Abingdon: Routledge.

Catherine A. Simon and Stephen Ward (Eds) (2020) Education Studies: A Student's Guide. Abingdon: Routledge.

Cathal Ó. Siochrú (Ed.) (2018) *Psychology and the Study of Education: Critical Perspectives on Developing Theories*. Abingdon: Routledge.

British Education Studies Association (BESA)

Many of the editors and contributors to the Education Studies book series are members of the British Education Studies Association. Formed in 2005, BESA is an academic association providing a network for tutors and students in Education Studies. It holds an annual conference with research papers from staff and students; there are bursaries for students on Education Studies programmes.

The website offers information and news about Education Studies and two journals: *Educationalfutures* and *Transformations*, a journal for student publications. Both are available without charge on the website: https://educationstudies.org.uk/

Abbreviations

The following abbreviations are used in the text:

ACM	Association for Computing Machinery
APC	Anti-Precarity Cymru
BIS	Business, Innovation and Skills (Dept of)
BAME	black, Asian and minority ethnic
BMA	British Medical Association
CA	Capability Approach (to disability)
CIBA	Centre for Information Behaviour and the Evaluation of Research
CILIP	Chartered Institute of Library and Information Professions
CNAA	Council for National Academic Awards
COLA	Cost of Living Adjustment
CPD	Committee of Directors of Polytechnics
DFE	Department for Education
DIY	do it yourself
DLHE	Destination of Leavers from Higher Education
DWP	Department for Work and Pensions
ECA	Early Career Academic
ECU	Equality Challenge Unit
EU	European Union
FAHE	Further and Higher Education Act (1992)
FHEA	Fellow of the Higher Education Academy
GP	general practitioner
HE	higher education
HEI	higher education institution
HESA	Higher Education Statistical Agency
HMG	Her Majesty's Government
IAPT	Improving Access to Psychological Therapies
ICT	information and communication technologies
IWGB	Independent Workers Union of Great Britain
IPPR	Institute for Public Policy Research
L&T	learning and teaching

LEA	local education authority
LTA	Learning, Teaching and Assessment
NHS	National Health Service
NSS	National Student Survey
OASP	online academic self-presentation
OECD	Organisation for Economic Co-operation and Development
OFS	Office for Students
PSF	Professional Standards Framework
QAA	Quality Assurance Agency
QTS	Qualified Teacher Status
RCP	Royal College of Psychiatrists
REF	Research Excellence Framework
RIBA	Royal Institute of British Architects
STEM	science, technology, engineering and mathematics
TEF	Teaching Excellence Framework
UCU	University and College Union
USS	Universities Superannuation Scheme
WHO	World Health Organisation
WBL	work-based learning

1 Higher education
Change, churn and challenges

Brendan Bartram

Introduction

In many countries around the world today, higher education (HE) is a topic that is more than occasionally in the news. This is certainly the case in the UK, for a wide variety of reasons – there are more institutions than ever before awarding degrees, and more students studying for them at both undergraduate and postgraduate levels. This expansion in numbers and participation has been accompanied by questions about funding and management methods, growing expectations from stakeholders (e.g. regarding employability, mental health care, etc.), and increased scrutiny from government, the media and, indeed, wider society. HE itself is in part responsible for some of this growth in attention, as universities increasingly gaze inwards at themselves in an attempt to make sense of and reflect on the changing landscapes within which they operate. This academic interest has resulted in a global expansion of journals and research centres focused on the policy and practice of HE (Tight, 2018).

This mass expansion has unsurprisingly produced an increasingly diverse university sector in the UK. Though there are commonalities when it comes to certain policy trends and pressures (e.g. the Teaching Excellence Framework [TEF], Research Excellence Framework [REF]), the sector as a whole is arguably more diverse and divided than ever before. Around 10 years ago, I described higher education as 'an educational sector that lacks even a unified sense of purpose and identity' (Bartram, 2009: 308), a description which perhaps applies even more now than it did then. Some commentators (e.g. Scott, 2018) suggest that this lack of consensus constitutes a contemporary crisis of meaning, though such assertions might be misplaced – in one respect, such alarmist descriptions are neither contemporary nor quite accurate: a glance through history shows us a fairly consistent ongoing struggle with defining the purpose of HE in changing social circumstances. Nietzsche's *Anti-Education* from 1872 (2016), for example, conveys a strong sense of dismay about the changing nature of universities and the degraded form of education they were providing, focused on personality and character development at the expense of developing deeply critical minds. He goes on to criticise what he saw as a system too focused on expanding an impoverished utilitarian education to people who would be better off pursuing other goals – views which still resonate with some today. Over 100 years later, the title of Allan Bloom's 1987 book – *The Closing of the American Mind: How Higher Education Has Failed Democracy and Impoverished the Souls of Today's Students* – requires no explanation as to the nature of its central message. Looking back through history, Virginia Sapiro (2015) suggests that a discourse of crisis has in fact characterised university education for several hundred years now.

In a sense, then, change and churn in HE may just be constant symptoms of a system in perpetual flux, driven by competing and evolving philosophies, expectations and demands. Though some of the drivers of change may not be new, there are of course some distinctively modern elements influencing the pace, nature and scale of change. I would argue that the increasingly heterogenous nature of HE has to do with how individual institutions are positioned (and position themselves) in relation to a mixture of long-standing and contemporary priorities and tensions that can be conceptualised as a set of binary polarities. These polarities are often closely inter-connected and mutually influential, with important implications for how universities shape their identities and define their purposes, the kinds of courses they offer, the teaching and assessment regimes they provide and, indeed, the students they recruit.

Questions for discussion

- Before looking at the next section, what do you think some of these binary polarities might be?
- When you have discussed your ideas with others, compare them with the list below.
- Where would you place your own institution on the various continua, and what evidence would you draw on to support your decisions?
- Why have some of the terms below been placed in inverted commas?
- What additional polarities could there be?
- Are some of these terms essentially synonymous? If so, which ones, and why?
- Is there any room to argue that some of these aspects may not necessarily be mutually exclusive?

Possible polarities and continua:

Teaching intensive	Research intensive
'Traditional'	'Non-traditional'
Lower entry criteria	Higher entry criteria
'Vocational'	'Academic'
Pre-92	Post-92
Global focus	local focus
Widening participation	elitist
TEF bronze	TEF gold
TEF-focused	REF-focused
Recruitment-focused	rejection-focused
High ranking	Low ranking

One thing most current analyses of UK HE have in common is the broad agreement that the challenges and financial pressures universities now face are unlikely to diminish in the years ahead, and that these will have consequences for all those who work and study in HE. The Augar Review (DfE, 2019) will no doubt have far-reaching implications for HE in a number of important areas. These include such diverse issues as the sector's rebalanced relationship with further education (FE) colleges, the potential loss of funding for foundation degrees, extending student loan repayments from 30 to 40 years, and the possible threat of removing certain non-vocational courses from universities within the post-92 sector. These recommendations serve to heighten ongoing pressures associated with finance, fees and funding, and in the process amplify the competitive challenges and demands imposed on institutions by a system already heavily dominated by metrics and mechanisms such as the TEF and REF. The various data sources these frameworks draw on – particularly the National Student Survey (NSS) with regard to the TEF – have significantly increased institutional efforts to manage and enhance students' experience, satisfaction, wellbeing, engagement and employability, to say nothing of their academic outcomes and degree classifications. Some have suggested that these preoccupations have produced a managerialist audit culture which has practically fetishised the notion of competition in the sector (Bartram, 2020, Naidoo, 2018). Only time will tell, of course, what additional pressures and challenges will ensue as a result of Brexit, with already widely predicted reductions in research funding and collaborative opportunities.

Aims of the book

This book brings together a wide-ranging and stimulating selection of critical essays that explore current issues relating to the policy and practice of HE. It does this by including chapters which consider how staff and students experience aspects of working, learning and being at university. The contributions selected are deliberately wide-ranging in an attempt to provide higher-level undergraduate students of education with an imaginative set of varied theme-based analyses that will hopefully broaden their interests in the increasingly diverse and expansive field of HE. As different as the individual subjects the chapters cover are, they all engage with topical issues in the sector, from the current mental health 'crisis' at universities to the changing role of technology, the rise of precarity, the 'teaching excellence' conundrum and equality and diversity. Each chapter examines contemporary issues from the point of view of expert insiders, and provides students with discussion questions and topics that they may wish to select and explore further in their own assignments and education projects. The book is therefore a unique resource for students with strong interests in this important educational sector.

Overview of the chapters

Beth Sumner begins the book with an examination of changing notions of risk. The chapter explores the realities of studying at an English post-1992 university, examined through the lenses of institutional habitus and reputational affect. It draws on data taken from her doctoral study, which examined student biographies of transition at a post-92 Higher Education Institution (HEI) in the English Midlands. Binary ways of considering universities in terms of their pre- or post-92 status remain a common feature of the UK HE landscape. Consequently, reputation and league-table ranking continue to act as a proxy for quality, with 'working class students predominantly ending up in universities seen to be "second class" both by themselves and others', according to Reay (2018:10). This way of thinking prevails, regardless of the fact that there may be no systematic differences in teaching quality, or in the likelihood of obtaining a good degree classification. As Blackman (2017:14) suggests: 'we appear to be in a world based on snobbery and discrimination rather than evidence, which is socially damaging and could be producing worse educational outcomes overall'.

Sumner shows that despite acting as an educational 'sanctuary' and offering many students their first positive educational experience, the 'sticky residue' of attending a low-status HEI had wide-ranging effects on students' experiences and sense of self. The chapter explores the changing notions of risk that arise from studying at a post-92 HEI, seen initially by many as a 'safe' choice but which becomes a much riskier venture when attempting to make the transition into graduate employment.

Staying with the employment theme in the next chapter, Sinead D'Silva and Samantha Pugh consider the context of employability in higher education, reinforced through metrics like university rankings and the TEF. It focuses on the lived experiences of students as they decide on their various pathways from a STEM (science, technology, engineering and mathematics) degree. The research uses the theoretical framing of Margret Archer's 'Internal Conversations' to make sense of the reflexive actions of individuals. It presents the cases of Tony, who wanted to return home to the countryside; Jane, whose mental health became more important to her over the years and who wanted to choose an ethical career path; and Isaac, who wanted to be an engineer but picked his degree to boost his employability. D'Silva and Pugh argue that a blanket employability agenda, although beneficial to some, does not incorporate the lifestyle choices and experiences of individuals that mould their decision-making processes as they make their way through life. This exciting yet daunting point of transition is misunderstood through policy as objective, responding to market demands and skill shortages. Instead, the stories individuals share about their transitions from a degree to their lives as graduates are better explained through decision-making processes influenced by their personal concerns.

Following on from this, Bartram moves on to explore the topic of online academic self-presentation (OASP). A relatively small number of studies have to date examined this phenomenon, which sees academics routinely sharing and publicising their work online via platforms such as Academia. Edu and Research Gate, to name but a few. Studies that have been carried out tend to explore the extent of uptake and the perceived benefits and challenges entailed. This chapter touches on these elements but offers a more critical discussion of this less explored terrain – specifically, it examines the ways in which broader socio-cultural factors articulate with pervasive neo-liberal influences on HE to explain and understand the expansion of OASP. It begins with an exploration of the relationship between OASP and contemporary social trends, before moving on to examine how neo-liberal forms of competition in the academy become entwined with self-promotional tendencies influenced by contemporary celebrity culture.

In the next chapter, Mark Elliot continues the neo-liberal theme in his consideration of one of the most prominent contemporary issues in HE: the emergence of the student as consumer. He argues that HE policy in the UK since the Browne Review has recast students as consumers of educational services and universities as service providers, based on a belief that this approach will enhance both the performance of universities and the educational experience of students. UK HE has arguably been dominated by other neo-liberal reforms promoting competition. In 2011, for example, the coalition government simultaneously reduced the block grant to universities and increased tuition fees to a maximum of £9,000, thus increasing competition between universities to recruit students. In addition, the management of UK HE is dominated by the use of metrics to measure performance, perhaps most notably by the Teaching Excellence Framework introduced in 2017. Elliot's chapter explores how the use of competition and performance metrics in UK HE have served to entrench a construction of the student as consumer – a construction that may have damaging consequences for students and, indeed, for HE as a whole. Mark also considers alternatives to the student-as-consumer model, and how such approaches could be creatively subverted.

Bailey et al. explore the interface of technology and learning in the next chapter, focusing specifically on the ways in which students navigate information online and the challenges they face. Against a backdrop of literature from the past two decades, findings are presented from a recent observational study (employing screen-recording software and stimulated recall) of how students approach a writing-from-sources task, supplemented by interview transcripts and reflective accounts by librarians and academic writing teachers at a UK university. The chapter begins with a brief discussion of the role of information literacy in HE, before reviewing methods employed in previous studies on students' information search processes. Drawing on examples from screen recordings, the authors explore the challenges of a literature search, such as selecting useful keywords, filtering search results, over-reliance on familiar friends such as Google or Wikipedia and accessing full-text versions of journal articles. These processes not only require cognitive/technical skill but have an affective dimension too. Bailey *et al.* conclude by highlighting examples of good practice from their study and consider whether contemporary students are more information-literate than their counterparts in previous decades.

Staying with the broad theme of teaching and learning in the next chapter, Namrata Rao and Anesa Hosein examine academic diversity in contemporary UK academia, considering the possible implications of such diversity for approaches, practices and policies regarding learning and teaching (L&T). Whilst there is an acknowledgement of diversity among academic staff, they argue that the discussion on how this may influence L&T has remained relatively absent. Over the last 20 years, there have been calls to feminise the curriculum and, more recently, a movement from students asking for the curriculum to be decolonised by making it less male and Anglo-centric. The authors examine how else we can think about dismantling, diversifying and challenging current L&T curricular practices by harnessing the plurality of the academic staff body. They draw on a range of HE statistics to examine the extent of academic diversity to establish which aspects/characteristics of academic identity (gender, age, ethnicity, etc.) dominate British academic spaces and which of those identities are (un)intentionally being left out. The academic workforce in the UK is considered through a multitude of lenses to explore the nature of their academic contracts (full time or part time), the focus on academic work (teaching only, research only or teaching and research), age, gender, ethnicity, nationality and disability. Some of the key questions pertinent for HE environments in relation to these aspects are discussed; for example, what are the possible implications for the learning experience of students of exposure to a largely white and male-dominated academic workforce?

In Chapter Eight, Muddiman *et al.* move on to explore an additional workforce issue: competing narratives of precarity, flexibility and efficiency in HE. Although discussions of casualisation and precarity have become increasingly prominent in HE, with 54 per cent of UK academic staff on insecure contracts, the way this impacts working conditions and learning environments in universities is contested. Casualised working is often presented as a flexible arrangement benefiting staff and students, or as an unavoidable reality in austere times. However, there are concerns that this flexibility is asymmetrical, as workers often find themselves vulnerable, financially insecure and unable to make long-term plans. The material, psychological and social impacts on both staff and students in relation to teaching, research activities and wellbeing are outlined. The chapter examines how unions and grassroots movements have engaged with these issues through collective bargaining and creative outputs (e.g. #zinesagainstprecarity), emphasising the importance of both online and physical spaces. This is embedded in critiques of wider societal trends of the gig economy and zero-hours contracts. It concludes by exploring what is next for HE and precarity, setting out alternate visions of university life for staff and students.

In the next chapter, Hathaway and Rao turn their attention to one of the most contentious issues in HE in recent times – the Teaching Excellence Framework (TEF). Contemporary models of HE focus on developing various aspects of institutional excellence, teaching excellence being of course no exception. Empirical work on teaching and learning has contributed to defining measures of educational quality and to producing guidance materials aiming to support this. Such guidance sets out the standards, scholarly approaches, qualities and aspirations that those teaching in HE should adhere and aspire to. Contemporary discourse is awash with terms like 'student-centred', 'intellectual challenge' and 'co-production', which are now common parlance at institutional level and are increasingly ingrained in wider educational discourses. However, it could be argued that considerable detail is lost when translating such guidance and rhetoric into practice, raising questions about meanings and shared understandings in contemporary university learning spaces. Moreover, the detailed evidence base beyond the guidance is often unexplored. This chapter explores the research underlying such guidance and examines the dissonance between evidence and action through an analysis of the perceptions of university teachers.

In Chapter Ten, Clare Dickens picks up on a rather different but equally topical HE issue – student mental health. The scale of the mental health crisis at UK universities is allegedly revealed in a study by the Institute for Public Policy Research (IPPR) think tank. It shows that the number of students who disclosed a mental health problem in their first year rose fivefold to reach 15,395 in a decade. This narrative of crisis linked with increased disclosure is, however, open to question when we consider the supposed aim of campaigns such as *Time to Change* (2018) to reduce the stigma associated with mental health issues and calling for social action to talk and break the silence; and indeed previous high-profile calls for students to disclose their difficulties. It would appear, reflecting on the trend of increased disclosures, that there may not be a crisis at all but rather an indication of success measured against the narrative of previous aims and campaigns, and the crisis perhaps derives from how well equipped we are to actually respond. This chapter explores current thinking and policy initiatives in relation to students' mental health, examining how well equipped universities are to meet the challenges they face in this area in order to reconfigure themselves as health-promoting and supportive environments.

In an attempt to understand the broader HE policy context in the next chapter, Stephen Ward takes a historical perspective on the economic theories, philosophy and social policies which have affected knowledge in higher education over three broad phases: the medieval, the modern and the postmodern. The university has a long history with the first European universities established in the eleventh century in Bologna, Paris and Oxford under the auspices of the Roman Catholic Church. A section on the medieval university shows that many of their features exist in today's HE system. The 'modern' university emerged with the Humboldt University of Berlin in 1810 and became the model for the European and American universities of the nineteenth and twentieth centuries. Their underlying philosophy was based on Kant's German idealism in the search for truth, together with Humboldt's proposal that the university should be fully funded by the state and enjoy academic freedom in teaching and research. The current 'postmodern' university loses its independence and control of knowledge as it competes for student fees in the neo-liberal HE market. Knowledge as the search for truth is replaced by 'performativity' in gaining graduate employment. The chapter examines the underlying political context and concludes with a critique of the postmodern context for higher education.

The next two chapters examine issues of diversity and equity in HE. David Thompson and Stephanie Brewster firstly consider the notion of student diversity and work-based learning. There is an increasing emphasis on equality, diversity and inclusion and on graduate employability within HE. Work-based learning (off campus, on placement) is a key component of many undergraduate degrees, but for many students, factors such as ill health, disability and caring or work responsibilities can impact on their experience of work-based learning. Disabled people in particular are at a significant disadvantage in the workplace but stand to gain most from placements, if their learning can be maximised. This chapter starts with exploring the current position of work-based learning in HE, and then considers the implications for our diverse student population with a particular focus on disabled students. It goes on to discuss the authors' research, which includes the views of both students and HE staff. Students reported challenges including anxiety, confidence levels, familiarity with the setting, whether to disclose a disability to a setting, how health can impact on placement attendance, how strategies are employed to deal with challenges, and work–life balance. The conclusion makes some tentative recommendations for those supporting placement learning in HE in any capacity and who wish to maximise learning for all students. Ultimately, a goal for HE should be improving disabled students' employability rates to bring them more in line with non-disabled students.

And before considering what overall conclusions might be distilled from these wide-ranging contributions, Ruth Mieschbuehler in the penultimate chapter broadens the focus to consider how we might go about promoting what she sees as real equality in higher education. She argues that there is a need to reclaim a forgotten sense of what 'equality' means. This is equality as the right to be the same rather than the right to be different. Equality as difference is what many students, academics and managers in HE accept and promote. Treating people as equal to them means merely accepting and respecting differences. What was once a universal concept emphasising a common humanity has been replaced by a particular concept emphasising the respect that must be given to what are divisive elements of people's given identities. This is not a simple semantic change but a political change that undermines the universalising project of HE and indeed, the 'university'. The impact of this politicised, particularised view of equality is manifest throughout higher education. In policy terms, it means the creation of initiatives in institutions and classrooms to celebrate and even promote diversity. In terms of assessment, it is expressed in the adoption of relational comparisons of student attainment that are used to compare relative attainment levels between groups. Instead of seeing students who desire and deserve the best a university education can offer, they are presented in policies and practice as being easily differentiated into racial, cultural, class or gender-based groups. As the research discussed in this chapter reveals, the consequences of equality as diversity are often unwelcome to students. This divisive thinking may seem to empower various groups, but ultimately it denies all students the possibility of accessing the best university education, an education that embodies what Matthew Arnold called 'the best that has been thought and said'. Instead, education is rebuilt around fixed, particular identities. Recapturing real equality means restoring the forgotten 'absolute' sense of human equality and defending it along with 'absolute' standards which offer all students the ability to reach their human potential through access to a universal liberal education.

Conclusion

Higher Education is a diverse and expanding educational sector. Though a discourse of change and crisis in relation to HE is sometimes thought to be a modern phenomenon, it is clear that universities have always been subject to challenge and development, as new ideas and changing social contexts influence their policy priorities and day-to-day practices. As discussed, the chapters included in the book offer insights into a range of these matters; we hope that these accounts and analyses will give readers a much stronger understanding of some of the contradictions, complexities and challenges currently facing the sector.

Summary points

- Higher education has undergone significant expansion in recent times.
- This expansion has been accompanied by funding and management innovations, growing expectations from stakeholders and increased public and governmental scrutiny.
- Change and churn in HE may be constant symptoms of a system in perpetual flux, driven by competing and evolving philosophies, expectations and demands.
- This book offers varied insights into how current policies and priorities variously influence staff, students and practices in the sector.

Recommended reading

Frank, J., Gowar, N. and Naef, M. (2019) *English Universities in Crisis: Markets Without Competition.* Bristol: Bristol University Press.

Hayes, S. (2019) *The Labour of Words in Higher Education: Is it Time to Reoccupy Policy?* Leiden: Brill.

Strike, T., Nicholls, J. and Rushforth, J. (2019) *Governing Higher Education Today: International Perspectives.* Abingdon: Routledge.

Tong, V., Standen, A. and Sotiriou, M. (2018) *Shaping Higher Education with Students: Ways to Connect Research and Teaching.* London: UCL Press.

References

Bartram, B. (2009) Student Support in Higher Education – Understandings, Implications and Challenges. *Higher Education Quarterly*, 63(3), pp. 308–314.

Bartram, B. (2020) Queering the TEF. In K. Carruthers Thomas and A. French (Eds.), *Challenging the Teaching Excellence Framework: Diversity Deficits in Higher Education Evaluations.* Bingley, UK: Emerald Publishing.

Blackman, T. (2017) *The Comprehensive University: An Alternative to Social Stratification by Academic Selection.* Oxford: Higher Education Policy Institute.

Bloom, A. (1987) *The Closing of the American Mind: How Higher Education Has Failed Democracy and Impoverished the Souls of Today's Students.* New York: Simon and Schuster.

DfE (2019) *Post-18 Education and Funding: Independent Panel Report.* London: DfE.

Naidoo, R. (2018) The Competition Fetish in Higher Education: Shamans, Mind Snares and Consequences. *European Educational Research Journal*, 17(5), pp. 605–620.

Nietzsche, F. (2016) *Anti-Education* (Translator Damion Searls). New York: New York Review Books Classics.

Reay, D. (2018) Working Class Educational Transitions to University: The Limits of Success. *European Journal of Education*, 53(4), pp. 528–540.

Sapiro, V. (2015) *The Coming Crisis in Higher Education.* Decanal Valedictory Delivered Before the Faculty of the College of Arts and Sciences, Boston University, April 27. Available at: http://blogs.bu.edu/vsapiro/files/2016/06/Coming-Crisis-in-Higher-Ed-Sapiro-2015.pdf (accessed 19 August 2019).

Scott, P. (2018) *The Crisis of the University.* London: Routledge.

Tight, M. (2018) *Higher Education Research: The Developing Field.* London: Bloomsbury.

2 Changing notions of risk

The realities of studying in a post-92 university

Bethany Sumner

Introduction

This chapter explores the realities of studying at an English post-1992 university in relation to issues around institutional hierarchy and reputation. The chapter draws on data taken from a doctoral study which examined first-generation student biographies of transition at a case study post-1992 higher education institution (HEI) in the Midlands.

Binary ways of considering universities in terms of their pre- or post-1992 status remains a common feature of the higher education (HE) landscape (Blackman, 2017). Consequently an institution's reputation and league table ranking can act as a proxy for quality (Stich, 2012), and it is often the case that 'working class students predominantly end up in universities seen to be "second class" both by themselves and others' (Reay, 2018:10). A deficit way of perceiving newer universities seems to have prevailed, regardless of the lack of evidence that post-1992 HEIs offer diminished teaching quality or a lower likelihood of obtaining a good degree classification. As argued by Blackman (2017:14), 'we appear to be in a world based on snobbery and discrimination rather than evidence, which is socially damaging and could be producing worse educational outcomes overall'.

The findings from the doctoral study discussed in this chapter evidence the way in which inequality is maintained and perpetuated in the HE sector and the impact this can have on students' lived experiences. The chapter explores the changing notions of risk that arise from studying at a post-92 HEI, which may initially be viewed as a 'safe' decision (given the lower entry criteria and diverse student body) but which can become a much riskier choice when students attempt to make the transition into graduate employment.

The chapter begins with a brief overview of the background to English HE, exploring the history of the post-1992 university and examining the way in which institutional inequality has operated historically within the sector. The current HE context will be outlined, and the concept of 'student choice' briefly explored. The chapter will then move on to explore the lived experiences of students in the case study university and to examine the significance of these experiences in light of current policy developments and concerns about social justice. HE policy and university status differ across Scotland, Northern Ireland and Wales; discussions here focus exclusively on the English context.

Background – the history of the post-92 university

The term 'post-1992 university' is commonly used for HEIs, which were originally polytechnics and higher education colleges and which gained university status during 1992 as a result of the

Further and Higher Education Act (FAHE). Prior to 1992, HE in the UK followed a binary system, with polytechnic institutions and universities having separate titles, funding agreements and governance arrangements (Raffe and Croxford, 2015). Although they offered HE courses, polytechnics and colleges differed from universities in a number of ways. They generally focused on offering a range of vocational courses, produced less research and tended to be in urban locations. The 1992 FAHE (in theory) dissolved the binary system of polytechnics and universities by investing polytechnics with degree awarding powers and allowing them to assume the title of 'university' (McCaig, 2011). This immediately increased the number of universities by 50 per cent and effectively doubled the number of university students (Boliver, 2015).

Unsurprisingly, this new 'unified' system retained many characteristics of earlier stratification which affected the way in which institutions positioned themselves (Cooke, 2011). The 'older' institutions retained stringent entry requirements and traditional academic curricula, while the post-1992 universities continued to be associated with local and diverse student intakes and greater vocational provision. Consequently, the FAHE effectively moved HE from an explicit to an implicit two-tier system, which remained characterised by a hierarchy of status based on the institution's age, or the date it became a university. However, the stigma of being known as a 'new university' was not new. HEIs had been using their age as a way to convey superiority long before the development of the post-1992 university. For example, the medieval universities of Oxford and Cambridge were viewed as superior to their nineteenth-century red-brick rivals. Likewise, the 'new' universities such as Bath and York created during the Robbins expansion of HE in the 1960s were then seen as inferior to the traditional universities. They later became known as 'old' universities to distinguish themselves from the 'even-newer' post-92 institutions. Evidently, although the designations of 'old' and 'new' have applied to different universities at different times, these terms have remained synonymous with high and low status (Boliver, 2015).

Since the introduction of the 1992 Act, the English university hierarchy appears to have remained relatively stable. Research by Raffe and Croxford (2015) examined UCAS data between 1996 and 2010 in order to investigate whether the university hierarchy in England had weakened during this time period. The findings of this research indicated that institutional hierarchy had remained largely unchanged, with the researchers suggesting that status distinctions between pre- and post-1992 institutions had, if anything, become more pronounced. The study concluded that English HE stratification 'has been stable and resistant to pressures for change from expansion, institutional restructuring or the development of market arrangements' (Raffe and Croxford, 2015: 332).

Given the established stratification within the HE system, it is evident that the tag of being a former polytechnic can be difficult to shake off. The history of an institution has clear implications for notions of 'reputation' and 'prestige' which can make it challenging for newer universities to achieve parity of esteem with more traditional institutions (Boliver, 2015). This issue is exacerbated by the point that post-92 universities tend to have lower entry requirements and less selective practices than older elite HEIs such as Russell Group institutions. The Russell Group represents a self-identifying subset of 24 older 'leading' research-intensive universities (including Oxford University and University of Cambridge) which, since 1994, have utilised their self-defined 'world-class' status to successfully distinguish themselves as superior to other universities. Despite having no official status, the Russell Group exerts 'considerable influence on government policy by dint of its market share, reputation for excellence, lobbying power and prestigious alumni' (Harrison, 2011: 450).

Clearly, historical background and notions of prestige serve to inform judgements regarding the status (and therefore the quality) of universities (Boliver, 2015).

University status has implications for the social demographic of student bodies, with high entry criteria and social selectivity going hand in hand (Harrison, 2011), resulting in a lack of students from non-privileged social backgrounds studying in elite HEIs. Consequently, it seems that universities remain firmly embedded in the British class system, with students from advantaged backgrounds tending to concentrate in high-status institutions (Raffe and Croxford, 2015) whilst working-class students are more likely to be found studying within the more diverse and inclusive (in terms of their lower entry criteria and less elite ethos) post-92 universities (Strathdee, 2009). This class-based stratification has fuelled ongoing concerns about social justice and equality, meaning that concerns about participation now centre on 'who goes where and why' (Ball *et al.*, 2002: 354).

The role of ranking systems

Ranking systems such as league tables are a key factor in improving or maintaining university reputation and status. The English HE system has become increasingly market-driven over recent years, as government strategy has focused on putting 'students at the heart of the system' (BIS, 2011) and enabling student 'choice' through a number of marketised mechanisms such as league tables and, more recently, the development of the Teaching Excellence Framework (TEF). Since the initial introduction of league tables in the late 1990s and early 2000s, a significant number of university league tables have been published in England every year, by newspapers such as *the Times* and *the Guardian* and also by the *Complete University Guide*, which is a stand-alone organisation. These tables use data from a number of sources such as the National Student Survey (NSS – a student satisfaction survey for Level 6 students), graduate employment data, entry requirements and research activity and funding. The use of entry requirements as a proxy for quality is particularly problematic for post-92 HEIs, which tend to be less selective and have more diverse student intakes.

The use of league tables and other marketisation instruments has been justified by the discourse of expanding student 'choice'. Government policy documents continually suggest that increasing competition within the sector will drive up the quality of institutional provision by encouraging HEIs to be more responsive to the needs of their students. This reasoning assumes the position of students as rational consumers who are free to choose their institution of study based on a number of factors. However, as Harrison (2011) rightly points out, if student choices are impacted by long-standing institutional hierarchy and notions of status which are beyond the control of the institution itself, then this raises questions regarding the usefulness of a market rationale. This argument is supported by Raffe and Croxford (2015: 332), who state that:

> The assumption underlying market policies, that consumers base their HE choices on factors that institutions can change such as the content, quality and prices of their programmes, and not on factors beyond their control such as their history, and their past reputation, is questionable.

Furthermore, as pointed out by Brown (2011), the way in which university ranking systems make no allowances for context and assume all HEIs have similar student cohorts is problematic, as is the perpetuation of a narrow view of 'quality' in a diverse, mass system. As Brown states here: 'League tables indeed strengthen the market position of institutions that are already prestigious and well-funded, at the expense of those that may be seeking to build reputation by attending to the needs of students and employers' (2011: 16).

Given their limited funds and less advantaged student cohorts, arguably, it is the post-92 HEIs who do the most important work in terms of social justice, yet it appears that they are the most penalised by the ongoing marketisation of the English HE system. This is further evidenced by the way in which new universities tend to occupy lower league table positions whilst the highest positions are reserved for the most selective institutions.

Individual/group task

Reflect on how important university league tables were when deciding where you were going to apply to study – did you consult them? If so, what impact did they have on your decision making?

Consider what other factors influenced your choice. How do these factors compare to your peers?

Research methods and case-study context

The data discussed in the following sections of this chapter are drawn from a qualitative doctoral research study which explored first-generation student transitions in a post-92 university. It drew on in-depth, biographical interviews with 21 students who were at various stages of the student lifecycle, including applicants, current students and recent graduates. The participants were diverse in terms of their age, ethnic background and subject of study, but were all from working-class backgrounds.

The research utilised a case-study approach, and the case-study institution is a large, inner-city, post-1992 HEI. In the interests of anonymity, the institution will be referred to using the pseudonym 'Central'. Central has a relatively large student cohort of around 24,000 students studying across four faculties and two main campuses. Of those students, 24 per cent are mature, and the majority of students are full time (79 per cent), undergraduate (82 per cent), living within a 30-mile radius (69 per cent). As is typical of a post-92 university, the majority of the student body are from socio-culturally diverse backgrounds, and many are first-generation entrants. Around 98 per cent of the student body attended state schools. Like many newer universities, Central occupies a relatively low league table position, ranking just above 100 out of 131 in *The Sunday Times Good University Guide* (O'Leary, 2019). Central is located in an area which is highly populated by other universities, containing two post-92 HEIs, an elite Russell Group university and a semi-elite 'Plateglass' institution, all within a 15-mile radius. This means that competition for local students is fierce. The local HE field was able to act as a microcosm of the wider HE sector, which allowed the significance of institutional reputation and status to be explored in relation to the participants' experiences, which are discussed in the following sections.

Student choice

The Higher Education White Paper, *Success as a Knowledge Economy* (BIS, 2016: 11), stated that 'the most important outcome of higher education is finding employment' and research has shown that the majority of students enter HE to improve their employment prospects. For younger students, HE is often positioned as the next logical step in their education trajectory and is legitimised both by schools/colleges and also by wider policy discourse as the most 'acceptable aspiration' (Brown, 2011: 7). This was the case for the majority of the participants in the study, who saw university attendance as the most rational next step in their educational journeys.

It was evident that university status had varying degrees of influence when the participants were deciding where to study. The participants all made (unprompted) reference to the local HE hierarchy but responded to the relatively low positioning of Central in various ways. Interestingly, they generally placed limited importance on marketisation instruments such as league table position and outlined that although they were aware that Central occupied a lower position than the other universities located within the city, this was not a hugely important factor in their decision making. The majority of the participants within the study elected to study at Central because it was somewhere which 'felt right':

> I looked at league tables but I didn't give them much thought to be honest. It was more about the feel I got when I came on the open day, the open day here was really good and that swung it for me.
>
> (Abbie)

> I did look at them (league tables), but to be honest it was more (pause) more about how it felt and the facilities for me.
>
> (Danni)

In this way, the students' 'choosing' of Central as their place of study was mediated by their class background, which recognised Central as an institution which reflected similar dispositions and values to theirs (Stitch, 2012) and as such posed a lower level of risk. This allowed for a level of protection from the 'crisis' of feeling out of place, which is often experienced by first-generation students in more elite institutions (Reay *et al.*, 2005; Ostrove *et al.*, 2011).

Furthermore, the dismissal of performative ranking systems could be considered to be a strategy of self-protection to shield the participants from the emotional injury of studying at a low-status university. However, for some of the participants, the mention of league tables created a different reaction, invoking a sense of regret that they were studying at a relatively low-status institution. It became evident that, for some individuals, the division between 'high' and 'low' university status may have had a significant impact on their feelings of self-worth.

> I didn't want to come here originally, I wanted to go to a good university like Plateglass or Redbrick, that was the dream.
>
> (Emma)

> I wanted to go to Plateglass because it's like smart people go to Plateglass so I'm going to go there.
>
> (Karolina)

As seen in the above quotes, a 'good' university is generally considered to be a highly selective one (Blackman, 2017) where the most talented students study. This understanding has clear implications for students who study in non-selective, post-92 HEIs, who may then be positioned (both by themselves and others) as 'lacking' in ability and/or ambition. In the quote above, by stating that 'smart people go to Plateglass', Karolina is suggesting that 'less smart people go to Central', which has clear implications for her own self-image.

Other participants in the study expressed a sense of anger and frustration that the positive and transformative experience they had engaged in at Central was absent in the wider discourse concerning what was considered to be a 'good' university:

> I am proud to have said I come from Central University and I don't know how many students would say that, which is one of the issues I have with higher education at the moment is about the inequality of the status stuff, when I say Central University, not the Redbrick … then that gets a lot of negative reactions from people … If I was the education secretary tomorrow the first thing I would do, I don't know how … but I would try and disband the Russell group, because I don't, I don't believe in it … it goes against all my values.
>
> (Eddie)

In this way university ranking can be regarded as legitimising tacit processes of unequal valuation of both post-92 universities and their students. The findings from this research suggest that students respond to low university ranking and reputation in various ways but that studying in a low-status HEI can potentially have real and damaging effects on the students who study in these institutions.

The positives of a post-1992 context

Post-1992 universities are sometimes considered to offer a greater level of support (both academic and pastoral) to their students, which makes sense given the more diverse needs of their student bodies. The participants in this study credited the level of support offered by Central as being a key advantage to studying within a post-92 university. This 'support' was positioned as a desirable good by the participants that went some way to compensating for the lower reputational position of Central in local discourse:

> But to be honest with you I don't feel like Central was a bad mistake because I have friends that went to Redbrick and they don't have no support whatsoever [sic] but the support, the support system here is quite good.
>
> (Shamsun)

Furthermore, notions of friendliness, diversity and comfort featured in the majority of the participant narratives when discussing their experiences of studying at Central. The university appeared to offer a place of educational sanctuary where the participants (many of whom had previously had difficult educational experiences) felt safe and able to succeed in their studies and grow in confidence. Central's inclusive and diverse institutional context offered a place where the participants felt a sense of belonging, something which literature suggests first-generation students often struggle with (Spiegler and Bednarek, 2013). In this way. university study posed less of a threat to the participants' existing identity and sense of self:

> I really love it here yeah. I don't … I thought it would be like a massive step but I feel quite comfortable here, I feel like I know my way around and I feel comfortable.
>
> (Beccy)

I've become comfortable here, it's like my little home, it's like nice.

(Karolina)

Like Central is different. It opens a lot of doors as opposed to Plateglass. I feel like Plateglass is very closed in and prestige and it's all like (pause) I'm not saying Central doesn't have prestige students but it opens up for everyone, people with disabilities and people who you know are not that like (pause) I just feel like they welcome every single person here.

(Caprice)

The participants saw Central as being inclusive and welcoming, reflecting a demographic, and dispositions which aligned with their own. The welcoming and inclusive feel to the institution, coupled with its 'achievable' entry criteria, city-centre location and heavy investment in facilities positioned Central as an attractive choice for local and distance students alike. The way in which the participants in this study felt welcome and that they belonged within the university environment, despite being from 'non-traditional', first-generation backgrounds, is evidence of the important work undertaken by post-1992 universities. This was instrumental in allowing the participants to develop a sense of belonging at Central and facilitated them in successfully transitioning between home and university, combining strong connections to their family and home life with the development of a robust student identity. This key strength of the post-92 experience is rarely acknowledged in wider discourse and demonstrates the way in which newer universities play a critical role in promoting a sense of self-fulfilment for non-traditional students:

Uni for me was life changing, (pause) that's really corny but I think sort of my journey sort of before I came to university to when I graduated, the difference in myself was just incredible. So just sort of confidence building, person building, I suppose sort of finding out who I am … so I think university has allowed me to be, to find out who me is.

(Abbie)

It's given me a voice. I was the shyest person on the planet, I really was! I never used to speak to people … It's crazy when I think how far I've come.

(Afia)

Individual/group discussion task

What do you consider to be the most important benefits of university study? Is it solely about improved employment prospects, or is personal fulfilment and enrichment also important? Do you feel that enough focus is given to these areas in government policy?

The idea that Central was understood as offering a supportive space where the participants were surrounded by 'people like them' (Reay *et al.*, 2009) positioned this as a safe choice which was achievable (and thus less risky) and which did not disrupt their existing dispositions. However, studying at a low-status HEI meant the participants potentially risked being excluded from the benefits that an elite education can confer as they faced the reality of graduating with a devalued degree in an overcrowded graduate labour market. This issue will now be discussed in the following section.

Changing notions of risk – moving to employment

Both quantitative and qualitative research has shown that students who attend elite, selective universities are more likely to find it easier to achieve graduate-level employment and enjoy increased earnings upon graduation (Belfield *et al.*, 2018; Crew, 2015). Brown and Hesketh (2004) suggest that inequality within the HE sector and graduate employment markets has become more pronounced since the development of mass higher education. Previously, a degree in itself conferred value; however, the rapid growth in student numbers over the past few decades has meant that university status has become increasingly used as a way to distinguish between job applicants. Bourdieu (1986) suggests that for goods to have value, they need to be difficult to acquire; therefore a degree from a selective institution (which is more challenging to get into) can carry more symbolic value in labour market fields than a degree from a recruiting institution such as Central which is accessible to 'people without social value' (Bourdieu, 1993: 98 in Reay *et al.*, 2005: 163). In this way, graduates of post-92 HEIs are unfairly disadvantaged by the increasing number of graduates in the job market, as their degree confers less symbolic value in the competitive field of graduate employment.

This is compounded by the practices of graduate employers who continue to recruit from a narrow range of universities (Milburn, 2012), creating a vicious cycle which reinforces the reputation of high-status universities and perpetuates the status quo. The way in which university reputation has been used as a proxy for quality has, according to Strathdee (2009: 86), allowed elite employers to increasingly target graduates of selective HEIs because they view them as 'safe bets'. The lower status of newer universities in comparison to elite HEIs can mean that their graduates are at a disadvantage in graduate labour markets, which has clear implications for social mobility (Leathwood, 2004).

Brown *et al.* (2012: 136) discuss how the concept of a degree as a 'positional good' outlines the way in which graduates are positioned in graduate labour markets. It appears that the symbolic value of a degree is (at least in part) dependent on the hierarchical position of the awarding institution. When the 'quality' of the university (according to reputation and rankings position) is taken to reflect differences in the 'calibre' of student, this can obviously have significant implications for how they are positioned (and how they position themselves) in graduate employment markets. Accordingly, Central's relatively low position in the institutional hierarchy may have had a substantial effect on the participants' achievements after graduation because the symbolic value of their degree may have carried less value in the field of graduate employment than a degree from a more elite university.

The participants in this study had internalised the dominant narrative of university study 'opening doors' in relation to employment prospects, and many of the participants appeared to feel optimistic about their future. It was evident that the participants had entered into the field of HE fully believing in and 'actively pursuing the prize it offers' (Bourdieu and Wacquant, 1992: 19). However, levels of risk altered significantly depending on what stage of their student journey the participants were currently at. In comparison to the participants in their first year of study, those who were approaching graduation, or who had recently graduated, expressed growing concern about the risk they had taken by attending a low-status university:

> I wish I went to Redbrick … I think it's more like a prestigious university and employers value that I think.
>
> (Shamsun)

Despite high aspirations, some of the recent graduates who were interviewed had been unable to obtain graduate-level employment and were working in unskilled, minimum wage jobs. Other participants who were nearing graduation expressed concern at their ability to gain employment in the competitive graduate job market, leading some of them to plan to continue working in their existing employment, at least in the short term. For these participants, a strong element of self-blame was evident as they misrecognised structural limitations (such as a lack of local graduate employment and high competition for jobs) and instead blamed their own personal shortcomings. Some of the graduate participants in particular expressed a strong sense of frustration and concern that they had made the 'wrong choice' (both in terms of university and course choice), which appeared to be particularly detrimental to their wellbeing and happiness.

> Depending on what university you go to depending on what course you do it's very (pause) your job opportunities very much differ.
>
> (Joe)

> I do think maybe I'd have been, I'd have a better chance at getting a job if I'd gone to somewhere more prestige like Redbrick. I know employers really care about that, don't they. I feel like if I'd been to Redbrick my degree would be worth more.
>
> (Leah)

This regret appeared to undermine many of the positive aspects the participants had gained from their degree, such as the growth in confidence they had experienced from gaining educational success. The narratives of these participants reflected the way in which their lack of labour market success had caused them to internalise implicit messages regarding the diminished value of their qualifications. The way in which the positive and transformative experiences of the participants during their time as students did not easily translate to improved employment after graduation made studying at Central a risky venture.

It was evident that difficulty finding graduate-level employment can have a marked impact on an individual's self-esteem and can cause emotional injuries such as feelings of frustration, unhappiness and self-blame. In this way it can be suggested that the larger discourses of stratification in the HE field effectively became smaller discourses of injured identities (Stich, 2012) for students who struggle to achieve their graduate aspirations. For some of the graduate participants in this study, electing to attend university (but then being unable to achieve their aspirations after graduation) created significant emotional injuries. Their difficulties upon graduation led to a level of discontent with their life, which they had not experienced prior to undertaking university study:

> I just wonder if it's all for nothing, I felt so positive about the future when I graduated, because I never thought I'd get a 2:1, never. I really messed up second year so. But then I didn't really know where to go from there or what to do so it hasn't really worked for me.
>
> (Leah)

> I've really struggled to find a job that I actually want ... At times you feel like oh I've got a dream that I can't even really put to use, it's quite frustrating in a way. I don't want to be stuck in retail, like I did a degree and it's not really anything to do with my degree. We don't get paid for what we do, I feel really undervalued. I feel really undervalued.
>
> (Malisa)

Evidently the inequalities within the stratified HE system matter because status differences in universities are reflected in the positional advantage of their graduates within the labour market (Raffe and Croxford, 2015). Addressing this inequality is therefore imperative in terms of social justice and social mobility. Dominant discussions around issues of equality in HE have thus far focused on increasing the numbers of non-privileged students entering elite HEIs by using features such as contextual offers and outreach work. Whilst this is clearly important, strategies like this are tokenistic at best and are ignoring the bigger issue at play: the notion of university status itself. A key part of this challenge lies with employers who continue to favour graduates from elite institutions (Raffe and Croxford, 2015). If the diminished status of post-92 HEIs was really to be challenged, then concerns around 'who goes where' would become redundant altogether.

Individual/group discussion task

What changes do you think could be made to try and challenge the inequality within the HE sector?
Whose responsibility do you think this is?

Conclusion

This chapter has outlined the way in which institutional hierarchy serves to legitimise and perpetuate inequality within the HE sector. It has evidenced the way in which students' class background can structure their decision making, positioning the post-92 university as an achievable goal and a safe space, but one which carries significant risks in relation to graduate labour outcomes. The participant narratives which have underpinned discussions in this chapter have revealed that the post-92 environment can be welcoming, inclusive and diverse – a place of educational sanctuary. However, the non-employment related benefits of studying in a post-92 context are largely absent from the dominant discourse around post-92 universities, which commonly depicts them as offering 'second-rate' (Reay, 2018: 10), or 'crap' (Archer *et al.*, 2003), versions of HE.

Current government policy positions social mobility as one of the central goals of recent reforms within the sector, noting that 'higher education can be a powerful engine of social mobility' (BIS, 2011: 54). However, this rhetoric is at odds with marketisation mechanisms such as league tables which legitimise the continued devaluation of both the post-92 experience and degree. This chapter has argued that this devaluation is not only deeply unfair and profoundly inaccurate, but also has consequences for the students who study within these institutions. There is a clear need to challenge the stratification of the HE sector which continues to value some institutions over and above others at a high cost to those who study in 'low status' post-92 institutions. The research study discussed indicates that the post-92 experience is not a second-best form of university study but one that actually offers an important and worthy form of higher education. A system which legitimises privilege and inequality through mechanisms of marketisation, league table position and history is cruel and unfair to students who study in newer institutions. 'Worth' is not, and surely should not be, defined by status.

Summary points

- The 1992 FAHE Act aimed to dissolve the HE binary system by giving polytechnic institutions university status. However, stratification has remained an entrenched feature of the English HE system, and university reputation continues to operate as a proxy for quality. Marketised mechanisms such as league tables perpetuate this issue.
- Currently, universities remain polarised in terms of academic selectivity and the socio-economic make-up of their student bodies. Older 'elite' HEIs maintain high entry requirements and have a greater number of students from advantaged backgrounds, whilst newer post-92 universities have lower entry criteria and more diverse student bodies.
- The type of institution attended has clear implications in terms of graduate employability, with degrees from prestigious HEIs continuing to hold more value than those from less established institutions. Evidence suggests that graduate employers favour students who have attended elite institutions, leaving graduates from newer universities at a disadvantage. This can have a damaging effect on graduates from post-1992 universities and has important implications in terms of social justice.
- This chapter has argued that the hierarchical nature of HE needs to be challenged in order for the inequality which is rooted within the field to really be addressed.

Recommended reading

Bathmaker, A.-M., Ingram, N., Abrahams, J., Hoare, A., Waller, R. and Bradley, H. (2016) *Higher Education, Social Class and Social Mobility: The Degree Generation*. London: Palgrave Macmillan.

Bowers-Brown, T., Ingram, N. and Burke, C. (2019) Higher Education and Aspiration. *International Studies in Sociology of Education*, 28(3–4), pp. 207–214.

Clarke, M. (2017) Rethinking Graduate Employability: The Role of Capital, Individual Attributes and Context. *Studies in Higher Education*, 43(11), pp. 1923–1937.

Stich, A. (2012) *Access to Inequality: Reconsidering Class, Knowledge, and Capital in Higher Education*. Plymouth: Lexington.

References

Archer, L., Hutchings, M. and Ross, A. (2003) *Higher Education and Social Class: Issues of Exclusion and Inclusion*. London: Routledge Falmer.

Ball, S., Reay, D. and David, M. (2002) Ethnic Choosing: Minority Ethnic Students, Social Class and Higher Education Choice. *Race, Ethnicity and Education*, 5(4), pp. 333–357.

Belfield, C., Britton, J., Buscha, F., Dearden, L., Dickson, M., Van der Erve, L., Sibieta, L., Vignoles, A., Walker, I. and Zhu, Y. (2018) *The Relative Labour Market Returns to Different Degrees*. London: Institute for Fiscal Studies.

BIS (2011) *Students at the Heart of the System*. London: The Stationery Office.

BIS (2016) *Higher Education: Success as a Knowledge Economy*. London: The Stationery Office.

Blackman, T. (2017) *The Comprehensive University: An Alternative to Social Stratification by Academic Selection*. Oxford: Higher Education Policy Institute.

Boliver, V. (2015) Are There Distinctive Clusters of Higher and Lower Status Universities in the UK? *Oxford Review of Education*, 41(5), pp. 608–627.

Bourdieu, P. (1986) The Forms of Capital. In: J. Richardson, (Ed.) *Handbook of Theory and Research for the Sociology of Education*. New York: Greenwood.

Bourdieu, P. and Wacquant, L. J. D. (1992) *An Invitation to Reflexive Sociology*. Cambridge: Polity Press.

Brown, P. and Hesketh, A. (2004) *The Mismanagement of Talent: Employability and Jobs in the Knowledge Economy*. Oxford: Oxford University Press.

Brown, P., Lauder, H. and Ashton, D. (2012) *The Global Auction: The Broken Promises of Education, Jobs and Incomes.* Oxford: Oxford University Press.

Brown, R. (2011) The March of the Market. In: M. Molesworth, E. Nixon, and R. Scullion, (Eds.) *The Marketisation of Higher Education and the Student as Consumer.* Abingdon: Routledge.

Cooke, S. (2011) *Perspectives of the Learning Journeys of Students in English Higher Education.* Birmingham: University of Birmingham.

Crew, T. (2015) Beyond Graduation: The Trajectories of Graduates in North Wales. *People, Place and Policy,* 9(1), pp. 29–47.

Harrison, N. (2011) Have the Changes Introduced by the 2004 Higher Education Act made Higher Education Admissions in England Wider and Fairer? *Journal of Educational Policy,* 26(3), pp. 449–468.

Leathwood, C. (2004) A Critique of Institutional Inequalities in Higher Education. *Theory and Research in Education,* 2(1), pp. 31–48.

McCaig, C. (2011) Access Agreements, Widening Participation and Market Positionality: Enabling Student Choice? In: M. Molesworth, R. Scullion, and E. Nixon, (Eds.) *The Marketisation of Higher Education and the Student as Consumer.* Abingdon: Routledge.

Milburn, A. (2012) *University Challenge: How Higher Education Can Advance Social Mobility a Progress Report by the Independent Reviewer on Social Mobility and Child Poverty.* London: Cabinet Office.

O'Leary, J. (2019). Available at: https://www.thetimes.co.uk/article/good-university-guide-in-full-tp6dzs7wn (accessed 18 December 2019).

Ostrove, J. M., Stewart, A. J. and Curtin, N. L. (2011) Social Class and Belonging: Implications for Graduate Students' Career Aspirations. *Journal of Higher Education,* 82(6), pp. 748–774.

Raffe, D. and Croxford, L. (2015) How Stable Is the Stratification of Higher Education in England and Scotland? *British Journal of Sociology of Education,* 36(2), pp. 313–335.

Reay, D. (2018) Working Class Educational Transitions to University: The Limits of Success. *European Journal of Education,* 53(4), pp. 528–540.

Reay, D., Crozier, G. and Clayton, J. (2009) 'Strangers in Paradise?' Working-Class Students in Elite Universities. *Sociology,* 43(6), pp. 1103–1121.

Reay, D., David, M. E. and Ball, S. (2005) *Degrees of Choice: Class, Race, Gender and Higher Education.* Stoke-On-Trent: Trentham Books Limited.

Spiegler, T. and Bednarek, A. (2013) First-Generation Students: What We Ask, What We Know and What It Means: An International Review of the State of Research. *International Studies in Sociology of Education,* 23(1), pp. 318–337.

Stich, A. (2012) *Access to Inequality: Reconsidering Class, Knowledge and Capital in Higher Education.* Plymouth: Lexington.

Strathdee, R. (2009) Reputation in the Sociology of Education. *British Journal of Sociology of Education,* 30(1), pp. 83–96.

3 Transitioning from higher education
Stories from students in a STEM discipline

Sinead D'Silva and Samantha Pugh

Introduction

This chapter is a critical assessment of the context of employability, presented through the lived experiences of young people as they undertake processes of decision-making about their various pathways from a STEM (science, technology, engineering and mathematics) degree to their lives as graduates. It will lay out the context of employability as an agenda in higher education (HE), reinforced through metrics like university rankings and the Teaching Excellence Framework (TEF), and will attempt to locate the student within this discourse. The chapter draws on qualitative research that used Margaret Archer's (2003) theoretical framing of 'Internal Conversations' to make sense of the reflexive actions of individuals as they transitioned from the final year of their physics degree to their life 6 months after graduation. It presents the cases of Tony, whose priority was to return home to the countryside as he was not so bothered about employability; Jane, whose mental health became more important to her over the years and who wanted to choose an ethical career path; and Isaac, who engaged diligently with employability and got a graduate scheme in his desired field.

Through the cases, we find that a uniform employability agenda, although beneficial in some ways, does not incorporate the lifestyle choices and experiences that mould decision-making processes as people make their way through life. Furthermore, it does not ascribe any relationship with the precarious situations in which young people may find themselves. This exciting yet daunting point of transition is misunderstood by policy makers as a linear progression into work directly related to degree discipline, wherein the graduate is assumed to respond to market demands and skill shortages. Instead, the stories individuals share about their transitions from a degree to their lives as graduates are better explained through decision-making processes influenced by personal concerns and subsequent projects and practice. These concerns reflect some of the challenges students, and particularly young people, may face when considering their graduate futures. In presenting these stories, it is hoped that the notion of 'success' as a graduate is critically engaged with and even challenged, as doing so can help confront barriers to seeing young peoples' futures in a range of ways. The chapter intends to encourage those interested in graduate futures to think beyond the 'education to work' linear pathway and embrace the multitude of possible future selves alongside questioning the structural expectations directed at graduates.

Understanding employability and graduate futures

There appears to be a love–hate relationship with the employability agenda in HE in England. On the one hand, it is understood as positive for the individual and society as a whole. It is suggested that it will help promote individual worth based on achievement, social and economic wellbeing (Knight and Yorke, 2004) and will enhance education in learning, teaching and assessment (LTA) practice (Pegg *et al.*, 2012). This view is often based on the belief that skills-focused education begets a capable workforce and citizenry and in turn a stronger economy. In some ways, this perspective over-emphasises the importance of the economy, or rather the 'knowledge economy'. Therefore, on the other hand, there are concerns about endorsing a policy that places stress on a system within which the student is no longer a learner or one who engages with knowledge. Under such a system, students are treated as mere service users accessing a product in the market (Naidoo, 2003), posing a threat to the education system by granting the market power over knowledge, particularly by how the term is discursively framed (Boden and Nedeva, 2010; Dunn 2014). These debates on what appears to be the complexity of graduate futures seem to omit the graduates themselves.

Our concern thus is that the literature on employability has favoured policy, employers and staff notions of how best to understand and respond to graduate futures. It assumes that young people will take paths expected of them by broader structures – and their 'elders' in society. This is evident through acts such as the increase in funding for science subjects to fill a STEM skills gap, or the use of Destination of Leavers from Higher Education (DLHE – now Graduate Outcomes) statistics to act as a proxy for 'employability'. Such a framing places the onus of responding to economic situations on individuals and is often misrepresented as 'choice'.

This approach forgets that individuals possess the ability to negotiate the social world as human beings with constraints and enablements they might have in society and in relation to structures. Simultaneously, critical perspectives that draw on Bourdieu in relation to research on HE in the UK run the risk of treating structural constraints and enablements as deterministic, once again overlooking the individual's agential capacity (Reay, 2004). A key point of departure in thinking of graduate futures can be to locate this as a process of decision-making. Currently, employability is spoken about as being personal to the individual and thus their responsibility, while simultaneously demanding that the individual respond to external demands, particularly seen through policy (Boden and Nedeva, 2010; Brown *et al.*, 2003; Chadha and Toner, 2017; Sin and Neave, 2016). This makes the 'development' of employability rather paradoxical or perhaps a self-fulfilling prophecy. Thus, a shortcoming of graduate employability lies in viewing the transition to postgraduate life as homogenous across graduates. This research employed Archer's (2003) notion of Internal Conversations, which is a processual reflexive negotiation of the social world. That is, everyday decision-making is done through the process of identifying Concerns → Projects → Practice. Furthermore, this rests on the meta-philosophy of Critical Realism, which is ontologically and epistemologically constructed to balance the role of structure and agency in attempts to know the social world. This helps address the aforementioned problems in the structure–agency debate in knowing the social world.

Through this change in perspective, we can begin to view employability as a structure through which students consider how work and their lives around them interact. This perspective is thus more conducive to the development of the graduate sense of self.

Considering contrasting stories

Research was conducted with eight young people as they made their way from the final year of their degree programme to their lives 6 months post-graduation. It considered the various factors that influenced decision-making accounting for changes over time through a longitudinal study at four key points over 14 months. In this section, through three stories, we present the varying priorities each person had and the ways in which they viewed employability and eventually decided on pathways from their degree programme. They all saw their situations as successful, yet only one is seen as the 'correct' way to 'develop' employability, according to perceived wisdom on employability development.

Tony

Tony's pathway was constructed by decision-making that primarily relied on geography – or his desire to return home to the countryside – and serendipitous occurrences in his life. He decided to do a degree in a subject he liked as it would not restrict his options as he was afraid of being tied down to something for the rest of his life:

> *Tony:* It was something I enjoyed doing through A levels and I didn't really know what I wanted to do with my career. So I thought I'd do physics because I enjoy it and it offers a lot of opportunities. So there's plenty of career paths afterwards. I mean when I was coming around the open days a lot of the people I would be talking to would be trying to sell me on going into finance and things like that. And when you think of doing a physics degree you don't think of going into finance so it's just like there's such a broad range of things. [Interview 1]

Being honest about his decision to do a degree while in his final year also enabled Tony to speak about other factors that influenced his decision-making process. A crucial such factor was wanting to return to the countryside:

> *Tony:* I've never really lived in a city, so … I don't know, it's a lot more busy there's a lot more going on. There's always somewhere you can go out and go do something […] It's interesting just having all those options available for things to do. But then it is quite … I don't know. I enjoy the quiet. I don't know if that's because I've been brought up in the countryside but I do enjoy peace and quiet, which you don't get here. [Interview 1]

For Tony, doing a degree was a time dedicated to advanced study and achieving good results in the same. Underlying his concern was a consideration – perhaps inadvertently – of his potential future trajectory. Tony was clear that he did not make attempts to 'enhance' his employability or rather his CV as he wanted to use his time on his degree to learn. Curiously, Tony had in fact been dabbling in teaching experience to see if he would enjoy such work, which shows the embedded nature of employability in degrees. He eventually decided that at this stage in his life he did not want to teach as that too would hold him down. Returning home to ponder his future therefore became a key project for Tony, as perhaps his concern was really a need to consider a future that suited his lifestyle desire – one away from big cities.

It was this dedication to his personal concern, which translated into the practice of focusing on his degree. Simultaneous to this, Tony appeared to know that wanting to 'stay local' was not as unusual a worldview with regards to getting a job as employability often makes it out to be. This is

Table 3.1 Participant trajectories from final year to 6 months after graduation

Person	Career plan at university End semester 1	Career plan at university End Semester 2	Activity on graduating	Status 6 months post-graduation	Home or location prior to university	Location post-university
Tony	Interested in Information and Communications Technology (ICT) and teaching, applied for teaching scheme via career module	Undecided; not looking at jobs, but plans to attend career fair in April	Got a job via friend's father's friend through happenchance meeting at a tearoom (café)	Working on said job – big data SME	East Anglia (Rural)	Home
Isaac	Interested in arms and ammunition, robotics industries – Applying to graduate schemes	Got a graduate scheme offer – accepted in intended industry	6-week research placement at Yorkshire Urban university	Started graduate scheme	North Yorkshire	Greater Manchester
Jane	Academia, applying for Masters	Accepted onto Masters, but unsure of uptake; thinking about health physics	Temporary summer administration job at local pool	Temporary work at hospital; looking into health-related Masters course	Southern English Coast	Home

evident in the way he spoke about getting his job, which he himself seemed slightly unsettled about, given the discourse around the need for employability development at university:

> *Tony:* There wasn't a [formal employment] post, because it wasn't [based on] my work [experience] that I got the job so easily. I figured that they wanted me and for some reason quite badly. It just sort of fell into place; it wasn't anything I did. But I did get it easily so I figured they wanted me as badly as I wanted the job so I was quite at ease, they made me feel at ease about that.
> *Interviewer:* Yeah.
> *Tony:* I did tell you how I got the job right? About meeting in the tearoom so yeah. It was that meeting in the tearoom I think, I sent them 2 e-mails, had a skype call and a phone call, and they sent me a contract, that was all. [Interview 3]

Tony was happy with where he found himself in terms of employment, despite feeling that the future he laid out for himself was not something the employability agenda catered to or viewed favourably. His desire to return home resulted in an outcome that worked well for him and his situation, rather than compliance with a broader agenda to move where discipline-related graduate employment is available. This may not be the pathway that others in similar situations – that is, those coming from the countryside to cities – may opt for, but it worked well for Tony.

Questions for discussion

- What are the ways in which people may experience life differently based on where they grew up, or where they consider home? How might this have an impact on experience at university and transition from it?
- Considering people's futures after a degree, what factors might influence the decision to move away from home to go to university, and then to return?

Isaac

The trajectory taken by Isaac may be viewed as that of the ideal STEM graduate. He engaged with employability in multiple ways, including leading a sports-based society at university, undertaking part-time work, taking up industry-related modules, playing an instrument and engaging with associated employability and careers-related events. He eventually achieved a 2.1 and got onto a graduate scheme in a big defence company.

When asked what he thought about the world of work, Isaac appeared to reflect on what was expected of him by the employer, the language of which seemed to flow easily for him, once again hinting at the assumptions of the need to satisfy employers. He imagined how he might be able to prove his worth to an employer:

> *Isaac:* Um, I think you get encouraged about the degree, for a start. I don't know how many times I've heard the statistic of like, I've forgotten what it is. I think it's like 96 per cent of physics grads are either working or studying six months from graduation. It's like the highest degree. It's the degree that has that percentage as the highest. So that's always an encouraging statistic. [...] People are always saying that physics is a good degree to get employed from. You will

always find something, I think. Um, and then … I just think I've done quite a lot of stuff. Like quite a lot of extra stuff like starting [a sport society], doing part-time work, I think that's the sort of thing they say helps to get you employed. So that kind of boosts my confidence a bit, I think. [Interview 1]

Perhaps it is the case that employability development through degrees focuses on what employers and the market want and thus obscures the expectations of the potential employee. In so doing, the employee is expected to be an individual who sets himself/herself apart from the rest and surprises the potential employer. Simultaneously, they must conform to what the employer wants through not only certain degree qualifications or job requirements but also additional accomplishments, or what are more commonly called 'skills'. What is interesting about Isaac's path is that he went on to undertake an engineering-based role. His physics degree had kept his options wide, but Isaac also chose his degree deliberately as he felt it would add some prestige that he engaged with theoretical rather than practical-focused learning. Isaac was also motivated to do well in his work as he felt he took pride in it. But he also felt a sense of being an imposter in the engineering field. To overcome this, he planned to gain a new qualification to affirm his identity as an engineer:

Isaac: I suppose it would just be a, what's the word, confirmation, it would be a confirmation that I've achieved my goal of becoming an engineer rather than being a physicist. Because yeah so after I'd finished my physics degree I wanted to be an engineer and I've been hired now as an engineer. But I'm obviously not a competent engineer yet because I've just started on a graduate scheme but then when I've finished the scheme I might not necessarily be and then it will just be at some point in my career as an engineer I'll be like a good engineer. And I suppose going through the whole chartership process means there'll be like a defined time, when that happens then I'll know for certain I am now an engineer rather than kind of playing it by ear I suppose. [Interview 4]

Isaac's seemingly straightforward pathway brought no more security than anyone who did not take such a path. Isaac had to consider his future after the graduate scheme while participating in it. It appeared that there was never an end to making oneself relevant, and the possibility for feeling insecure about one's capacities in such a competitive job landscape heightens this feeling. Isaac does have a plan in place to circumvent this, but it reflects expectations outside of the individual that seem to be fixed.

Questions for discussion

- Why might Isaac be described as the 'ideal student' in terms of employability?
- What messages should HE be sending to employers about graduate employment?

Jane

Jane's process of transitioning from a degree incorporated her experience of living with depression while at university. Employability took a back seat in this sense as decision-making was dominated by other concerns. Jane's story bridges the link between personal, social and educational life at university and subsequently on to work.

Narrating her experience of the university over the years, she reflected on some emotional turbulence she went through:

> *Jane:* [In Year One] I was quite shy and I've got a boyfriend and stuff so I just didn't go out that much really. Which was my own fault. But yeah then eventually I came to terms with it and was like 'do I actually want to be doing that?' cause I did it a few times and it always ended badly [laughter] and I thought 'it seems like a waste of time to me' and it just makes me feel a bit shit really, the next day and stuff. Yeah, so eventually I kinda decided that I don't care if I don't live that way, like I've got other things that I enjoy. Um, in second year I just like suffered from depression a little bit, and that affected my study [...] [the year] was so awful, since then I got some medication and sorted myself out a little bit and Third Year has been good. [Interview 1]

This experience of depression made Jane postpone getting straight into a career as she instead focused on getting her degree done and taking up a job – any job – while returning home. Jane had previously doubted her capacity to undertake a job because of her experience of depression during her degree, where her confidence in herself was negatively impacted. A desire to take a pause from the pressures during her degree made her postpone the offers she received for a Master's programme. This defined how she made her decisions and was a concern that was personal to her. In addition to other pressures on young people, they must also consider their own expectations for themselves, which is often obscured. On completing her degree, Jane returned home where she found herself able to recuperate:

> *Jane:* Oh, it's a different era for me [laughter]. I'm like a completely different person, basically, to when I was at university.
> *Interviewer:* How do you mean?
> *Jane:* [...] I'm motivated to get where I want to go, even if it takes a bit longer and actually, I'm glad that it's going to take a bit longer because it means that I get to develop personally and I get to find my own interests within Science that I want to pursue, rather than rushing into finding a career that is going to pay me well or have a future. I'd rather take my time and find something that I actually really care about. [Interview 4]

There was another dimension to Jane's decision to delay deciding on a career path; she had an ethical approach to this process. She wanted to do something that contributed to the wellbeing of society, a view she developed during the course of her degree programme through interacting with social science electives. Combining this and her mental wellbeing, Jane used an approach that was tailored to her needs, one that was slow-paced and reflected her own particular sense of self as a graduate.

Questions for discussion

- What is the role of the university in supporting students' mental health and wellbeing?
- What are the contributing factors to a student's wellbeing during their time at university?
- What might be the effects of delaying deciding on a job or career path? Consider how these may be positive.

Discussion

Through these stories, it becomes evident that the logics of how employers and policy makers consider the futures of young people differ from how young people view their futures for themselves. Instead of the economic rationale, the process of making decisions varies greatly with the experiences people have. As has been demonstrated, even in instances where a linear trajectory has been followed – and perhaps as a result of this – the weaknesses and paradox of developing employability are revealed. That is, while employability is considered something the individual student is responsible for, they are also expected to cater to the expectations of policy makers and employers, which may create conflict with their own expectations for themselves and their lives. Thinking through the stories, there are two key ways in which young people transitioning from a degree might experience this process differently to how it is generally understood.

Awareness of the world around them and expectations of employer demands

Comparing the available literature and policy-based expectations with the stories, it can be suggested that the student is often misunderstood as unidimensional to suit agendas external to them. This does not account for the understanding people have of themselves and their surroundings. Young people appear to often negotiate and renegotiate their thoughts about their futures through employability provision coupled with moments of experience, such as the prolonged impact of Jane's mental health, which made her renegotiate a slower pace for her life; or Isaac's somewhat frantic applying for jobs having learnt of the near-approaching closing dates during a compulsory employability module in his final year. Contrary to policy expectations, individuals make decisions according to their evaluation of the complex world around them, including social, economic and political aspects. This research, and indeed work on employability, has shown how young people are aware of what is required of them by employers for better or worse (Ashley et al., 2015; Moreau and Leathwood, 2006; Tomlinson, 2008). This awareness amongst young people is poorly understood by policy makers, employers themselves and sometimes even universities. Such a view seeps into the practices and communications in the aforementioned structures when making decisions about possible future graduate selves and may omit opportunities for people should they not comply with linear pathways from particular degrees. This also has implications for HE as a failure to acknowledge alternate routes from a degree. Viewing the degree as preparing students primarily for the world of work can have a negative impact on provision (Boden and Nedeva, 2010; Dunn, 2014).

Another way in which young people's awareness of the world around them is sometimes ignored is through the perception of formality as the sole route to 'developing' an employable person. This obscures the social and cultural capitals at play when privilege is reproduced in society, a concern raised by a range of studies on the unequal HE landscape using Bourdieu's conceptual framework of the forms of capitals (Allen et al., 2013; Brown et al., 2016; Kalfa and Taksa, 2015; Reay, 2001; Reay, Crozier, and Clayton, 2010). It also denies a common practice of social life, namely informal interactions. Employability appears to assume only formal provision as enabling employment, while some young people are aware that the reality is not as straightforward. Whether it is being selected for jobs that have not been advertised, learning about specific course options and even gaining temporary work experience, it appears that social networks such as the family are crucial in securing, or supporting the securing of, employment. This was the case for the three participants presented.

Relatedly, given the emphasis placed on 'developing' employability, the stories revealed that young people often had high expectations of themselves in terms of demonstrating such ability and performing effectively at work. They were generally aware of the demands placed on them and so employability was sometimes unconsciously embedded in their actions. Yet, although young people may progress onto a graduate scheme, most schemes run for 2 years, and afterwards the individual must be prepared either for the uncertainty of not being offered a contract, or to ask themselves whether they are willing to stay on with their current employment. Here, we must ask what effect has on people, and the implications of a precarious work future. Thus, people begin to identify alternatives to an expected trajectory from their degree discipline. With more people getting degrees, young people may feel that it is now necessary to have a degree to be able to access jobs. There may, therefore, be many who do not intend to continue onto a path defined by their degree. This was evident in the current research in the way young people reflected on their options. For example, physics was undertaken because of the breadth of options for graduates, and, in the case of Jane and Isaac, it also held an unspoken quality of being a theoretically demanding degree and superior to other sciences.

The role of lifestyle choices and experiences

In this section, the factors are less structurally implicated than those mentioned in the previous section, though they are nevertheless impacted by external factors. Personal motivation and lifestyle choice are more important in employment and career futures than is recognised in the wider literature. Students do not view university solely as a means to an economic end but also seek to relate their selves and personalities to what they do in terms of their futures (Tomlinson, 2016). Often, people consider their citizenry, lifestyle and future selves as important and not limited to careers, such as in the case of Jane, who saw education as fulfilling a higher purpose. Therefore, although people live individualised lives, within the constraints and enablements of the existing capitalist system potentially reproducing power relations in society, they nonetheless transform, and are transformed by, the world around them. These interactions take place in many ways. For instance, in engaging with 'other' activities – co-curricular and extra-curricular – students could potentially help influence their graduate prospects (as in Tomlinson, 2008). Yet participants did not undertake them primarily to influence their employment prospects, as a majority of studies tend to assume, but rather as attempts to socialise, or as an opportunity to try new activities or hobbies. Considerations that such activities make one more employable were seen as secondary, or a bonus. Rather than harnessing this to improve notions of citizenship, to which HE arguably ought to contribute, the time spent at university is misunderstood as a manufacturing warehouse, with various appendages of employment-readiness being attached to students. Universities need to move away from functioning as 'bubbles' and work as structures that enable interaction with wider populations and create an active citizenry (Holton, 2015a; Reay, Crozier and Clayton, 2009).

Another way in which experience influences decision-making is through people's emotional relationship with geographies and their expectations for themselves. This research focused on graduate prospects in terms of decision-making about employment and career futures. However, it is evident that in many cases, geography was a factor influencing graduate prospects. That means it was not just about finding the right job, but also achieving personal fulfilment regarding location. While the role of geography has been discussed previously in the process of leaving home to go to university (Donnelly and Gamsu, 2018; Duke-Williams, 2009; Holdsworth, 2009; Holton and Riley, 2013) as well as potential immobility in this regard (Hinton, 2011; Holton, 2015b), there is little to no work on the role of geography in transitions from a degree, whether to work or otherwise. This research is a starting point that presents such a practice.

Conclusion

Uncertainty has become an internalised aspect of everyday life, and complies with Archer's (2003) argument that late modernity forces the individual to be perpetually reflexive. As a result, and given continued labour-market changes, it would be disingenuous to consider uptake of employment as solely determined by job availability. Each of the participants' lives shows that it is not possible to supply a one-size-fits-all approach to education and employability. These young people had plans for their lives which subtly incorporated this insecurity. This stands in contrast to the idea of a linear trajectory to work that HE and policy appear to assume, according to literature on the same and relevant documents.

As we consider looking forward, it is imperative to sustain a critique of the ways in which policy is implemented and constructed. According to Brooks (2018), who offers a critique of academic work on how policy understands students, the recent construction of policy verges on a more sinister treatment of students that co-opts the vocabulary of vulnerability and paternalistic caring and becomes part of how policy is structured in the UK. It very much buys into the social justice vocabulary, though with little to no intended change towards social justice. In this way, in order to confront the issue of employability, and arguably issues relating to HE, it is helpful to maintain a balance between considering the impact of structure and actor. Once again, it is necessary to confront policies on their objectives within their contexts, their intended consequences and how they are experienced, all while maintaining a critique of the very purpose and role of HE in society.

Summary points

- Young people make decisions through a consideration of their own situations. They must be supported to think through them rather than having trajectories prescribed for them.
- The accountability of job access cannot be solely placed on young people and universities; not only are there additional personal concerns and lifestyle choices associated with future trajectories, but employers too have a defining role in these outcomes.
- There is no definite linear trajectory from a degree as people may choose a common-sense pathway or opt for a range of other options. It is important to approach these different trajectories with equal support.

Recommended reading

Burke, C. and Christie, F. (Eds.) (2018) *Graduate Careers in Context: Research, Policy and Practice*. Abingdon: Routledge.

D'Silva, S. and Pugh, S.L. (2020) Understanding the Factors that Can Influence Student Career Decision Making. *Prospects Luminate*. Available at: https://luminate.prospects.ac.uk/understanding-the-factors-that-can-influence-student-career-decision-making (Accessed 19 February 2020).

Hordósy, R. and Clark, T. (2018) 'It's Scary and It's Big, and There's No Job Security': Undergraduate Experiences of Career Planning and Stratification in an English Red Brick University. *Social Sciences*, 7(10), pp. 173–93.

Pegg, A., Waldock, J., Hendy-Isaac, S. and Lawton, R. (2012) *Pedagogy for Employability*. York, UK: Higher Education Academy.

References

Allen, K., Quinn, J., Hollingworth, S. and Rose, A. (2013) Becoming Employable Students and 'Ideal' Creative Workers: Exclusion and Inequality in Higher Education Work Placements. *British Journal of Sociology of Education*, 34(3), pp. 431–52.

Archer, M. (2003) *Structure, Agency and the Internal Conversation*. Cambridge: CUP.

Ashley, L., Duberley, J., Sommerlad, H. and Scholarios, D. (2015) *A Qualitative Evaluation of Non-Educational Barriers to the Elite Professions*. London: Social Mobility and Child Poverty Commission.

Boden, R. and Nedeva, M. (2010) Employing Discourse: Universities and Graduate Employability. *Journal of Education Policy*, 25(1), pp. 37–54.

Brooks, R. (2018) The Construction of Higher Education Students in English Policy Documents. *British Journal of Sociology of Education*, 39(6), pp. 745–61.

Brown, P., Hesketh, A. and Williams, S. (2003) Employability in a Knowledge-Driven Economy. *Journal of Education and Work*, 16(2), pp. 107–26.

Brown, P., Power, S., Tholen, G. and Allouch, A. (2016) Credentials, Talent and Cultural Capital: A Comparative Study of Educational Elites in England and France. *British Journal of Sociology of Education*, 37(2), pp. 191–211.

Chadha, D. and Toner, J. (2017) Focusing in on Employability: Using Content Analysis to Explore the Employability Discourse in UK and USA Universities. *International Journal of Educational Technology in Higher Education*, 14(33), pp. 1–26.

Donnelly, M. and Gamsu, S. (2018) Regional Structures of Feeling? A Spatially and Socially Differentiated Analysis of UK Student Im/mobility. *British Journal of Sociology of Education*, 39(7), pp. 961–81.

Duke-Williams, O. (2009) The Geographies of Student Migration in the UK. *Environment and Planning*, 41(8), pp. 1826–48.

Dunn, B. (2014) Skills, Credentials and Their Unequal Reward in a Heterogeneous Global Political Economy. *Journal of Sociology*, 50(3), pp. 349–67.

Hinton, D. (2011) 'Wales Is My Home': Higher Education Aspirations and Student Mobilities in Wales. *Children's Geographies*, 9(1), pp. 23–34.

Holdsworth, C. (2009) 'Going Away to Uni': Mobility, Modernity and Independence of English Higher Education Students. *Environment and Planning*, 41(8), pp. 1849–64.

Holton, M. (2015a) Adapting Relationships with Place: Investigating the Evolving Place Attachment and 'Sense of Place' of UK Higher Education Students During a Period of Intense Transition. *Geoforum*, 59, pp. 21–9.

Holton, M. (2015b) 'I Already Know the City, I Don't Have to Explore It': Adjustments to 'Sense of Place' for 'Local' UK University Students. *Population, Space and Place*, 21(8), pp. 820–31.

Holton, M. and Riley, M. (2013) Student Geographies: Exploring the Diverse Geographies of Students and Higher Education. *Geography Compass*, 7(1), pp. 61–74.

Kalfa, S. and Taksa, L. (2015) Cultural Capital in Business Higher Education: Reconsidering the Graduate Attributes Movement and the Focus on Employability. *Studies in Higher Education*, 40(4), pp. 580–95.

Knight, P. and Yorke, M. (2004) *Learning, Curriculum and Employability in Higher Education*. Abingdon: Routledge.

Moreau, M. and Leathwood, C. (2006) Graduates' Employment and the Discourse of Employability: A Critical Analysis. *Journal of Education and Work*, 19(4), pp. 305–24.

Naidoo, R. (2003) Repositioning Higher Education as a Global Commodity: Opportunities and Challenges for Future Sociology of Education Work. *British Journal of Sociology of Education*, 24(2), pp. 249–59.

Pegg, A., Waldock, J., Hendy-Isaac, S. and Lawton, R. (2012) Pedagogy for Employability. *Higher Education Bulletin*, 1, pp. 1–58.

Reay, D. (2001) Finding or Losing Yourself? Working-Class Relationships to Education. *Journal of Education Policy*, 16(4), pp. 333–46.

Reay, D. (2004) 'It's All Becoming a Habitus': Beyond the Habitual Use of Habitus in Educational Research. *British Journal of Sociology of Education*, 25(4), pp. 431–44.

Reay, D., Crozier, G. and Clayton, J. (2009) 'Strangers in Paradise'? Working-Class Students in Elite Universities. *Sociology*, 43(6), pp. 1103–21.

Reay, D., Crozier, G.. and Clayton, J. (2010) 'Fitting in' or 'Standing Out': Working-Class Students in UK Higher Education. *British Educational Research Journal*, 36(1), pp. 107–24.

Sin, C. and Neave, G. (2016) Employability Deconstructed: Perceptions of Bologna Stakeholders. *Studies in Higher Education*, 41(8), pp. 1447–62.

Tomlinson, M. (2008) 'The Degree Is Not Enough': Students' Perceptions of the Role of Higher Education Credentials for Graduate Work and Employability. *British Journal of Sociology of Education*, 29(1), pp. 49–61.

Tomlinson, M. (2016) Student Perceptions of Themselves as 'Consumers' of Higher Education. *British Journal of Sociology of Education*, 38(4), pp. 450–67.

4 'Academics online'

Self-promotion, competition and celebrification

Brendan Bartram

Introduction

As discussed in the introduction, change has always been a fundamental and pervasive feature of higher education (HE), though few would dispute that the last two decades have been particularly characterised by an increase in both the speed and number of changes the sector has seen. Technological developments have, of course, been central to many of these changes, and one particular technological innovation relates to the proliferation and spread of academic social media – digital platforms that allow university researchers and lecturers to present themselves and their work online. Ubiquitous brands like Facebook, Twitter, Academia.Edu and ResearchGate are commonly and increasingly used by academics around the globe to curate an online presence (Lupton, 2014). A relatively small number of studies have examined this phenomenon of online academic self-presentation (OASP). Those that have tend to explore the extent of uptake and the perceived benefits and challenges entailed. Lupton's (2014) study is in fact one of few to explore academics' views on the varied affordances and problems associated with OASP. Key benefits identified by the participants included broadening their academic networks, disseminating and sharing research easily and quickly, and accessing and providing support to colleagues with similar interests. The challenges noted were equally wide-ranging, varying from concerns about privacy and the blurring of professional and personal boundaries, to the time-consuming nature of curating an online presence and the perception of obligation that was contributing to intensified work pressures as digital public engagement becomes an additional professional expectation. Many of the participants echoed how these pressures may be felt more acutely by early-career and temporary staff aware of the need to survive in an increasingly competitive domain. One participant acknowledged the role of the broader neo-liberal climate in this respect, and its effects:

> We are the perfect neo-liberal subjects, eager to take on more work (i.e. work about work) to succeed. We have simply internalized labor, and social media propel that predatory, self-inflicted affliction.
>
> (p. 27)

This chapter intends to offer a critical discussion of this less explored dimension – specifically, the ways in which broader socio-cultural factors articulate with pervasive neo-liberal influences on HE to explain and understand the expansion of online academic self-presentation. It begins with an exploration of the relationship between OASP and contemporary social trends, before moving on to examine how neo-liberal forms of competition in the academy become entwined with self-promotional tendencies influenced by celebrity culture.

Question for discussion

- To what extent do you agree with the advantages and disadvantages identified above, and can you think of further ones?

OASP and social trends

As suggested, the increasing dominance of the internet (David Marshall, 2010) – and the proliferation of new social media technologies that afford increased means of presenting ourselves to the wider world – is an obvious part of the explanation for the growth in OASP. It is now almost 20 years since Castells first discussed the relationship between the internet and network society:

> the internet is the fabric of our lives. If information technology is the present-day equivalent of electricity in the industrial era, in our age the internet could be linked to both the electrical grid and the electric engine because of its ability to distribute the power of information throughout the entire realm of human activity. Furthermore, as new technologies of energy generation and distribution made possible the factory and the large corporation as the organizational foundation of industrial society, the internet is the technological basis for the organizational form of the Information Age: the network. (Castells, 2001:1)

Curating our network presence has thus become firmly embedded in broader social trends towards increased online self-presentation, as all of us engage more and more with connective technologies in all areas of our lives. Facebook, Twitter, YouTube, LinkedIn and the plethora of dating sites have normalised and increased our opportunities to present, perform and promote our professional, social, cultural and sexual identities online. David Marshall argues that we have in fact now reached the point where 'the public self is constantly worked upon and updated in its online form to both maintain its currency and to acknowledge its centrality to the individual's identity, which is dependent upon its network of connections to sustain the life of the on-line persona' (2010: 42). Van Dijck echoes this idea, pointing out that platforms such as Facebook and LinkedIn have 'pushed the art and science of mass self-communication to a new level' (2013:210). This idea of a new level is arguably reflected in the use of the term 'post-digital' by Jandrić et al. (2018:893) to imply a certain redundancy in continued binary divisions of on- and offline realities:

> We are increasingly no longer in a world where digital technology and media is separate, virtual, 'other' to a 'natural' human and social life. This has inspired the emergence of a new concept – ' the postdigital' – which is slowly but surely gaining traction in a wide range of disciplines.

In this sense, it could be argued that the internet has not simply enabled new means of self-presentation and promotion, but has also begun to reshape these notions and, perhaps as importantly, to reshape social expectations of our behaviour in this domain. Several psychological studies see our online presentations and performances simply as extensions of basic human needs to make good impressions on other people 'by drawing others' attention to one's strengths, accomplishments and importance' (den Hartog *et al.*, 2018: 2). Den Hartog *et al.* and several other studies (e.g. Hart *et al.*, 2016) have pointed out that these needs will be experienced more acutely by certain personality types, with narcissists particularly inclined to engage in online self-promoting activities. Taylor and Strutton (2016) present evidence to support this, reporting a correlation between high Facebook usage and strong narcissistic traits, for example, with higher usage leading to amplified desires for online self-promotion. Stepping aside from the narcissistic angle, Goffman's theory of self-performance (1959) provides a useful lens for examining online self-presentation. His model highlights a tri-partite set of discursive needs – expressive, communicative and promotional – and it is easy to see how all of these needs can be as easily accommodated by our online presentations as through our face-to-face interactions.

As such, then, OASP can be located within a view of fundamental human needs that may naturally be stronger among certain individuals, and which may in general have been heightened by the widespread availability of new media technologies that encourage us to engage more in forms of online self-presentation. Given the focus of this chapter specifically on online *academic* self-presentation, however, it is worth considering what the literature reveals about the extent to which HE itself may be partly responsible for promoting this growth.

The neo-liberalised university – competition, managerialism and performativity

With regard to understanding OASP, Barbour and Marshall (2012) offer a five-fold categorisation of online academic selves or performances. These are described as:

- the formal self;
- the networked self;
- the comprehensive self;
- the teaching self;
- the uncontainable self.

The formal self concerns the non-interactive self-representation often displayed on institutional websites; the networked self is a more interactive performance often involving academic blogs, for example; the comprehensive self-integrates both academic and more personal online self-presentations. Hammarfelt *et al.* (2016) comment that while these three 'selves' potentially reach a large and diverse audience, the presentation of teaching selves tends to be aimed specifically at pedagogic interactions with students. The final category relates to academics who choose not to engage with forms of OASP and thus run the risk of incurring 'an uncontainable self' as they exercise limited control over how their online academic identity is displayed. Hammarfelt *et al.* (2016:2–3) suggest an additional category which they term 'the quantified academic self':

> This self-representation focuses on achievement, reputation and reach, and is interactive, extra-institutional, and primarily directed towards an academic audience (narrowcast). It focuses on professional accomplishment, which makes it different from the comprehensive self, and

research is the main focus, not teaching. The construction of the quantified self is best described as semi-automated; profiles are usually, but not always, created by researchers themselves but algorithms automatically collect data on publications, citations, and social media mentions from several platforms.

This particular self-representation resonates throughout the literature, where it is frequently tethered to discussions of the neo-liberalised university, and the ways in which it creates a climate that drives ever greater OASP. Various authors discuss the many and varied forms of competition pervading contemporary higher education. Naidoo (2018:1) suggests universities are now 'locked in a competition fetish', as they struggle for positional advantage in a system characterised by status wars and competitive mechanisms. Though she acknowledges that academic rivalry is far from a novel concept, Naidoo argues that recent reforms and policies have elevated forms of competition to new heights – institutions compete for status and influence in a context where 'the transformation of HE into a global commodity has resulted in HE itself becoming an industry for revenue generation' (4). The rise of excellence policies and rankings has served further to intensify these competitive market pressures, and an audit culture has ensued to gauge and monitor influence and position. Lund (2018:1–2) sums up the effect of this situation:

> The market-like dynamics shaping academic culture have, it would seem, instigated a form of perpetual competition where the aim is not to maximise human potential, but to gain advantage over others.

Such arguments highlight the central role of performativity in this audit culture. Ball (2012: 19) defines performativity as

> a powerful and insidious policy technology that is now at work at all levels and in all kinds of education and public service, a technology that links effort, values, purposes and self-understanding to measures and comparisons of output. Within the rigours and disciplines of performativity we are required to spend increasing amounts of our time in making ourselves accountable, reporting on what we do rather than doing it.

Duffy and Pooley (2017:1) discuss how increased labour market precarity in a progressively market-driven HE context only adds to these performative pressures, amplifying the needs of individual lecturers to engage in self-promotional practices. The authors discuss the sharp rise of academic social media and suggest that this expansion reflects and drives the self-branding imperatives many academics experience and engage in. Echoing Ball's analysis of performativity, they identify the articulation between the surrounding competitive climate and individual academic behaviour. Again, referring specifically to Academia.edu, they describe how:

> the site's fixation on analytics reinforces a culture of incessant self-monitoring – one already encouraged by university policies to measure quantifiable impact.

(1)

As suggested in the introduction, these pressures are potentially experienced more acutely by younger and less experienced academics who have not yet been able to build the reputational ballast required for cementing their ambitions in this fiercely competitive climate. However, as Jandrić (2014:299) comments, even more established professionals are rarely entirely safe in this environment:

> In the world of global precarious academia, where obtaining a tenured university position is equal to winning a medium-prized lottery, there are hundreds of people hungry for my position. I know exactly who they are – up to very recently, I was one of them. I must tick more boxes than they do, or I will be replaced.

Pressure to demonstrate 'impact' has of course become a prominent theme in HE research, particularly in the UK, where it is one of the guiding principles behind the research assessment methodology employed in the national REF (Research Excellence Framework) evaluation. Naidoo (2018:4) explains how UK institutions are now required 'to demonstrate the "impact" of their research beyond academia'. The concept has thus firmly embedded itself within 'the metric tide' (Wilsdon *et al.*, 2015) that has overwhelmed the HE zeitgeist, and academic social media only 'amplify and accelerate the logic of self-branding among scholars' (Duffy and Pooley, 2017:2) – scholars who are ever more mindful of their need to demonstrate and measure their individual impact in a system which demands and defines output as 'measurable deliverables' (Luka *et al.*, 2015:181). In this sense, many academic social media sites offer sets of easily quantifiable features by displaying how many papers an academic has produced, how many times they have been read/downloaded/cited and the number of fellow academics who follow their work. Such measures serve once again to embed 'an economization of subjectivity where the self ... becomes part of an entrepreneurial logic' (Scharff, 2015: 110) – a logic which perhaps reinforces pressures towards self-promoting gaming in the political economy of academic popularity. Hammarfelt *et al.* (2016:1) discuss this gaming logic, noting again how the various points and score systems displayed on many academic platforms explicitly encourage 'the gamification of quantified academic selves', in the process intensifying and commodifying 'the competitive nature of scholarship ... and academic outputs', and potentially leading to 'goal displacement and cheating'.

Lund's work (20182) certainly supports the above accounts. She argues that the competitive context described above not only heightens the needs academics experience to present and promote themselves and their work, but also normalises academic boasting – 'boasting can be considered a central driving force in neo-liberal universities .... Boasting is an increasingly visible, encouraged and expected practice in contemporary academic life, shaping the ways in which academics present themselves and interact'.

These practices may be further promoted by what some commentators refer to as the *network effect*. Boudreau and Jeppesen (2015) discuss the concept of online networks as business platforms whose value increases in proportion to network size; in other words, the more users or 'complementors' (buyers and sellers) a network has, the greater its collective value for all, and the greater the incentives to assert an online presence. This conceptualisation is clearly anchored in a business ontology and resonates strongly with ideas which are central to this chapter. The authors acknowledge this in their own discussion of networks which may not be explicitly commercial. When considering motivations for network engagement outside of business environments, they explain that

> signaling and reputational motivations – as when individuals signal capabilities through their work activity, outputs, and accolades ... are a plausible driver of mounting investments and

development activity as platforms grow larger. This is because greater numbers of platform participants provide a larger audience to which complementors may signal, and potentially greater incentives to do so. (1761)

However, they also recognise that network expansion may sometimes only further amplify challenges to 'stand out' in the already crowded market-place:

We theorize that … platform growth will face an opposing negative effect, as many independent, competing complementors will vie for limited attention and any one signal may degenerate with growing noise and confusion. (1762)

Question for discussion

- One of the key arguments above is that academic social media intensify the competitive climate in HE – is there a case for arguing that this is beneficial in any way at all?

When competition and celebrity collide

The suggestion thus in much of the literature is that the current HE context is not only responsible for increasing OASP, but that it also potentially – relating to Goffman's theory of self-presentation – elevates self-promotional needs over expressive and communicative ones. Fullick (2013:546) concurs, arguing that 'self-presentation reinforces and re-inscribes the tendency toward promotionalism that permeates contemporary economic, cultural, and social life'. The literature suggests that these pressures to self-promote might be further increased by a convergence of the competitive turn and what might be described as the 'celebrity turn': individual needs to demonstrate professional impact driven by corporate esteem imperatives collide with increased socio-cultural appetites for individualised attention and 'fame'. Cashmore (2006) identifies this close articulation between market and celebrity culture. Through this lens, the academic thus becomes a self-commoditising producer and product, hungry to demonstrate and publicise their professional worth and status. Several authors highlight how 'these changes in the culture, economics and technologies of university life help to explain the new prominence of celebrity/academic co-mingling' (Duffy and Pooley, 2017:3). Driessens (2013:3) suggests that this convergence is unsurprising since 'celebrity has become a defining characteristic of our mediatized societies'. He discusses the concept of 'celebrification', a process which increasingly sees ordinary people transformed into celebrities. He uses the term 'academostars' (p.5) to denote this process among academics. This concept is reiterated widely across the reading; Smyth (2017) refers to the emergence of 'academic rockstars', for example, while Brøgger (2016) notes the thrill of fame academics experience from OASP. Furedi (2010:493) discusses the ascendancy of celebrity culture in highly critical terms, describing how 'even the ivory tower of higher education has been brought into the frame. Universities are encouraged to embrace this culture and the shameless self-promoter has been rebranded as a celebrity academic'. David Marshall (2010:45) explains how online celebrity culture plays a particularly important role in fostering powerful representational regimes that 'articulate a way of thinking about individuality and producing the self through the public world' that have gained strong traction.

One aspect of this discussed to some degree in the reading concerns how this culture of academic self-promotion relates to issues of class and gender. Several studies suggest a strongly gendered dimension, with men more likely to engage in OASP. Duffy and Pooley (2017) suggest that this relates to broader social norms that mean men are more inclined to engage in self-promoting activities and self-aggrandisement. This is supported by Scharff's (2015:109) study which found women much more reluctant to self-promote because it was perceived to 'conflict with normative expectations that women are nice and modest and gives rise to dilemmas in the performance of femininity'. Lund's (2018) work also suggests that self-promotion and boasting are connected to the performance of what she describes as a global masculinity – competitive, successful, dominant and institutionally desirable. From a class perspective, Reay's (2015:14) work raises interesting questions about the extent to which social background might also strengthen the need for assertive self-promotion:

> Even if you are a supposedly middle-class academic, you are still having to guard against this devaluation. You risk being seen less of a scholar, and certainly less of an intellectual if you have tried to hold on to your working class habitus too overtly. For those of us uneasy hybrids who have ended up in academia, there is always hyper-vigilance, and a constant watching out for danger – we have become over-adrenalised academics.

Conclusion

Clearly, the discussion here will be challenged by some for taking a rather critical view of something that in many ways is, of course, a very positive technological advancement. I acknowledge this perspective and the many benefits offered by the online digital platforms mentioned throughout this chapter. I should also declare my personal enthusiasm for aspects of OASP, and I recognise the ways in which I too have benefitted from sharing my own work online and accessing that of others. In short, the usefulness of OASP is not in question, and as a phenomenon, OASP is unquestionably here to stay, embedded within modern social practices that reinforce our online digital habits and enable our identity performances. As many studies have suggested, OASP enables us to fulfil basic human needs for self-expression, communication and connection. However, as this discussion has also illustrated, it is difficult to ignore a pressing need for further reflection and research on the ways in which OASP appears to be increasingly tethered to neo-liberal influences that position it – and indeed, us – within a potentially corrosive amalgam of individually and collectively competitive status pressures. In a sense, OASP risks becoming an arena that resembles a performative panopticon, with 'over-adrenalised players/actors' locked in an endlessly competitive cycle of mutual viewing, surveillance and display. As one of the participants in Lupton's (2014: 27) study suggested, it is important that we further scrutinise OASP to control its potential for becoming a 'predatory, self-inflicted affliction', as individual gains become enmeshed in institutional status wars and game-playing – all the more so when, as discussed above, issues of career stage, class, gender and potentially race may mean the playing field is decidedly uneven.

Summary points

- Recent years have seen the proliferation of academic social media – digital platforms that allow academics to present themselves and their work online.

- While they offer many benefits for individual academics and institutions, there are a number of more problematic issues associated with their use.
- Many studies suggest that growing pressure on academics to promote their work is heightened by the competitive nature of contemporary HE policy. These neo-liberal pressures may be further amplified by the nature of the mediatised societies we now live in.

Questions for discussion

- What are your own views on the relationship between academic social media and issues of race, class and gender?
- If you were to carry out some research on this topic, can you think of a suitable angle, title and set of underpinning research questions?

Recommended reading

Jordan, K. (2019) From Social Networks to Publishing Platforms: A Review of the History and Scholarship of Academic Social Network Sites. *Frontiers in Digital Humanities.* Available at: https://www.frontiersin.org/articles/10.3389/fdigh.2019.00005/full (accessed 27 February 2020).

Rasmussen Neal, D. (2012) *Social Media for Academics: A Practical Guide.* London: Chandos Publishing.

References

Ball, S. (2012) Performativity, Commodification and Commitment: An I-Spy Guide to the Neoliberal University. *British Journal of Education Studies*, 60(1), pp. 17–28.

Barbour, K. and Marshall, D. (2012) The Academic Online: Constructing Persona Through the World Wide Web. *First Monday*, 17(9). Available at: https://firstmonday.org/ojs/index.php/fm/article/download/3969/3292doi:10.5210/fm.v0i0.3969 (accessed 27 February 2020).

Boudreau, K. and Jeppesen, L. (2015) Unpaid Crowd Complementors: The Platform Network Effect Mirage. *Strategic Management Journal*, 36(12), pp. 1761–1777.

Brøgger, K. (2016) The Rule of Mimetic Desire in Higher Education: Governing Through Naming, Shaming and Faming. *British Journal of Sociology of Education*, 37(1), pp. 72–91.

Cashmore, E. (2006) *Celebrity Culture.* Abingdon: Routledge.

Castells, M. (2001) *The Internet Galaxy: Reflections on the Internet, Business, and Society.* Oxford, UK: Oxford University Press.

David Marshall, P. (2010) The Presentation and Promotion of the Self: Celebrity as Marker of Presentational Media. *Celebrity Studies*, 1(1), pp. 35–48.

Den Hartog, D., De Hoogh, A. and Belschak, F. (2018) Toot Your Own Horn? Leader Narcissism and the Effectiveness of Employee Self-Promotion. *Journal of Management*, 46(2), pp. 261–286.

Driessens, O. (2013) The Celebritization of Society and Culture: Understanding the Structural Dynamics of Celebrity Culture. *International Journal of Cultural Studies*, 16(6), pp. 641–657.

Duffy, B. and Pooley, J. (2017) 'Facebook for Academics': The Convergence of Self-Branding and Social Media Logic on Academia.Edu. *Social Media and Society*, 3(1), pp.1–11.

Fullick, M. (2013) 'Gendering' the Self in Online Dating Discourse. *Canadian Journal of Communication*, 38(4), pp. 545–562.

Furedi, F. (2010) Celebrity Culture. *Society*, 47(6), pp. 493–497.

Goffman, E. (1959) *The Presentation of Self in Everyday Life.* New York: Anchor Books.

Hammarfelt, B., de Rijcke, S. and Rushforth, A. (2016) Quantified Academic Selves: The Gamification of Research Through Social Networking Services. *Information Research*, 21(2), pp. 1–13.

Hart, W., Adams, J. A. and Burton, K. A. (2016) Narcissistic for the People: Narcissists and Non-Narcissists Disagree About How to Make a Good Impression. *Personality and Individual Differences*, 91, pp. 69–73.

Jandrić, P. (2014) If You Can't Beat Them, Join Them. In: Giroux, D. and Karmis, D. (eds), *Défaire Refaire L'Université Essai de Tout Dire.* Quebec: Les Cahiers de l' Idiotie, pp. 294–303.

Jandrić, P., Knox, J., Besley, T., Ryberg, T., Suoranta, J. and Hayes, S. (2018) Postdigital Science and Education. *Educational Philosophy and Theory*, 50(10), pp. 893–899.

Luka, M., Harvey, A., Hogan, M., Shepherd, T.. and Zeffiro, A. (2015) Scholarship as Cultural Production in the Neoliberal University: Working Within and Against Deliverables. *Studies in Social Justice*, 9(2), pp. 176–196.

Lund, R. (2018) The Social Organisation of Boasting in the Neoliberal University. *Gender and Education*. Available at: https//:doi: 10.1080/09540253.2018.1482412 (accessed 27 February 2020).

Lupton, D. (2014) 'Feeling Better Connected': Academics' Use of Social Media. *News and Media Research Centre*. Canberra: University of Canberra.

Naidoo, R. (2018) The Competition Fetish in Higher Education: Shamans, Mind Snares and Consequences. *European Educational Research Journal*. Available at: https://doi.org/10.1177/1474904118784839 (accessed 27 February 2020).

Reay, D. (2015) A Working-Class Hero is Still Something To Be: Problematising Social Mobility. Available at: https://www.academia.edu/13647866/A_Working_class_Hero_is_still_something_to_be_Problematising_Social_Mobility (accessed 27 February, 2020).

Scharff, C. (2015) Blowing Your Own Trumpet: Exploring the Gendered Dynamics of Self-Promotion in the Classical Music Profession. *The Sociological Review*, 62(1), pp. 97–112.

Smyth, J. (2017) *The Toxic University – Zombie Leadership, Academic Rockstars and Neoliberal Ideology*. London: Palgrave.

Taylor, D. and Strutton, D. (2016) 'Does Facebook Usage Lead to Conspicuous Consumption?' The Role of Envy, Narcissism and Self-Promotion. *Journal of Research in Interactive Marketing*, 10(3), pp. 231–248.

Van Dijck, J. (2013) 'You Have One Identity': Performing the Self on Facebook and LinkedIn. *Media, Culture and Society*, 35(2), pp. 199–215.

Wilsdon, J., Allen, L., Belfiore, E., Campbell, P., Curry, S., Hill, S. and Johnson, B. (2015) *The Metric Tide: Report of the Independent Review of the Role of Metrics in Research Assessment and Management*. London: HEFCE.

5   Higher standards and better-informed students or false promises and 'gaming' the system?

Competition, metrics and the consumerisation of students in UK higher education

Mark Elliot

Introduction

One of the most prominent contemporary issues in higher education (HE) in the UK has been the emergence of the student as consumer. HE policy in the UK since the Browne Review (2010) has recast students as consumers of educational services, with universities redefined as service providers. Those responsible for such policies claim that this approach will enhance both the performance of universities and the educational experience of students (BIS, 2011). A commitment to market competition and the use of performance metrics are two key constituents of neoliberalism. In recent times, UK HE has arguably been dominated by neoliberal reforms promoting both competition and the use of performance metrics. In 2011, the coalition government simultaneously reduced the block grant to universities and increased tuition fees to a maximum of £9,000 (BIS, 2011), thus increasing competition between universities in recruiting students. In addition, the management of HE in the UK is now dominated by the use of metrics to measure performance. The reliance on metrics has increased recently after the introduction of the Teaching Excellence Framework (TEF) in 2017. This chapter aims to explore how the use of competition and performance metrics in UK HE have contributed to the emergence of the student as consumer and how critics argue that these developments may have had damaging consequences for students and for HE as a whole. Finally, alternatives to the student-as-consumer model are considered.

The wider higher education context

The emergence of the phenomenon of student as consumer has taken place within the broader historical context of a reconceptualisation of the role of HE itself (Naidoo and Williams, 2015 and Ward in this volume). Since the mid-twentieth century there has been a gradual move away from conceiving of HE as a public good that is worthy of public funding, towards a conception of HE as a primarily economic private good through which individuals can improve their position in the labour market (Williams, 2016). For example, the Robbins Report (1963) can be interpreted as conceiving of HE for the first time as an economic good rather than a cultural public good (Williams, 2016), and Prime Minister James Callaghan questioned the role of HE as a public good in the late 1970s

(Macfarlane, 2015). As Naidoo and Williams (2015:209) put it, 'there has been a shift from HE as a collective good to a conception of HE as a private good conferring benefit chiefly upon individuals who are expected to contribute to its costs'.

The reconceptualisation of students as consumers is often attributed to the neoliberal policies of Margaret Thatcher's governments from 1979 onwards (Macfarlane, 2015). However, it can be argued that this process started much earlier. The term 'student as consumer' was used as early as 1969, and the subject received some investigation from HE scholars in the 1960s (Macfarlane, 2015). Nevertheless, the student-as-consumer phenomenon has gained particular momentum since the Browne Review (2010) paved the way for universities to charge students tuition fees of up to £9,000 per year. Subsequent HE policy (BIS, 2011) explicitly referred to students as 'customers' or 'consumers', and normalised the use of consumerist language when stating, for example, that students would seek out the university courses that offered them the best 'value for money'. The recasting of students as consumers of educational services and universities as service providers was consolidated by the inclusion of universities and students under the Consumer Rights Act of 2015. In addition, universities have become obliged to publish data in a variety of metrics, such as the National Student Survey (NSS) and the TEF, that are designed to measure performance and rank institutions accordingly. Such measures have contributed to the 'sector-wide valorisation of the student-consumer, their service experience and their satisfaction' (Nixon *et al.*, 2018:929).

The 'neoliberal transformation' of HE

Neoliberalism 'has retained a central position in academic accounts that attempt to make sense of the changing nature of the [HE] sector' (Erickson, Hanna and Walker, 2020) and is a useful conceptual lens though which to view recent developments in UK HE (O'Leary and Cui, 2020). Naidoo and Williams (2015:209) state that HE in the UK has undergone a 'neoliberal transformation'. Central to this transformation has been the key role neoliberalism has played in the consumerisation of HE and its students (Ball, 2012; O'Leary and Cui, 2020).

It is acknowledged here that neoliberalism can be seen as 'vague and conceptually overburdened' (Downs, 2017:59). Nevertheless, there is some consensus regarding the dominance of neoliberalism and its key characteristics. Neoliberalism has become the dominant political and economic ideology, with its commitment to free-market economics since the demise of communism (Lynch, 2015). Morrisey (2015) argues that neoliberalism has become hegemonic and, in so doing, has become accepted as common sense. Barnett (2010:272) supports this view and claims that neoliberalism's position has changed over time from being 'an ideology into hegemonic common sense'. Harvey (2005) also argues that neoliberalism has become accepted as common sense. He theorises that, in order to become unquestioningly and uncritically accepted as common sense, an idea must contain concepts that appeal instinctively. In the case of neoliberalism, the key concept that has this type of appeal is that of 'freedom'. Barnett (2010:270) describes 'freedom' as 'an intuitively appealing concept'. In this context, freedom applies to individual freedom of choice, free markets, free trade and entrepreneurial freedoms. Brown (2015:10) also argues that neoliberalism has become dominant by consistently disseminating the idea that 'all conduct is economic conduct, all spheres of existence are framed and measured by economic terms and metrics, even when those spheres are not directly monetized'. According to Brown (2015:176) the values of free-market competition and metrics come to be used in every area of life and thus 'construe the human itself as exclusively *homo economicus*'.

Under neoliberal government administrations, rather than HE being seen as something that the state would spend money on, it is conceived of as a potential contributor to the state's exchequer. HE is regarded as a potential generator of revenue, with universities defined as providers of saleable educational services (Lynch, 2015). Neoliberal governments, such as the recent Coalition and Conservative administrations, perceive HE as a commodity and are likely to allow private, for-profit providers to enter the market. Ball (2012:29) refers to this as the 'commodification of educational practice', with Lynch (2015:191–192) arguing that higher education has become seen as a 'tradable service' and a 'marketable commodity'. Collini (2012) is also critical of the neoliberal assertion that the principal role of universities is to make a contribution to the national economy, boost economic growth and help graduates to achieve higher salaries, believing that universities can justifiably be concerned with learning and scholarship for their own sake. Naidoo and Jamieson (2005) also conclude that the value of higher education is now measured by numbers in terms of how many students are recruited, how many students secure well-paid jobs, how much research and consultancy revenue is generated and how well institutions fare in league tables. Education that has no market value is trivialised and subordinated (Lynch, 2010). Molesworth *et al.* (2009:280) conclude that 'the overriding criterion by which we measure the value of HE is its contribution to the economy. This is what we refer to as the neo-liberal university'.

As noted above, two of the central tenets of neoliberalism that have played an important role in the consumerisation of HE and its students are competition and the use of metrics to measure performance. This is to say that the market has the overriding ideological influence on how education is organised and managed and that 'every action, interaction and behaviour is one that is mediated as a market transaction with economic value that is subject to a process of quantification' (O'Leary and Cui, 2020:143). Advocates of this approach argue that both students and HE in general will benefit from market competition and the use of metrics such as the TEF and the National Student Survey (NSS). Critics suggest that their dominant influence can have negative consequences.

Competition

Naidoo (2016) argues that the introduction of a market-based system that throws universities into competition with each other is part of a wider 'competition fetish' that exists within higher education: 'there appears to be a modern-day magical belief that competition in higher education will provide the solution to all the unsolved problems of higher education' (p.1). Furedi (2009) makes the point that HE has long since embraced the concept of competition. Universities have always competed with each other for resources and funding, whilst individual academics have often engaged in rivalries whilst attempting to grow their own reputations. However, Furedi (2009) argues that the type of market-driven competition that increasingly characterises HE in the UK is somewhat different. The key, and potentially 'disturbing', difference is 'the attempt to recast the relationship between academics and students along the model of a service provider and a customer' (p.2). The use of competition contributes towards the reconceptualisation of the student as a consumer of educational services. Competition is reified 'as the central feature of human relations' (Macfarlane and Tomlinson, 2017:10). Increasingly, competition has been placed at the heart of the governance and management of HE. Universities compete with each other for students 'in a higher education sector where funding follows the student and the forces of competition replace the burdens of bureaucracy in driving up the quality of academic experience' (BIS, 2011:24). Competition-based systems also exist *within* universities as academics are encouraged to improve recruitment and retention of students and score highly on internal teaching evaluation and student satisfaction surveys (BIS, 2011).

Naidoo (2016) invokes the work of Bourdieu when explaining that competition becomes seen as 'doxa'. A doxa is something that becomes normalised and accepted as common sense or 'an unquestionable orthodoxy that operates as if it were the objective truth' (Naidoo, 2016:1). Competition is considered to be a fair and naturally occurring phenomenon. 'To question competition is to be insane' (p.1). The current policy framework is based on the arguably doxic premise that competition between, and within, higher education institutions will produce an HE system that is more efficient and effective and fairer for students (Naidoo and Jamieson, 2005; Molesworth *et al.*, 2009; Brown and Carasso, 2013). As Naidoo and Jamieson (2005:270) put it:

> The underlying assumption is that higher education services that are below standard will be rejected, thus forcing higher education providers to improve or lose out on 'customers' and revenue. The student-consumer thus emerges as the focus of competition and a modernizing force that will bring about increased efficiency, diversity and flexibility to the higher education sector.

However, Brown and Carasso (2013) problematise the claim that competition will inevitably lead to a fairer and more effective system of HE. The assertion that the student as consumer will reject education services that are below standard is flawed because the true value of the services provided cannot be evaluated at the time they are provided. Education is what has been termed a 'post-experience' good (Tomlinson, 2017:717). This means that any outcomes, desirable or otherwise, associated with the so-called consumption of educational services are unlikely to be apparent for many years (Brown and Carasso, 2013). In other words, 'higher education remains a future-orientated (post-experience) good: it is one which students more likely invest in rather than immediately consume. Its value, therefore, is assessed in terms of longer-term impact rather than immediate fulfilment' (Tomlinson, 2017:717). Nobody could be in the position necessary to make a judgement about the quality, suitability or utility of education at the time of 'purchase' in the same way as they could about the purchase of a less complicated product or service (Brown and Carasso, 2013).

In addition, competition can have an arguably negative effect on the way universities function internally. Halffman and Radder (2015) believe that a permanent state of competition between and within universities has altered their social fabric and created a culture of mistrust. Universities compete with each other for students and researchers for funds, while departments within the same university are pitted against each other in the knowledge that those who do not recruit successfully could be closed. The perceived need to recruit students and to do well in rankings, league tables and internal or external student satisfaction surveys can lead to resources being diverted away from academic activities such as learning and teaching and towards managerial and administrative functions such as marketing, enrolment and a variety of student support services and facilities designed to make the institution more competitive. Despite this investment, it may paradoxically be the case that consumerist students choose institutions not as a result of their educational credentials but because of their attraction to restaurants, sports facilities and the image of 'an attractive student life' (Halffman and Radder, 2015:168). Nixon *et al.* (2016) develop this point when they argue that intense competition for students can lead to universities making false promises that result in unrealistic expectations from students. This in turn can result in students who experience 'intense dissatisfaction when entering a mass HE sector and encountering a reality that is not the idealised fantasy shaped and potentially intensified by university promotional communications' (Nixon *et al.*, 2016:934).

The 'metricisation' of higher education

The management and governance of UK HE are increasingly dominated by the use of performance metrics such as the NSS, the Research Excellence Framework (REF) and the TEF. Burrows (2012) argues that HE and academic life in the UK are now shaped and controlled by the perceived need to perform highly in these metrics and refers to this process as 'metricisation'. Spence (2018) and Parker (2018) also argue that HE in the UK is overwhelmingly characterised by the importance of performing well in the relevant metrics. Academics working in the UK may now be amongst the most surveilled groups in history as their work can be measured and evaluated by more than 100 different scales and indices (Erickson *et al*, 2020). Those in favour of the use of metrics to manage and govern HE claim that their use will result in increased accountability and transparency. For example, the Higher Education and Research Bill (BIS, 2016) lays out plans for the introduction of the TEF and claims that it will be part of 'a transparency revolution, enabling students to make informed choices between institutions and courses that meet employers' needs' (p. 2). Muller (2018a:1) argues that supporters of metrics-based systems have 'the belief that making such metrics public assures that institutions are actually carrying out their purposes'.

However, many scholars are critical of the extent to which metrics have come to dominate academic life. Whilst the use of metrics is ostensibly about transparency and accountability, critics argue that their real purpose is to consolidate the reframing of students as the consumers of educational services provided by universities (Collini, 2018). Many scholars are critical of the extent to which metrics have come to dominate the HE landscape. According to Burrows (2012), metrics now dominate the management of HE in the UK after a steady growth in their use dating back to the mid-1980s. Muller (2018:4) believes that society has developed an obsession with quantifying human performance which he calls a 'metric fixation'. This term refers to a situation whereby organisations presuppose that there is a connection between measurement and performance. A belief develops that if something can be measured, it can be improved (Muller, 2018). Porter (2018:527) also suggests that metrics have become overly important in what he calls 'the fetishization of quantification'. Porter (2018) argues that metrics have become so important partly because there is a belief that 'measurement is tantamount to science' but, in reality, their uses are often administrative and political rather than scientific. Burrows (2012) continues to make the argument that academic life is increasingly defined by these 'metric assemblages'. His key assertion is that the most important metrics have taken on a life of their own and are now responsible for shaping, constructing, influencing and controlling academic life. These metrics have taken academic life to a place 'beyond the audit culture' and are part of a 'hegemonic project' where there 'develops an ability not just to mimic, but to enact competitive market processes' (Burrows, 2012:357).

A recurring theme in critiques of the use of metrics is that their use has superseded the importance of experience, expertise and professional judgement. Proponents of the use of metrics believe 'that it is possible and desirable to replace judgement, acquired by personal experience and talent, with numerical indicators of comparative performance based on standardized data' (Muller, 2018a:1). Porter (2018) concurs with Muller (2018) when asserting that metrics have superseded the importance of expertise and experience. Ball (2012) also agrees with this sentiment when arguing that the so-called productivity measured by metrics is given priority over professional judgement. Spence (2018:1) accepts that the management of teaching and research is necessary but is critical of an HE system that 'privileges an instrumental ethos of measurement'. Both Muller (2018) and Spence (2018) conclude that metrics can be useful to measure and improve performance but should be used alongside, not instead of, professional judgement, expertise and experience. This conclusion is reached, at least in part, because in HE, 'not everything that is important is measurable, and much that is measurable is unimportant' (Muller, 2018:18). Collini (2012) agrees that it is very difficult, or impossible, to measure some of the aspects of higher education that really matter. For example, how can the ability of students to think critically be measured effectively?

Developing a 'metric fixation' can have further negative consequences for HE and its students. There is the likelihood of institutions and individuals trying to 'game' the system in order to achieve higher scores in the metrics and the potential for innovation, creativity and criticality to be stifled when people are asked to work to 'pre-established numerical goals' (Muller, 2018a:1). Muller (2018) points to the work of American social psychologist Donald Campbell and British economist C.A.E. Goodhart, who in 1975 independently published research which posited that an over-reliance on metrics would be likely to lead to the measures being corrupted and data distorted. This is likely to occur when the measurement itself becomes more important than what it is purporting to measure (O'Leary and Cui, 2020). Data may be distorted in order to enhance performance in the metrics. In HE, for example, a decision could be made to measure only that which is easy to measure such as attendance, contact hours or the mean mark of a module. Furthermore, Muller (2018) argues that the pursuit of improved scores in the metrics may lead to lower academic standards. Writing about HE in the US, Muller (2018) argues that more students are entering universities who are not ready for degree-level study. These students are expensive for universities as they require additional resources to develop the skills necessary to study at university level. However, a university's ranking may be dependent on measures such as the number of students who successfully graduate and the number of students who graduate with what are referred to in the UK as 'good degrees' (a 1:1 or 2:1 classification). The result of the pressure to do well in the metrics can be that the academic standards required for progression and graduation are lowered, and pressure is placed on academics by administrators and managers to ensure that the requirements of their modules and courses are easier to fulfil. It can be argued that the increasing importance placed on improving performance in the metrics sends a clear message to all stakeholders 'that what matters most is measurable outputs, devaluing the university as an independent space for thinking' (Nixon *et al.*, 2016:929).

Ultimately, Erickson *et al.* (2020:4) view the process of metricisation as harmful and argue that it can be responsible for people 'changing their behaviours and developing expectations to adapt to the systems of measurement that they live within'. In addition, the metricised audit culture is 'suffocating' and prioritises the purpose of providing students with skills that are supposedly needed to enhance their position in the job market over education for any other purpose (e.g. for its own sake, for developing critical thinking skills or for social benefit – Erickson *et al.* 2020:4). Lynch (2015) concurs when she claims that the continual focus on measured performance constantly and harmfully directs students towards concentrating on their own economic self-interest and the extrinsic rewards of qualification acquisition. Erickson *et al.* (2020:4) conclude that 'cultures of audit and measurement are grotesquely distorting the very activities that they seek to scrutinise'.

Pockets of resistance

It seems unlikely that the neoliberal transformation of HE will slow any time soon. Despite the critiques discussed above, competition and metrics seem likely to continue to underpin the management and governance of HE in the UK. Whilst policy makers profess to place 'students at the heart of the system' (BIS, 2011), critics claim that the reframing of students as consumers is likely to lead to dissatisfaction, disengagement and an inferior educational experience. Some notable pockets of resistance to the neoliberal transformation do exist in the UK. These projects reject the notion that students are consumers of educational services in favour of treating students as collaborative partners.

One of the most prominent anti-consumerist projects took place at the University of Lincoln. The 'Student as Producer' (Neary *et al.*, 2014) project seeks to actively oppose what it sees as a neoliberal system that promotes a consumerist model of HE which has overseen cuts to the public funding of HE, the imposition of student tuition fees and a resultant increase in student debt. Neary and Saunders (2016:2) describe the project as

> an act of resistance to the current policy framework being imposed on universities in England and around the world and, as such, is a critical response to attempts by national governments to create and consolidate a consumerist culture and impose high levels of debt among undergraduate students.

The project sees HE repurposed to counter the hegemonic neoliberal model of the university that has emerged in recent times. Employing critical pedagogy based on the work of Freire (1968), amongst others, the project intends to empower students to understand and take action against the exploitative, discriminatory capitalist system and promote social justice (Maisuria and Cole, 2017). The project aligns to the key principles of 'popular education' outlined by Johnson (1979 in Maisuria and Cole, 2017:613). These principles are developing a critique of the current system, establishing alternative educational objectives, using education to change the world and providing educational opportunity for all (Maisuria and Cole, 2017).

A key aspect of the project is the use of research-engaged teaching and learning (Neary *et al.*, 2014). This approach means that 'students learn primarily by engagement with real research projects, or projects which replicate the process of research in their discipline. Engagement is created through active collaboration amongst and between students and academics' (p.10). The use of this collaborative approach aims to ensure that students are actively involved in, and have ownership of, the production of knowledge that is of genuine academic value. From the outset, a key objective of the project was to ensure that students 'became part of the academic project of the university … rather than passive consumers of information' (Neary *et al.*, 2014:9).

A Higher Education Academy report on the 'Student as Producer' project references the work of Healey and Jenkins (2009). Healey has been responsible for projects that aim to combat the rise of student consumerism and to make explicit connections between research and teaching within universities (e.g. Healey *et al.*, 2014). These projects also promote collaboration between staff and students and wish to see students treated as partners in the learning process. These projects aim to achieve student engagement through working in partnership with students in teaching and learning (including assessment), research and inquiry, scholarship of teaching and learning and curriculum design. In keeping with the Lincoln project, the 'Students as Partners' project conceptualises students as active participants in their teaching and learning rather than passive consumers of knowledge. Healey *et al.* (2014) argue that recent HE policy promotes a passive, consumerist approach to learning which emphasises achieving quantifiable results rather than having any concern for a pedagogical process that may involve creativity, innovation and unexpected outcomes that cannot be measured quantitatively (Healey *et al.*, 2014).

Conclusion

HE in the UK has arguably undergone a neoliberal transformation in recent times. The use of competition and performance metrics have played a crucial role in this transformation and have contributed to the reconceptualisation of students as consumers of educational services and universities as educational service providers. Government policy (e.g. BIS, 2011) claims that competition will improve standards by driving out sub-standard providers and enhancing the quality of education experienced by students. Proponents of the use of metrics to measure performance in HE claim that they will increase transparency and accountability and empower students to make more informed choices regarding their education.

However, the claim that competition will result in an improved educational experience for students is rejected by critics who argue that the value of a university education cannot be evaluated at the time it is being provided and is something that students invest in for the future (Tomlinson, 2017). Furthermore, universities desperate to recruit students may divert resources away from academic activities to administrative and managerial functions such as marketing. Finally, universities which try to recruit students with shiny new facilities and the promise of 'an attractive student life' (Halfmann and Radder, 2015:168) may cause students to have unrealistic expectations. When these expectations are not fulfilled, students may become dissatisfied, disenchanted and disengaged.

Critics of the increasingly dominant use of metrics to measure performance argue that their purpose is to consolidate the recasting of students as consumers of educational services rather than increasing transparency and accountability (Collini, 2018). Further critique suggests that the use of quantitative performance measures has become fetishised and valued more highly than professional expertise and experience (Muller, 2018). It is also argued that many important facets of HE, such as the ability to think critically, cannot be measured effectively using quantitative methods (Collini, 2012). Most concerning, perhaps, is the assertion that pressure placed upon universities and their staff to perform well in the metrics may lead to the system being gamed by the lowering of academic standards and an unwillingness to innovate, thus decreasing the quality of education provided and 'devaluing the university as an independent space for thinking' (Nixon *et al.*, 2016:929). Pockets of resistance to the neoliberal transformation of HE exist in the form of innovative and subversive projects that aim to treat students as partners and collaborators rather than passive consumers. Given the pressure on all universities to recruit students and to perform well in the metrics, the extent to which such projects can achieve their aims and become part of the mainstream in the long term remains to be seen.

Summary points

- Policy makers claim that competition between universities to recruit students will drive up academic standards and that the use of metrics to measure performance will make HE more transparent and accountable.

- Critics claim that intense competition between universities can lead to unrealistic promises being made to students and resources being diverted away from academic activities to administrative functions. The perceived necessity to perform well in the metrics can lead to a gaming of the system that results in lower academic standards.
- Innovative projects have attempted to reconceptualise the student as a partner and collaborator in academic enterprise rather than a consumer of educational services.

Questions for discussion

- Should HE be considered a collective public good and, therefore, publicly funded?
- Is competition between universities a good thing for students and HE as a whole?
- Do you feel that the use of metrics in HE improves transparency and accountability?
- What steps could universities take to resist student consumerism?

Recommended reading

Bartram, B. (2020) Queering the TEF. In A. French and K. Carruthers Thomas (Eds.), *Challenging the Teaching Excellence Framework: Diversity Deficits in Higher Education Evaluations*. Bingley, UK: Emerald Publishing.

Naidoo, R. (2018) The Competition Fetish in Higher Education: Shamans, Mind Snares and Consequences. *European Educational Research Journal*, 17(5), pp. 605–620.

Scott, P. (2018) *The Crisis of the University*. London: Routledge.

References

Ball, S. (2012) Performativity, Commodification and Commitment: An I-Spy Guide to the Neoliberal University. *British Journal of Education Studies*, 60(1), pp. 17–28.

Barnett, C. (2010) Publics and Markets: What's Wrong with Neoliberalism? In S.J. Smith, R. Pain, S.A. Marston, and J.P. III Jones (Eds.), *The Sage Handbook of Social Geography*. London: Sage.

BIS (2011) *Higher Education: Students at the Heart of the System*. London: Department for Business Innovation and Skills.

BIS (2016) *Higher Education and Research Bill*. London: Department for Business Innovation and Skills.

Brown, R. and Carasso, H. (2013) *Everything for Sale? The Marketisation of UK Higher Education*. London: Routledge.

Brown, W. (2015) *Undoing the Demos: Neoliberalism's Stealth Revolution*. Cambridge, MA: The MIT Press.

Browne, J. (2010) *Securing a Sustainable Future for Higher Education: An Independent Review of Higher Education Funding and Student Finance*. London: Her Majesty's Stationary Office.

Burrows, R. (2012) Living with the H-Index? Metric Assemblages in the Contemporary Academy. *The Sociological Review*, 60(2), pp. 355–372.

Collini, S. (2012) *What Are Universities For?* London: Penguin.

Collini, S. (2018) *Speaking of Universities*. London: Penguin.

Downs, Y. (2017) Neoliberalism and the Value of Higher Education. In T. Rudd and I.F. Goodson (Eds.), *Negotiating Neoliberalism: Developing Alternative Educational Visions*. Rotterdam: Sense.

Erickson, M., Hanna, P. and Walker, C. (2020) The UK Higher Education Senior Management Survey: A Statactivist Response to Managerialist Governance. *Studies in Higher Education*. Available at: https://doi.org/10.1080/03075079.2020.1712693 (Accessed 21 April 2020).

Freire, P. (2000) *Pedagogy of the Oppressed*, 30th Anniversary Ed. New York: Continuum.

Furedi, F. (2009) Introduction to the Marketization of Higher Education and the Student as Consumer. In M. Molesworth, E. Nixon, and R. Scullion (Eds.), *The Marketization of Higher Education and the Student as Consumer*. London: Routledge.

Halfmann, W. and Radder, H. (2015) The Academic Manifesto: From an Occupied to a Public University. *Minerva*, 53(2), pp. 165–187.

Harvey, D. (2005) *A Brief History of Neoliberalism*. Oxford: Oxford University Press.

Healey, M., Flint, A. and Harrington, K. (2014) *Engagement Through Partnership: Students as Partners in Learning and Teaching in Higher Education*. York: HEA.

Healey, M. and Jenkins, A. (2009) *Developing Undergraduate Research and Inquiry*. York: HEA.

Lynch, K. (2010) Carelessness: A Hidden Doxa of Higher Education. *Arts and Humanities in Higher Education*, 9(1), pp. 54–67.

Lynch, K. (2015) Control by Numbers: New Managerialism and Ranking in Higher Education. *Critical Studies in Education*, 56(2), pp. 190–207.

Macfarlane, B. (2015) *Freedom to Learn: The Threat to Student Academic Freedom and Why It Needs to Be Reclaimed*. London: Routledge.

Maisuria, A. and Cole, M. (2017) The Neoliberalization of Higher Education in England: An alternative is possible. *Policy Futures in Education*, 15 (5), pp. 602–619.

Molesworth, M., Nixon, E. and Scullion, R. (2009) Having, Being and Higher Education: The Marketisation of the University and the Transformation of the Student into Consumer. *Teaching in Higher Education*, 14(3), pp. 277–287.

Morrisey, J. (2015) Regimes of Performance: Practices of the Normalised Self in the Neoliberal University. *British Journal of Sociology of Education*, 36(4), pp. 614–634.

Muller, J. (2018) *The Tyranny of Metrics*. Princeton: Princeton University Press.

Muller, J. (2018a) The Tyranny of Metrics: The Quest to Quantify Everything Undermines Higher Education. *The Chronicle of Higher Education*, 64(20), pp. 1–7.

Naidoo, R. (2016) The Competition Fetish in Higher Education: Varieties, Animators and Consequences. *British Journal of Sociology of Education*, 37(1), pp. 1–10.

Naidoo, R. and Jamieson, I. (2005) Empowering Participants or Corroding Learning? Towards a Research Agenda on the Impact of Student Consumerism in Higher Education. *Journal of Education Policy*, 20(3), pp. 267–281.

Naidoo, R. and Williams, J. (2015) The Neoliberal Regime in English Higher Education: Charters, Consumers and the Erosion of the Public Good. *Critical Studies in Education*, 56(2), pp. 208–223.

Neary, M. (2010) Student as Producer: A Pedagogy for the Avant-Garde. *Learning Exchange*, 1(1). Available at: http://studentasproducer.lincoln.ac.uk/files/2014/03/15-72-1-pb-1.pdf (Accessed 21 April 2020).

Neary, M. and Saunders, G. (2016) Student as Producer and the Politics of Abolition: Making a New Form of Dissident Institution? *Critical Education*, 7(5), pp. 1–23.

Neary, M., Saunders, G., Haygard, A. and Dericott, D. (2014) *Student as Producer. Research-Engaged Teaching: An Institutional Strategy*. York: HEA.

Nixon, E., Scullion, R. and Hearn, R. (2018) Her Majesty the Student: Marketised Higher Education and the Narcissistic (Dis)Satisfactions of the Student-Consumer. *Studies in Higher Education*, 43(6), pp. 927–943.

O'Leary, M. and Cui, V. (2020) Reconceptualising Teaching and Learning in Higher Education: Challenging Neoliberal Narratives of Teaching Excellence Through Collaborative Observation. *Teaching in Higher Education*, 25(2), pp. 141–156.

Parker, M. (2018) *Shut Down the Business School: What's Wrong with Management Education*. London: Pluto Press.

Porter, T.M. (2018) The Fetishization of Quantification. A Historian Explores the Dark Side of Metric-Based Performance Evaluation. *Science*, 359(6375), pp. 527–527.

The Robbins Report. (1963). *Higher Education (Cm 2154)*. London: HMSO.

Spence, C. (2018) 'Judgement' Versus 'Metrics' in Higher Education Management. *Higher Education*, 77, pp. 761–775.

Tomlinson, M. (2017) Conceptions of the Value of Higher Education in a Measured Market. *Higher Education*, 75(4), pp. 711–727.

Williams, J. (2016) A Critical Exploration of Changing Definitions of Public Good in Relation to Higher Education. *Studies in Higher Education*, 41(4), pp. 619–630.

6 Weaving through the web

How students navigate information online in the twenty-first century

Carol Bailey, Hazel Bowley and Jodi Withers

Introduction

With university libraries moving to a predominantly online domain, students have become more reliant on the use of digital resources to find, evaluate and use source material for their assignments. This requires not only a range of devices and programmes but also an advanced level of information literacy, defined by the Chartered Institute of Library and Information Professions (CILIP, 2018: 8) as 'the ability to think critically and make balanced judgements about any information we find and use'.

Not all students arrive at university with the necessary skill set. To address this issue, the academic community requires a better understanding of students' capabilities. This chapter will, therefore, investigate the processes employed by students to search online for appropriate sources. Against a backdrop of literature from the past three decades, we present findings from a recent observational study (employing screen-recording software and stimulated recall) of how students approach a writing-from-sources task, supplemented by interviews with librarians at a post-1992 UK university.

We chose an observational method to counteract the response bias sometimes seen in surveys and interviews. A convenience sample of 33 students was recruited from across the university. The participants (7 male, 26 female) ranged in age from 18 to 60 and were studying Health (12), Business (8), Social Sciences (4), Performing Arts (3), Science (2), Education (2), Humanities (1) and Computer Science (1). Table 6.1 shows the breakdown of participants by Generation (X, Y or Z) and by study level as defined by the UK Framework for Higher Education Qualifications.

Participants were invited to group recording sessions in a non-specialist IT lab and given approximately 45 minutes to respond to the following prompt: 'Compare the advantages and drawbacks of reading on paper/online, using published research to support your points and giving your own opinion'. Their on-screen activity was captured using the screen-recording software Snagit®, and their essays were uploaded to the text-matching software Turnitin. A few days after the recording session, participants were invited to individual feedback meetings where they discussed their feelings about academic writing and how the recording data compared with their normal searching and composing strategies. We also interviewed six university librarians to triangulate their insights with the screen recordings and student interview data.

We discuss three aspects of our participants' search for sources: where they searched, how they searched and which sources they selected. We compare our findings with data from larger studies conducted over the past three decades and suggest how some of the information literacy challenges students face could be addressed.

Table 6.1 Participants by generation and study level

	FHEQ Level 3 (pre-degree)	FHEQ Level 4 (first-year undergraduate)	FHEQ Level 5 (second-year undergraduate)	FHEQ Level 7 (masters)
Generation Z (born 1997–2012)	2	4	1	0
Generation Y (born 1981–1996)	0	7	1	5
Generation X (born 1965–1980)	1	3	3	4
Baby boomer (born 1946–1964)	0	0	0	2

Where students search for sources

Technology has rapidly evolved over the last few decades, meaning that the majority of academic sources are now accessible online. This wealth of electronic information requires students to have an awareness of the available resources and the technical ability to search them. However, librarian interviews indicated that many lack this knowledge. Schools may not have libraries or include information literacy in the curriculum. Some international students originate from regions where there is no reliable electricity supply, let alone computer access. With many of our students coming from low socio-economic backgrounds, one cannot assume that they have regular access to a home computer. The myth of the 'digital native' has been strongly contested (Bennett *et al.*, 2008), as has the concept of the 'Google generation' (CIBER, 2008). Many of our participants expressed a preference for print over electronic resources, suggesting that they are not representative of the stereotypical generational divides.

Questions for discussion

- What IT skills have you developed since starting your degree? Which do you think are most important for new students to focus on?

Although 33 students participated in our study, 1 performed no searches during the recording session and two accidentally deleted their recordings, so we report below on the findings from 30 participants. They used a range of search tools, either for navigating to other sites (e.g. using the address bar to find Google) or to search directly for information. Seven different tools were used including LibrarySearch (LS), Google, Google Scholar (GS), Bing, databases, the address bar (AB) and the search tool within websites (see Table 6.2 for an overview). Of the participants, 12 used only one tool for all their information searches, 10 accessed two, 7 used three and 1 individual used four separate tools but demonstrated low proficiency. There was an obvious preference for LibrarySearch, Google and Google Scholar over databases: 25.52 per cent of literature searches were carried out using LibrarySearch, the university's library discovery tool.

There are various instances of participants struggling to navigate the university website in search of the library catalogue. For example, a level four Generation Y participant navigated from the

Table 6.2 Direct searches by search tool

	Count	Percentage of Total
Address bar	19	6.21
Bing	21	14.48
Database	13	8.97
Google Scholar	28	19.31
Google	34	23.45
LibrarySearch	37	25.52
Within Website	3	2.07
Total	145	100

student portal to 'subject resources' before going to the student homepage on the university website and following a link from there back to the 'subject resources' page; they then clicked on 'databases A–Z' and finally selected the library catalogue – a process lasting three minutes. A similar phenomenon was observed a decade ago by CIBER (2008: 10): 'People in virtual libraries spend a lot of time simply finding their way around: in fact they spend as much time finding their bearings as actually viewing what they find'. It is possible that participants were confused by the number of pathways to the library discovery tool, or by the fact that it may look different/be differently labelled in various university apps or webpages. Mobile-enabled browsing would also have an effect on the navigation between sites and sources as it alters not only the appearance of the website but also the configuration of menus. Six participants mentioned that under normal circumstances they would use a mobile device during the search process; in their case, the desktop configuration would have had slightly different functionality from what they were used to. Search preferences can be somewhat dependent on which technology we generally use.

Whilst our participants preferred LibrarySearch for their information searches, Google was very popular, totalling 23.45 per cent of literature searching; when also considering navigational searches, it can be seen that Google was the most popular overall. This aligns with previous research by Salehi *et al.* (2018). Since its inception, the appearance of the Google homepage has been consistently simple and plain. One aspect of this is the single search bar, which library discovery tools have begun to adopt (Georgas, 2014; Greenberg and Bar-Ilan, 2017). Another aspect is that there is less to distract people from their search, unlike some of the competing search engines (e.g. Bing) which include news articles, images and website links on their homepage. Bing was the default search engine on the PCs used in the study, so participants may have been using it passively (as the path of least resistance), not as their search tool of choice.

While some participants interacted with Google Scholar via the 'scholarly articles' links on a Google results page, 8 participants carried out 28 direct searches actively using Google Scholar. These participants were studying at FHEQ levels three to seven and represented Generations X (3), Y (4) and Z (1). Google Scholar's usefulness is dependent on the library catalogue, as it carries out the role of a meta-search engine. Students may not be aware that it is linking to sources subscribed to by their institution and that they would not be able to access these sources otherwise (Greenberg and Bar-Ilan, 2017).

Databases offer more advanced options for narrowing down search results; however, proficient use requires a high level of expertise. Six participants (three Gen. X/level seven and three Gen. Y/

level four) carried out 13 database searches. According to our librarians, few students use databases or are even aware of the tools specific to their subjects. In this case, four of the participants who accessed databases were from health-related courses, where library skills workshops are regularly embedded in the syllabus. The databases they accessed were relevant to the essay prompt rather than to their degree subject, indicating a willingness to adapt their skill set (though not always proficiently) to unfamiliar tools.

In a few cases, participants searched within websites that were not appropriate sources of information for their query. For example, one (Gen. X, level seven) participant searched in direct.gov for 'advantages of reading paper or online' and 'advantages of reading', while others used the university homepage search bar to look for sources. This suggests a lack of understanding about information architecture (Georgas, 2014).

How students search for sources

The way in which our participants approached searching in the context of the writing task varied enormously. Some participants began the writing task by searching for and reading sources – in two extreme cases, managing to write only a few words in the allotted time. Other participants began by writing their own thoughts on the topic, before searching for sources to back up their ideas. A third approach was to treat the search function as a reference resource, turning to it throughout the task for ideas and information. One very common pattern was that of returning to results from a previous search; we observed 82 cases (across 27/30 participants) of students interrupting their reading or writing to go back for more information.

In total, our participants made 123 fresh searches. These included:

- 91 instances where participants typed a word, phrase or sentence into a search box;
- 21 instances where participants acted on a search-engine suggestion, for example, the 'some people ask' or 'related searches' links, or began typing a search term and used the predictive text drop-down to complete it;
- 6 instances of Boolean search;
- 5 instances of known-item searching (pasting a reference or title into the search box).

The average number of searches per participant was 4.1, with a minimum of one fresh search and a maximum of 10.

Many studies (e.g. Holman, 2010) have noted a preference for natural-language queries, whereby searchers type a whole phrase, sentence or question rather than breaking the query into keywords. A large survey of first-year undergraduates in Canada found that respondents had difficulty in eliminating non-significant words from a search term (Mittermeyer and Quirion, 2003). Including non-significant words may limit the number of search results, while missing out significant words can result in many irrelevant hits. Interestingly, while students' tendency to employ natural-language queries in library tools is often attributed to their habitual use of Google, the practice was identified as early as 1989 by Marchionini, in a study of novice search strategies when using a full-text electronic encyclopaedia on CD-ROM.

A preference for natural-language searching was evident among our participants, with 10 typing the essay title 'compare the advantages and drawbacks of reading on paper/online', or a close variant. There was an inverse relationship between use of the essay title and age/study level, with students of a lower age and study level being more likely to reproduce the essay prompt. While we cannot infer too much from this (given our sample size and distribution), this finding does reflect other studies which suggest that natural-language searching is more prevalent among less experienced learners, or that older searchers may be more familiar with keywords, having used them to search print resources such as encyclopaedias and book indexes (Marchionini, 1989).

Search strings varied in length from 1 word ('online') to 12 ('what are the advantages and drawbacks of reading on paper and online'). Queries of 3–8 words long were most common, irrespective of study level or Generation. While many participants drew exclusively on the wording of the task prompt (as reported by Marchionini, 1989 and Georgas, 2014), several expanded their search through use of synonyms. Examples include

> *pros and cons*
> *how we read*
> *paper versus digital*
> *print vs digital*
> *screen vs paper*
> *advantages of ebooks*
> *benefits of reading online*
> *the difference between published and online reading*

Only two students (both level seven, Gen. X) employed Boolean operators (the limiters AND, OR and NOT, used to restrict or expand a search, e.g. 'reading/AND/advantages and disadvantages/AND/paper'). Participants used Boolean almost by default as presented on the Advanced Search page of the databases *Education Research Complete* and *Academic Search Complete*. Georgas (2014: 509) describes such use as 'passive', and it is worth noting that neither participant selected the OR/NOT operators or limited their search by field (e.g. title/abstract). Our librarians had mixed perspectives on Boolean searching, with one feeling that the strategy appealed to certain types of student while others said they taught it more at higher levels: 'PhD students tend to be better [i.e. more experienced at searching], so I'll go into the Boolean stuff and the wildcards and the more advanced techniques, if I feel that they are with me' (Librarian 4).

> Will Boolean ever totally go away? Probably not, but I think there will be less use for it … what we want is for students to get access to the relevant resources as easily as possible, without having to learn in detail about Boolean logic … I'm sure that natural searching will continue to improve and ultimately Boolean will be used less and less.
>
> (Librarian 6)

One way in which search engines – and, to an increasing degree, library discovery tools – make it easier to access relevant resources is through 'suggestions'. These include the 'people also ask' drop-down and 'searches related to' links in search engines such as Google or Bing; the Did You Mean (DYM) feature, which compensates for spelling mistakes in many tools; and predictive auto-complete in search boxes. In our study, only nine participants (five Gen. X, three Gen. Y and one Gen. Z) made use of the latter feature, many preferring to type search terms themselves even when the autocomplete function returned a viable suggestion. In most cases, autocomplete predictions were helpful and saved time; for example, one participant typed 'reading online' and selected 'vs print' from the GS drop-down. In a couple of cases, autocomplete proved a distraction. For example, one student was googling 'online or paper' and accepted the suggestion 'IELTS online or paper based' then added 'which is better' and scanned the results before moving on.

We were interested to note how participants' choice of search tool influenced their results. This appeared to be affected to some degree by what content was indexed by the tool, and by its ability to deal with punctuation and spelling issues. For example, LS returned relatively few results for queries replicating the task prompt 'paper/online'. This may be due to a known bug involving use of the / character. The query 'reading paper online' returned very different results according to search tool. Bing prioritised results about reading newspapers, including an essay-mill website. Google also listed results about newspapers, as well as an advert for online psychic readings. LS and GS, however, included nothing about newspapers in their top pages. One reason may be that GS indexes primarily academic sources, and it is possible that academic writers eschew 'paper' as a synonym for 'newspaper'. LS indexes some less academic material (including newspaper content), but comparative searches for 'reading paper online' and 'reading (paper OR newspaper) online' return noticeably different results, suggesting that LS does not treat *paper/newspaper* as synonyms.

Spelling mistakes had an equally significant impact on participants' search success. Two interesting examples are 'advantages of reading on paper' and 'advantages and drawbacks of reading on paper/online'. Google and Bing handled these with a DYM suggestion, while in both cases displaying results for the intended search. GS also offered a DYM alternative, but displayed results for the original (misspelled) search term. LS offered no DYM suggestion and no results – a failure compounded by the fact that the spellcheck function was not enabled on the University's default browser. While there is a DYM feature in LS, it activates only when a search returns fewer than 15 results – which is unlikely to happen with multi-word search terms. Lack of spelling intelligence is a serious drawback for library discovery tools (Holman, 2010). When spelling errors lead to few or no results in the library tools, students tend to assume that the library holds no articles on the subject, and resort to less academic sources of information.

Given the different ways search tools handle queries, one might assume students would vary their search methods according to which tool they were using. This proved not to be the case. Instead, participants often replicated their search term across different platforms, subsequently modifying it where a query proved unsuccessful, or as their train of thought developed and they needed fresh ideas for their essay. For example:

(LibrarySearch) advantages of readng [sic] on paper
(Google) advantages of reading on paper
(Google) stats of people reading online vs paper
(Google) people reading online vs paper

This confirms the findings of Holman (2010) and Asher *et al.* (2013), whose participants exhibited the same syntax and behaviour patterns across both search engines and library tools. While our librarians stress the importance of a structured approach to searching, in the recordings (possibly due to the 45-minute time constraint), participants appeared to be employing a more fluid, unplanned approach, described in other studies as 'hit-and-miss' (Mittermeyer and Quirion, 2003:

7), 'erratic' (CIBER, 2008: 32), 'haphazard' (Holman, 2010: 22) and – more positively – 'heuristic' and 'interactive' (Marchionini, 1989: 64).

We were curious to learn whether our participants would look beyond the first page of search results for each query. Our librarians observe that students often expect immediate answers to search queries: 'because they can't see something on that first page they're like well that hasn't found anything so I'm gonna try something else' (Librarian 3). This is borne out by many studies; for example, 598/649 of the sources used by students in the study by Asher *et al.* (2013) were located on the first page of hits. In the main, our participants conformed to this pattern: only 6/30 participants loaded a further results page. This occurred during searches performed in LS (six), databases (three), GS (two) and Google (one), suggesting that participants were less satisfied with the relevance rankings of the more academic search tools. However, it is difficult to generalise from this finding. Our participants were operating under severe time constraints; in cases where an individual found a satisfactory number of sources on the first page, they would be unlikely to search for more, a phenomenon termed 'satisficing' by Prabha *et al.* (2007). In cases where no/ few relevant results were returned, participants appear to have trusted the search tool's relevance ranking/algorithm (Asher *et al.*, 2013) and proceeded to modify their search or try another tool. The research by Lowe *et al.* (2018) suggests that searchers are right to trust relevance rankings and that these are reliable for natural-language as well as Boolean searches. However, scrolling beyond the first page of results is not the only indicator of 'search persistence' (Lowe *et al.*, 2018). We noted five instances where participants (two Gen. X students) searched for a source they had found cited elsewhere, by pasting the reference into a search box a practice sometimes known as 'citation mining' or 'chaining' (Hsin *et al.*, 2016). We also observed several instances of participants exploring links from a source they had already selected.

What sources students select

Being able to discern between sources that are credible and accurate and those that are not is an essential skill for successful undergraduate and postgraduate study. Raven (2012) found that the sources undergraduates expected to use (e.g. Google and newspaper articles) differed significantly from the sources academics wanted them to use (journals and library website). What constitutes a 'quality' academic source, however, is a matter of debate even in the academic community, so it is unsurprising that students have great difficulty in establishing whether a source is fit for purpose (Hampton-Reeves *et al.*, 2009). Research suggests that the most important criterion from a student's perspective is 'access ... access ... access' (Burton and Chadwick, 2000: 117) and that other considerations, such as the importance of scholarly peer-review, are somewhat secondary.

Our screencasting data collection method allowed us to observe the participants' actions when browsing their search results and record which sources they selected. A source was deemed 'selected' if a search result was clicked on in order to view the source. In total, our 30 participants made 173 selections. A variety of source types were viewed by participants, ranging from essay-mill webpages (4) to more esoteric sources such as conference papers (2) and ERIC records (3). Table 6.3 provides an overview of the sources accessed. Two source types are significant in terms of being accessed the most frequently: journal articles and webpages. Taken together, these two comprised over 80 per cent of the source selections, with others (books, textbooks, newspaper articles, etc.) being selected in very small numbers by a minority of students.

Table 6.3 Count of sources selected by source type

Source Type	Count of Participants	Count of Visits	Percentage of Total
Book	3	4	2.31
Book chapter	1	1	0.58
Conference paper	2	2	1.16
ERIC record	2	3	1.73
Handout/leaflet	1	2	1.16
Journal	1	3	1.73
Journal article	24	72	41.62
Master's dissertation	1	1	0.57
Newspaper article	1	1	0.57
Periodical	6	10	5.78
PowerPoint slides	1	1	0.57
Report	1	1	0.57
Textbook	1	1	0.57
Webpages	16	71	41.04
		173	100

Table 6.4 Proportion of source types accessed by students at each study level

Level	Journal Articles (%)	Webpages (%)	Other Sources (%)
Level 3	6	74	20
Level 4	42	38	20
Level 5	49	27	24
Level 7	50	36	14

The number of sources selected by individuals ranged from 0 to 16; the average number of sources accessed was 5.77. Journal articles were selected the most often (72 selections).

We examined source-type selection by study level (see Table 6.4) and by Generation. Only 6 per cent of the sources viewed by level three students were journal articles, with 74 per cent of their sources being webpages. In comparison, 50 per cent of the sources accessed by level seven students were journal articles. Levels five and seven alone accessed journals and conference papers, all sound scholarly sources, whereas levels three and four drew on more informal or perhaps more familiar sources, such as periodicals, newspaper articles and textbooks.

This in itself is not surprising; level three students have spent very little time in tertiary education, being in the first year of their degree, whereas level seven students have navigated their way through several years of undergraduate and postgraduate study. However, we found a significant difference between the proportion of journal articles and webpages accessed by participants at levels three and four. This is interesting, as the majority of level four participants were also in their first year of tertiary study. The extent to which research skills are embedded into modules might account for this. One librarian described a level four module which required students to analyse four journal articles, giving them a greater awareness that such sources are important. Her experience suggested that lecturers have a large influence on the sources that students use, and on their uptake of library services.

The frequency at which different source types are accessed of course does not tell us anything about the quality of those sources and the reasoning behind participants' choices. However, we can infer something about their decision-making processes from the actions captured on screen. For example, participants' use of filters to refine their searches could be indicative of their source evaluation criteria. Prior studies have found that students make minimal use of filters (e.g. Georgas 2014). Only 8 of our 30 participants used filters. Six participants used them multiple times, sifting their searches by date, source type (e.g. peer-reviewed journals), availability (e.g. 'online'), and database (e.g. 'all Ebsco databases'). This suggests that the use of filters was part of their usual search strategy and that there was some awareness that certain features are desirable. The most frequent filters used were date and source type (both used eight times).

However, not all filter use was effective. The heaviest single user of filters (seven occurrences) applied them in an increasingly desperate way over an eight-minute period in order to improve the relevance of search results returned by the query 'what are the advantages and drawbacks of reading on paper and online'. This returned 6,082 results, but none that were relevant. They applied date, subject and source-type filters and even modified their search phrase, but with no positive outcome. Another student apparently misunderstood the filter field and attempted to use it as a general search bar.

Webpages

Just over half (16) of the participants visited a webpage, and only 4 relied solely on them for information. Our participants visited a wide range of webpages in the course of their research. As Table 6.5 shows, only one fifth of webpages accessed were 'academic' in nature, having an .edu or ac.uk domain name.

The majority of webpages accessed were of non-academic standing. The titles of webpages ranged from the frankly bizarre (e.g. the Bing newsfeed webpage entitled 'Jesus was a Greek'; the website 'psychicsofa.com') to well-known online essay mills.

Most of the webpages accessed were superficially relevant to the research task. It is easy to see how students would have perceived titles such as LinkedIn's 'Why print books are better than ebooks' and blurtit.com's 'What is the advantage of paper?' as being potentially useful.

Table 6.5 Categories of webpages visited

Webpages Visited	Count of Participants	Count of Visits	Percentage of Total
Academic	4	13	18.30
Blog	8	15	22.13
Commercial	5	7	9.86
Essay mill	2	4	5.63
Forum	8	9	12.68
General	12	20	28.17
Social media	2	3	4.23
Webpages – overall	16	71	100

However, these webpages would not rate highly against any source evaluation criteria for quality. Despite some webpages being presented in a pseudo-academic manner by the inclusion of authors' names, credentials and a bibliography (e.g. lifehack.org, answers.com), their real purpose is to churn out articles with titles that are optimised to attract traffic to the website in order to increase online advertising revenue. Such websites are known as 'content farms' (McCreadie *et al.*, 2012). This strategy is also adopted by essay mills, which offer advisory, blog-type articles on a range of academic topics, designed to lure students to their sites. Essay mills were visited by two participants, one of whom was surprised to learn at interview that such sites existed or were deemed inappropriate for academic use. One librarian explained:

> Students who aren't doing as well … overwhelmingly favour those online resources, the popular resources … not necessarily Wikipedia: things like Buzzfeed, not-well-known magazines, blog-posts – which are fine in a certain context … but Buzzfeed's not going to cut it if you're talking about whether exercise can improve mental health … it's clickbait-esque in terms of these titles that pull you in, things that sound like they're going to be the answer to your assignment …
>
> (Librarian 3)

Only one 'Wiki' was accessed. It should be noted that Wikipedia did not stand out in the results pages for any of the searches we recorded. However, it is possible that being observed changed participants' behaviour (the Hawthorne effect). In her study examining the research expectations of undergraduates and professors, Raven (2012) wondered whether her survey respondents chose the sources they thought the researchers would want them to select, rather than the sources they would use in real life. This is borne out in our study by the Turnitin reports from two essays which showed that our participants had copied from sources they did not access using the monitored computer. Access to these sources can only be explained by the use of an additional mobile device.

There were a few instances of more credible sites being read, the website for the Migraine Trust being one (the participant was searching for information to support their point that using screens could trigger headaches). However, the preponderance of poor-quality, content farm–type websites suggests that our participants' grasp of what constitutes a 'quality' source was somewhat tenuous, and that their preference was for simply written sources, with titles that superficially appear to be relevant. This view could be countered by the encouraging fact that most students did not spend significant amounts of time on these websites, in many cases navigating away soon after accessing them.

Questions for discussion

- At what age do you think the art of critically evaluating information sources should be introduced? Did you learn about this in school?

Journal articles

In the hierarchy of scholarly sources, journal articles are considered to be the 'gold standard'. They are peer-reviewed and reflect current thinking in a discipline. Although there is a tacit expectation that students will engage with them during their undergraduate study, undergraduates are not their primary readership. The density and complexity of the discourse in journal articles presents a challenge: students surveyed by Hampton-Reeves *et al.* (2009: 21) reported that they found research papers 'sometimes ... too complex to be understood'. One librarian commented that the academic or technical language of journal articles might be a barrier for some.

Most of our participants (24/30) accessed journal articles and, encouragingly, the articles selected were broadly relevant to the essay prompt. One of the more pertinent articles, a 2018 literature review entitled 'Screen and Paper Reading Research – A Literature Review' was accessed by seven participants. The articles were drawn from disciplines as diverse as cognitive psychology, information and library studies and dance education. A less useful choice was a 2017 *Neuropsychologia* theoretical article 'Why are digits easier to identify than letters?' However, the participant only read the abstract before (correctly) discarding and moving on to select more useful sources.

Eight participants experienced problems accessing the full text of journal articles they had selected. In only one instance was this because the library did not subscribe to a full-text copy. In others, participants appeared unsure of where to access the text. One librarian explained:

> When students start to use a different database it sometimes throws them because they don't look the same ... If you look on an EBSCO database, there's a link that says PDF full text; if you're on SCOPUS it says 'view at Publisher', so it's knowing that there's a different wording...
>
> (Librarian 4)

As Holman noted in 2010, there is currently no standard practice across databases and other library tools. In two cases, the library results page directed participants not to the specific article but to the journal/issue: one level five (Gen. Z) student who was directed to the journal homepage (to access an article published in 2014) spent over two minutes searching the current issue (2019) and then the entire ACM digital library. We saw similar levels of search persistence (contradicting the assumption that students always go for the easy option) in other participants; for example, a level four (Gen. X) student spent 2 minutes 15 seconds unsuccessfully navigating authentication barriers to a *Wall Street Journal* article. Viewing the recordings was a somewhat discomforting experience as we witnessed several instances where the full text link was obvious (to us) but the student could not find it; for example, one participant spent 1 minute 18 seconds trying to access a 1992 article from the paywalled journal website instead of using Google Scholar's full-text links to open access repositories. Other barriers to accessing academic sources included an article being slow to load, broken links in the reference list of an online journal article and two-stage cookie preference pop-ups from ProQuest. As CIBER (2008: 30) note, 'Any barrier to access: be that additional log-ins, payment or hard copy, are too high for most consumers and information behind those barriers will increasingly be ignored', driving students to less credible information sources.

Conclusion

Our findings are limited by the sample size and distribution, by the fact that participants were self-selecting and the fact that being observed may have altered their behaviour. They were also working under time constraints and not in their natural environment. While we cannot generalise from our small sample, it is fair to say that we observed an amazing diversity in skill levels and approaches to searching. We witnessed many examples of good practice, as well as instances where students would benefit from help. To quote an earlier study, 'user behaviour is very diverse ... One size does not fit all' (CIBER, 2008: 10).

Our results do reflect findings from previous, larger studies of information behaviour. In their literature review, Williams and Rowlands (2007) found no evidence of change in young people's searching expertise across generations; on the contrary, research dating from the early 1990s identified difficulties in formulating appropriate search terms and a tendency to repeat the same search rather than explore synonyms. Marchionini (1989) noted a preference for natural-language searching in the 1980s, before the World Wide Web became publicly available. And the importance of training students to evaluate the information they access has long been recognised (Burton and Chadwick, 2000).

It is beyond the scope of this chapter to examine in depth how best to tackle the challenge of information literacy in HE. However, we would like to summarise three key recommendations from the literature:

- Discovery tools must continue to standardise and simplify their interfaces (CIBER, 2008) and meet students' expectations regarding natural-language searches and the ability to deal with spelling/syntax mistakes (Holman, 2010). Otherwise, people will not use them.
- Such improvement will allow librarians and other information literacy developers to focus on teaching critical and evaluative skills rather than search techniques (Hampton-Reeves *et al.*, 2009; Lowe *et al.*, 2018). As the accessibility and abundance of information expands, the ability to evaluate it becomes increasingly vital (Asher *et al.*, 2013).
- Several studies point to increased collaboration between academic staff, librarians and students as the way forward (Yevelson-Shorsher and Bronstein, 2018). Librarians in the research institution comment that students are more likely to make use of their services if these are signposted by teaching staff, and especially in cases where an assignment has been set which requires students to make use of specific databases or to search for a particular source type.

We should perhaps not be surprised that the information literacy needs of our participants proved to be the same as those reported in previous decades. Information literacy is not a skill set we are born with but one we develop over time, with practice and guidance. To quote one of our librarians:

> I suppose it's a meta-problem, isn't it – finding things, looking critically, being a critical person – it's not just about library catalogues, it's a human skill, and those human skills are 'forever' problems, aren't they? Every new generation is going to have to face the same problems, so maybe there's not like a silver bullet ... but we can still try ...
>
> (Librarian 2)

Summary points

- Students are willing to use the library discovery tool, but sometimes have problems locating it.
- Key factors in Google's popularity are its simple interface and tolerance for natural-language search terms/spelling errors.
- Skill levels and approaches to searching are very diverse, but individuals tend to use the same approach across multiple platforms.

- The choice of search tool determines results to a large extent.
- Students appear to be more effective at judging the relevance than the credibility of the sources they select.
- Search skills appear higher among students on courses where these are foregrounded in an assignment and where there is good collaboration between academic and library staff.

Questions for discussion

- Where do you prefer to search for information? Why? Has this chapter made you reflect on how you might alter your search approaches in the future? If so, how?
- Who or what has helped you develop your information literacy skills?
- What more do you think your institution could do to help learners in this regard?

Recommended reading

O'Dochartaigh, N. (2012) *Internet Research Skills*. London: SAGE Publications Ltd.
Perruso, C. (2016) Undergraduates' Use of Google vs. Library Resources: A Four-Year Cohort Study. *College and Research Libraries*, 77(5), pp. 614–630.

References

Asher, A., Duke, L. and Wilson, S. (2013) Paths of Discovery: Comparing the Search Effectiveness of EBSCO Discovery Service, Summon, Google Scholar and Conventional Library Resources. *College and Research Libraries*, 74(5), pp. 464–488.

Bennett, S., Maton, K. and Kervin, L. (2008) The 'Digital Natives' Debate: A Critical Review of the Evidence. *British Journal of Education Technology*, 39(5), pp. 775–786.

Burton, V. and Chadwick, S. (2000) Investigating the Practices of Student Researchers: Patterns of Use and Criteria for Use of Internet and Library Sources. *Computers and Composition*, 17(3), pp. 309–328.

CIBER (2008) *Information Behaviour of the Researcher of the Future*. London: UCL.

CILIP (2018) *Definition of Information Literacy*. London: Information Literacy Group.

Georgas, H. (2014) Google vs. the Library (Part II): Student Search Patterns and Behaviors When Using Google and a Federated Search Tool. *Portal: Libraries and the Academy*, 24(4), pp. 503–532.

Greenberg, R. and Bar-Ilan, J. (2017) Library Metrics – Studying Academic Users' Information Retrieval Behavior: A Case Study of an Israeli University Library. *Journal of Librarianship and Information Science*, 49(4), pp. 454–467.

Hampton-Reeves, S., Mashiter, C., Westaway, J., Lumsden, P., Day, H., Hewertson, H. and Hart, A. (2009) *Students' Use of Research Content in Teaching and Learning: A Report for the Joint Information Systems Council (JISC) 2009*. Lancashire: Centre for Research-Informed Teaching.

Holman, L. (2010) Millennial Students' Mental Models of Search: Implications for Academic Librarians and Database Developers. *The Journal of Academic Librarianship*, 37(1), pp. 19–27.

Hsin, C., Cheng, Y. and Tsai, C. (2016) Searching and Sourcing Online Academic Literature: Comparisons of Doctoral Students and Junior Faculty in Education. *Online Information Review*, 40(7), pp. 979–997.

Lowe, M., Maxson, B., Stone, S., Miller, W., Snajdr, E. and Hanna, K. (2018) The Boolean is Dead, Long Live the Boolean! Natural Language versus Boolean Searching in Introductory Undergraduate Instruction. *College and Research Libraries*, 76(4), pp. 517–534.

Marchionini, G. (1989) Information-Seeking Strategies of Novices Using a Full-Text Electronic Encyclopedia. *Journal of the American Society for Information Science*, 40(1), pp. 54–66.

McCreadie, R., Macdonald, C. and Ounis, I. (2012) Map Reduce Indexing Strategies: Studying Scalability and Efficiency. *Information Processing and Management*, 48(5), pp. 1–16.

Mittermeyer, D. and Quirion, D. (2003) *Information Literacy: Study of Incoming First-Year Undergraduates in Quebec*. Montreal: Conference of Rectors and Principals of Quebec Universities.

Prabha, C., Connaway, L., Olszewski, L. and Jenkins, L. (2007) What is Enough? Satisficing Information Needs. *Journal of Documentation*, 63(1), pp. 74–89.

Raven, M. (2012) Bridging the Gap: Understanding the Differing Research Expectations of First-Year Students and Professors. *Evidence Based Library and Information Practice*, 7(3), pp. 4–31.

Salehi, S., Du, J. and Ashman, H. (2018) Use of Web Search Engines and Personalisation in Information Searching for Educational Purposes. *Information Research*, 23(2), pp. 1–13.

Williams, P. and Rowlands, I. (2007) *The Literature on Young People and Their Information Behaviour: Work Package II*. Available at: http://citeseerx.ist.psu.edu/viewdoc/download?doi=10.1.1.643.8970&rep=rep1&type=pdf (accessed 15 January 2020).

Yevelson-Shorsher, A. and Bronstein, J. (2018) Three Perspectives on Information Literacy in Academia: Talking to Librarians, Faculty and Students. *College and Research Libraries*, 79(4), pp. 535–553.

7 Academic diversity and its implications for teaching and learning

Anesa Hosein and Namrata Rao

Introduction

In the last 20 years, there have been calls to 'feminise' the university curriculum, and more recently a movement has been stirred by students to 'decolonise' it to make it less male and Anglo-centric (Le Grange, 2016). These calls have been made to ensure that the curriculum is appropriate for the diverse staff and student bodies in higher education (HE). There is now increasing diversity among staff and students in Western higher education institutions (HEIs) which reflects the social diversity currently existing in the Western world. Whether this diversity is reflected in teaching and learning processes is questionable, and it is not prominent in extant literature (see e.g. Kinchin *et al.*, 2018). In this chapter, we will examine the notion of academic diversity in HE and consider the possible implications of such diversity for students' learning experiences and for their academic role models. To examine the diversity of academics, we will use the UK as a case study and draw on demographic data collected by the UK's Higher Education Statistical Agency (HESA) in 2015–16.

Why is it important to examine academic diversity?

It is the policy in most HEIs, particularly in the UK, to increase diversity within academia among both students and academic staff (Bhopal, 2019). In the UK, the Equality Act was updated in 2010 to ensure that staff and students were protected against discrimination in employment or access to education in any of nine characteristics (see Table 7.1).

Ely and Thomas (2001) suggest that there are three perspectives that organisations such as HEIs can employ in increasing the diversity of academic staff:

- Integration-and-Learning Perspective: HEIs see academic diversity as a valuable resource that can be utilised to help them achieve their missions or goal.
- Access-and-Legitimacy Perspective: HEIs are aware that their incoming student body is diverse and want to match the diversity of their academic staff.
- Discrimination-and-Fairness Perspective: HEIs are morally persuaded that there should be more diverse academics in order to be fair and eliminate discrimination. It is a perspective that aligns most closely with the rationale for the 2010 Equality Act.

Throughout this chapter, we look at how HEIs are meeting some of the equality characteristics from the 2010 Equality Act and consider what this means in terms of the Ely and Thomas perspectives, particularly in respect of Integration-and-Learning.

Table 7.1 Protected characteristics based on the 2010 Equality Act

Protected characteristics
Age
Race
Sex
Disability
Gender reassignment
Marriage or civil partnership
Pregnancy and maternity
Sexual orientation
Religion and belief

The landscape of academic diversity

Using the HESA statistics, academic diversity was examined across seven characteristics. Four of these (age, sex, race and disability) were selected because they were based on the protected characteristics of the Equality Act (see Table 7.1). The other three are selected based on employment characteristics: the academic employment role, mode of employment and teaching qualification. For most academics, their *academic employment* role relates to teaching and/or research. This generates three forms of employment: teaching only; teaching and research; research only. Academics can sometimes have none of these roles; for example, they might have a management/leadership role, but this is rare. *Mode of employment* refers to the type of contract an academic may have, such as full-time or part-time. We will examine each of these factors separately when considering the curriculum and the student learning experience.

Age

In the UK, the majority of academics are between 36 and 55 years (Table 7.2). The population of young academics is relatively small because employers generally require a qualification at doctoral level (except perhaps in professional programmes such as acting and nursing). This means that the earliest a person may have an academic contract will be around 25 years.

Having mainly academics in the middle age groups has some advantages as well as some disadvantages. The main advantages being that if these academics were in academia prior to their mid-30s, they would possibly be more experienced teachers who can create an engaging learning environment. However, this group of academics may be out of touch with the experiences of new undergraduates, or unlikely to bring experiences and examples that resonate with new undergraduates. For example, younger academics are closer in age to the average undergraduate and hence may be perceived as more likely to remember their experience as undergraduates and to empathise with students (Muzaka, 2009; Weinkle *et al.*, 2020). Secondly, they may be perceived as being more approachable, and hence students may find it easier to engage with them outside of timetabled classroom hours. However, the disadvantages are that young academics may not be seen as credible, and if they have not worked outside of universities may lack the real-world experience of

Table 7.2 Diversity in academic staff based on key
characteristics (HESA 2015/2016)

Characteristics	Diversity in staffing (%)
Age	
35 and under	29
36–55	53
Over 55	19
Sex	
Female	46
Male	54
Race	
White	78
Ethnic minorities	14
Unknown	8
Disability	
With disability (declared)	4
Without disability	93
Unknown (undeclared)	3
Nationality	
UK	70
EU	18
Non-EU	13
Mode of employment	
Full-time	67
Part-time	33
Employment role	
Teaching only	27
Research and teaching	48
Research only	24
Other	1

the variety of skills graduates need in non-academic employment (Crozier and Woolnough, 2019). This lack of real-world experience may make it difficult for the young academic to relate theory to practice.

Discussion point

What do you think are the advantages of being taught by younger academics?

Gender

Although 51 per cent of the UK population is female, there are more male than female academics (see Figure 7.1) and this is not unique to the UK. The need to feminise the curriculum is often called

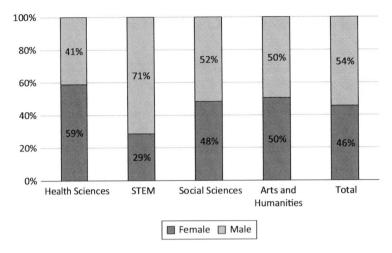

Figure 7.1 Distribution of academics across the disciplines by gender.

for because of the lack of women authors in the extant literature and female perspectives in the curriculum. This is because universities historically were typically male-oriented, with male academics doing most of the disciplinary research which fed into the curriculum (Peters, 2015). Except for the Health Sciences, male academics tend to dominate the disciplines (Figure 7.1). For example, there are less than a third of female academics in the science, technology, engineering and mathematics (STEM) disciplines.

In the last few years, a more even balance has been achieved, with just under half of the academics in universities being women (46 per cent). However, in some disciplines, the curriculum and research are still lacking in female-oriented perspectives. For example, Caroline Criado-Perez (2019) has demonstrated that male-dominated disciplines such as STEM have often omitted female perspectives and have produced outcomes that are relevant only to men, such as crash dummies being only of the male physique. In other disciplines such as history and literature there is an over-reliance on male perspectives as these are what are published, and women's voices are lost or marginalised (Greene and Kahn, 2003). The research that informs teaching in many disciplines is still dominated by men (Figure 7.2). This research is also more likely to be cited and hence creates a dominance in the field. Following the reasoning of Criado-Perez (2019), having a relatively equal number of women and men in teaching may mean that women's ideas and thoughts are more likely to be brought to the fore and women may recognise gaps in the curriculum that men may overlook.

Ethnicity and race

In most nations, there are dominant ethnicities in the population, and there is an expectation that the make-up of HE should reflect the ethnic distribution in the population. The UK has a predominantly white population; the 2011 census indicated a white population of 86 per cent with ethnic minorities at 14 per cent. To some extent, this is reflected in the academic staff distribution – with 14 per cent of ethnic minorities and 78 per cent white. The percentage of white academic staff is lower than in the population; however, there is 8 per cent of the academic staff population for which the ethnicity

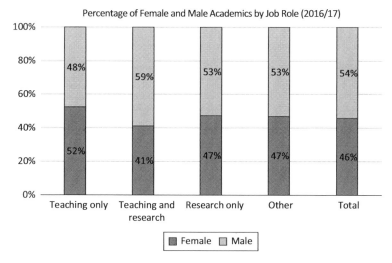

Figure 7.2 The distribution of academic job roles by gender (based on HESA statistics 2016/17).

is unknown. Perhaps more importantly, however, is the extent to which the curriculum is shaped by different ethnicities. Traditionally, the Global South has imported curriculum and educational policies from the Global North. This means that UK curricula may be heavily biased towards contexts and literature that reflect a white British perspective. Global South countries may, therefore, not highlight their perspective within the curriculum and therefore not allow for cross-pollination of educational ideas/curriculum between countries (Le Grange, 2016). Also, as students are increasingly becoming global citizens and migrant workers, it is important that different perspectives are shared and incorporated in the curriculum so that it reflects different cultures and ethnicities. For this reason, attempts have been made to make the curriculum more internationalised and globalised to enable graduates to recognise issues in the Global South as well (Leask, 2005).

Disability

In the UK, only four per cent of academic staff have a declared disability. This means that students often do not encounter many HE teaching staff with a disability. In the UK population, 16 per cent of working-age adults have a disability (DWP, 2014). The WHO suggests this is normal for most populations – they have estimated that about 15 per cent of the world's population has some form of disability (WHO, 2018). Thus, the figures within HE suggest that there is an under-representation of staff with disabilities. Not seeing or knowing staff with disabilities in HE will mean that there are arguably insufficient role models in higher education to make young disabled people aspire to academia or to recognise it as an inclusive space where individuals who have disabilities are welcome and included. However, some people with physical disabilities may have challenges that are difficult for the university to accommodate. Universities that offer distance-learning and online programmes can tackle some disability issues related to mobility, visual learning and so on.

Discussion point

Do you think that universities are excluding people with disabilities because they do not pro-actively cater for them?

If disabled staff are under-represented in HE, then academic staff may have little first-hand experience in understanding how academic practices and activities (such as assessments, group projects) need to be adapted for both academic staff and students with disability needs. Further, there may be some students and academics who may not recognise that they have a disability. In the absence of other individuals with similar disabilities, there may be a lack of appreciation of the spectrum of disabilities, which may consequently lead to their disability not being recognised. Often issues such as dyslexia and dyscalculia, for example, are sometimes discovered much later in life, and students need to be guided to recognise this at a much earlier age to ensure that their participation in HE is not affected (Battistutta *et al.*, 2018). Having academic staff with disabilities can make it possible for those students with disabilities to disclose them and, by gaining support, to be able to enjoy a good university learning experience. It is perhaps appropriate within teaching to highlight and include literature and discoveries from people with disabilities in the curriculum to make students (particularly those who have not declared a disability) aware that disabilities should not hamper their outcomes.

Nationality

In the UK, over a quarter of academics are from overseas (see Figure 7.3); however, this data obscures the fact that some academics from overseas have become British citizens. Unsurprisingly, a majority of academics are classified as British citizens (70 per cent). The largest percentage of

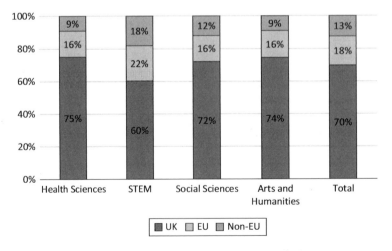

Figure 7.3 Distribution of academics by nationality and discipline.

migrant academics comes from the European Union (EU). Again this is not surprising, as the EU promotes freedom of movement to their member states (UK was a member state until January 2020), and academics from different parts of the EU can currently be employed without a visa – applying for which can otherwise be expensive and time-consuming (Foote *et al.*, 2008).

Although the population of non-EU countries makes up about 93 per cent of the world's population, the percentage of non-EU academics in the UK is only 13 per cent. The EU population in the world in contrast is just under 6 per cent, but 18 per cent of academics in the UK come from the EU. This demonstrates that having easy flows of people through immigration schemes can influence the diversity of academics based on their nationality in countries such as the UK. Further, the geographical proximity as well as population size and knowledge of language may also influence the in-flows of different nationalities into academia in some countries.

However, in 2016, the UK opted to leave the EU, and from January 2021, the right of freedom of movement to the UK from EU countries will no longer apply. This means EU academics will no longer have priority over those from other nations, and it remains to be seen whether this will affect the distribution of nationalities in UK universities. As English is the lingua franca, UK universities may in future attract more English-speaking migrant academics to create an internationally diverse staff body. Kinchin *et al.* (2018) found that the curriculum was enhanced by the presence of international academics, as they were able to bring first-hand real-life examples of their international context to the classrooms. Through this, international academics were able to offer different perspectives which enabled students to learn more about being global citizens and develop their intercultural competence.

Discussion point

What sort of data may be missed out if academics are classified as British citizens but may have been naturalised here?

Academic employment role

In the UK, female academics tend to have more teaching-only roles in comparison to male academics, who tend to have more research-only contracts. Interestingly, male academics have a higher percentage of research and teaching contracts (Figure 7.2). Traditionally, universities have had academics who did both teaching and research. inspired by the Humboldtian idea that research and teaching are linked (Josephson *et al.*, 2014; see also Chapter 11 in this volume). However, increasingly, universities across the world have staff that focus on teaching-only or research-only roles. Those staff who only do research may do some teaching, but this tends to be restricted to guest lectures in a course rather than leading and contributing fully to a course. Most UK staff have both research and teaching contracts (48 per cent). There is an argument that academic staff need to have *research-informed teaching* (Jenkins and Healey, 2005). This is where teaching is informed from the literature about the field (this is sometimes called *scholarship*) or by incorporating their own research into their teaching. Students on courses where lecturers incorporate their own research are perhaps more likely to have cutting-edge insights into what is occurring in the field, particularly as they may know about findings even one to two years before they are published. However, some of this research may be too advanced for a new student to understand, although one can argue it is the lecturer's job to make knowledge comprehensible to all levels. Further, these lecturers may only be willing to speak about their specialist research areas. On the other hand, teaching-only staff would perhaps read from a wide variety of literature and be able to share a breadth of recent research in their subject area with students (Hosein, 2017).

Mode of employment

Academic contracts in the UK are either full-time or part-time. Overwhelmingly, most of the full-time contracts are held by men, whilst most part-time contracts are held by women (see Figure 7.4). Most academics tend to be full-time (67 per cent); however, academics with caring responsibilities or particular life-style preferences may opt for a part-time contract. Alternatively, some universities may only have the finances for part-time contracts. There are several perceived advantages for students in having a full-time academic; in particular, a student may be more likely to find the academic on campus and hence have better access. However, this might be a misconception, as some full-time academics may be travelling for research and may not even *be* on campus. Having part-time academics teaching students may often lead to students having limited access to these staff. However, such part-time academics often have more than one job, which then allows them to draw on their experiences to enrich the learning experience of their students.

It might be suggested that full-time academics are more committed to their job, and hence to their students, but this is not always true; Maynard and Joseph (2006) show that part-time academics may be just as committed. It is possible that part-time academics might be more enthusiastic about their job and meeting their students as they only see them a few times in the week and might provide a more engaging classroom. Black female and white female academics were more likely to have part-time contracts (see Figure 7.5).

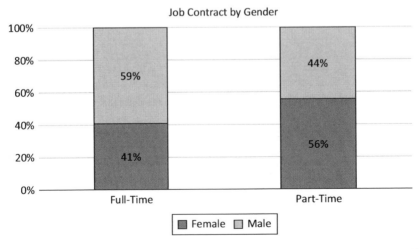

Figure 7.4 The distribution of contract type by gender (based on HESA statistics 2016–17).

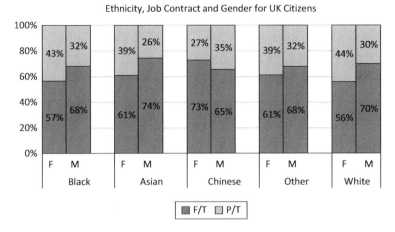

Figure 7.5 The distribution of ethnicity, gender and job contract type of UK citizens.

Discussion point

What might be the impact on your learning experience of having lecturers who are part-time as opposed to full-time?

Why do you think female academics tend to have more part-time jobs?

Teaching qualification

In both primary and secondary schools, teachers are normally required to have a teaching qualification (QTS). This helps teachers to understand approaches to teaching and how students learn in order to tailor their teaching to meet the needs of their students. In HE, there is no requirement to have a formal teaching qualification. However, within the last two decades, there has been a move to get more HE teachers qualified, or to have some training in teaching. HE teachers are hence likely to take a postgraduate certificate in learning and teaching in higher education, which usually earns them the status of Fellow of the Higher Education Academy (FHEA). This is accreditation for teacher training at this level. Across all universities, just over 54 per cent of teaching staff have a teaching qualification (see Table 7.3). Whilst just under half of the teachers are untrained, this statistic is probably not as bad as it looks. Normally, staff who have less than 3 years' experience are required to take the teaching qualification. Those with over 10 years' experience may well be experienced teachers who have had informal training, but untrained teachers may not be aware of different approaches to teaching and may thus replicate approaches they were accustomed to. That said, they may now be willing to innovate and try different approaches that can make teaching and learning interesting and effective.

Staff who have a teaching-only contract are less likely to have a teaching qualification than those with research and teaching, as well as those who are part-time. This may mean that in those disciplines which have teaching-only staff, those staff may feel less confident in trying out different approaches, and this may affect the learning experience of students in those disciplines.

Table 7.3 Teaching qualifications distribution in England

Teaching qualification	
Has teaching aualification	54%
No teaching qualification	29%
Not known	17%
Job role (of known qualification)	
Teaching only	57%
Research and teaching	70%
Employment mode (of known qualification)	
Full-time	71%
Part-time	56%

Characterising diversity in the disciplines

We have briefly looked at how gender might influence teaching in the disciplines. We now explore how the diversity of academic teaching staff can influence the teaching of disciplines in more detail. This is sometimes referred to as an 'intersectionality approach' (Crenshaw, 1991). We first look at the diversity of staff across the disciplines with respect to age and then nationality.

Age and discipline

Generally, the STEM disciplines tend to have younger academics, which may reflect how the disciplines recruit (see Figure 7.6). In the STEM disciplines, it is common for students to start their PhD directly after graduating with a bachelor's degree and hence have younger academics start teaching at around 26 years old, usually after the completion of a PhD. However, in other disciplines such as the Social Sciences, most academics tend to work outside the university, and then later in life they return to do a PhD or teach within a university. There are advantages and disadvantages of being taught by a young academic.

Undergraduates in the Social Sciences may have a better understanding of the range of opportunities available to them because they are often taught by older and more professionally experienced academics, whilst those in STEM degrees may have the comfort of being taught by younger staff whom students potentially perceive to be more approachable (Muzaka, 2009; Weinkle *et al.*, 2020). Thus, students in STEM degrees need to ensure they grasp the opportunities that are afforded by visiting and guest lecturers who provide these real-life experiences to understand how they can use their skills and understanding in contexts beyond university. Those students in the Social Sciences, on the other hand, need to recognise that although they may have an initial reticence to engage with their lecturers because of difference in ages and experience should try to seek out informal opportunities to help build a rapport that can make learning enjoyable.

Nationality and discipline

As noted previously, the UK has a large migrant academic population. We now explore which disciplines are more likely to benefit from this. In the STEM disciplines, just under half of academics

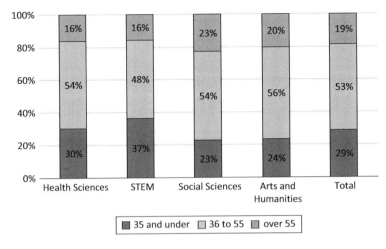

Figure 7.6 Distribution of academics by age and discipline.

(40 per cent) are migrants (Figure 7.3). The primary reason for this is that there is a shortage of STEM graduates in the UK, and academics from different regions of the world are often brought in to sustain programmes. In terms of intercultural and global understanding, this means that STEM students may be able to gain more from this diversity. As the percentage of non-EU academics in STEM is relatively high (18 per cent), it also means that they are less likely to get a primarily Euro-centric view of the world and may increase their understanding of the problems and challenges facing different regions of the world. The Health Sciences and Arts and Humanities have the least diversity in academic staff in terms of nationality, and their students may get a primarily British view of concepts. However, in disciplines such as Medicine (and other vocational subjects), this is perhaps needed as students need to be registered with the local State board to ensure they are eligible to practise and hence need to be familiar with local standards and regulations (see e.g. Hosein and Harle, 2017). Migrant academics may of course be less familiar with these. However, it may potentially limit such students' mobility if their learning is restricted to a mainly British context.

Secondary data analysis

The approach used to analyse the data in this chapter has been secondary data analysis. Secondary data analysis by its nature indicates that it is data that has been collected previously for a different purpose and is now being analysed for another purpose. For HESA, the data collected is census data, in that it is not a sample of the population of HEIs in the UK but rather a sample of the full population. Therefore, using statistical analysis to infer what the population is like is no longer nec-essary as we have access to the data for the entire population. However, one of the frustrations of secondary data analysis is that sometimes the data that is needed is not always available or was not collected, or the researcher would need more permissions to access it (Hosein, 2019). For example, the intersectional data on teaching qualifications and discipline is not freely available. Thus, further inspection of how diversity can affect teaching is sometimes affected by the avail-ability of accessible, good-quality data. Additionally, we have only analysed quantitative data, which can only provide an understanding of what is happening; we are therefore left to make inferences about why this might be the case or what the consequences of this might be. This is where qualitative data is often most useful in generating empirical evidence of the why, and to see what it looks like on the ground. Educational research arguably requires both to get a holistic view of the issue being explored.

Discussion point

What sort of qualitative data do you think you would need to understand the consequences of academic diversity for teaching?
What quantitative data do you think is needed to give us a better understanding of the diversity of academic staff?

Challenges and opportunities due to disciplinary diversity

What do these results mean for a university or a student? The diversity of the academic team means that there are more serendipitous incidents that enable students to learn about issues from different perspectives, as academics may bring in their own personal and professional perspectives (Kinchin *et al.*, 2018). However, in some academic systems, these personal perspectives may be supressed, and universities may need to encourage academics to share their personal stories to encourage a more enriched curriculum for the student. Hence, beyond the knowledge that is provided in lectures, academics from diverse backgrounds can bring additional and contextual knowledge to sessions. The perspective that they add based on their background is the value-added element to the lecture. Further, students encountering academics from diverse backgrounds may be able to adjust their unconscious bias, for example, recognising that STEM academics can be women as well. Students should also be proactive and seek out academics' diverse perspectives as these staff can provide a unique contribution to the dialogue of the discipline. For example, students in the Education discipline can ask international academics about their views on streaming/setting in classrooms in their home countries. We need to be wary, however, of reducing academics to their distinguishing attributes; we should recognise them as whole individuals who may have a number of intersectionalities that do not by themselves represent all of the people who share the same characteristics. However, students can interact with a wider range of academics to broaden their horizons and their critical thinking.

Conclusion

The HESA statistics allowed us to examine the diversity of academia and from this make some inferences about how diversity may affect student learning experiences and the curriculum. Without this data, it would be impossible to understand the disparities between disciplines as far as protected characteristics are concerned. In some countries, this data is not collected, but most Western countries have a national statistical agency which will collect similar data. However, if we are trying to examine diversity, then it is imperative that there are also good data collection methods available to track changes in academic diversity.

Throughout the chapter, we have noted that academic diversity appears to reflect the population, which suggests that institutions are trying to reflect fairness in their recruitment. However, in some disciplines, there may be a need to demonstrate greater academic diversity to increase access and reflect the backgrounds of their students, by increasing the number of women academics in STEM subjects, for example. We have argued, however, that by considering an integrating-and-learning perspective, students may be exposed to more diverse perspectives and a more internationalised, inclusive and enriched curriculum.

Summary points

- Academic diversity varies across disciplines.
- Academic diversity of gender, ethnicity and disability is mainly reflective of the general population, but this may limit the diversity of the curriculum.
- Integrating and learning from diversity can provide a richer and better curriculum for all students.

Recommended reading

Bhopal, K. (2019) Gender, Ethnicity and Career Progression in UK Higher Education: A Case Study Analysis. *Research Papers in Education*, pp. 1–16. Available at: https://doi.org/10.1080/02671522.2019.1615118
Hosein, A. and Rao, N. (2019) International Student Voice(s) - Where and What Are They? In: S. Lygo-Baker, I. Kinchin and N. Winstone (Eds) *Engaging Student Voices in Higher Education: Diverse Perspectives and Expectations in Partnership*. Cham: Springer International Publishing, pp. 71–87.
Vos, M., Çelik, G. and de Vries, S. (2016) Making Cultural Differences Matter? Diversity Perspectives in Higher Education. *Equality, Diversity and Inclusion: An International Journal*, 35(4), pp. 254–266.

References

Battistutta, L., Commissaire, E. and Steffgen, G. (2018) Impact of the Time of Diagnosis on the Perceived Competence of Adolescents with Dyslexia. *Learning Disability Quarterly*, 41(3), pp. 170–178.
Bhopal, K. (2019) Gender, Ethnicity and Career Progression in UK Higher Education: A Case Study Analysis. *Research Papers in Education*, pp. 1–16. Available at: https://doi.org/10.1080/02671522.2019.1615118 (accessed 30 March 2020).
Crenshaw, K. (1991) Mapping the Margins: Intersectionality, Identity Politics, and Violence Against Women of Color. *Stanford Law Review*, 43(6), pp. 1241–1299.
Criado-Perez, C. (2019) *Invisible Women: Exposing Data Bias in a World Designed for Men*. London: Chatto and Windus.
Crozier, S. and Woolnough, H. (2019) Is Age Just a Number? Credibility and Identity of Younger Academics in UK Business Schools. *Management Learning*. Available at: https://doi:10.1177/1350507619878807 (accessed 30 March 2020).
DWP (2014) Official Statistics: Disability Facts and Figures. Available at: https://www.gov.uk/government/publi cations/disability-facts-and-figures/disability-facts-and-figures (accessed 9 March 2020).
Ely, R. and Thomas, D. (2001) Cultural Diversity at Work: The Effects of Diversity Perspectives on Work Group Processes and Outcomes. *Administrative Science Quarterly*, 46(2), pp. 229–273.
Home Office (2010) *Equality Act*. London: The Stationery Office.
Foote, K., Li, W., Monk, J. and Theobald, R. (2008) Foreign-Born Scholars in US Universities: Issues, Concerns and Strategies. *Journal of Geography in Higher Education*, 32(2), pp. 167–178.
Greene, G. and Kahn, C. (2003) Feminist Scholarship and the Social Construction of Woman. In: G. Greene and C. Kahn (Eds) *Making a Difference*. Abingdon: , pp. 14–49
Hosein, A. (2017) Pedagogic Frailty and the Research-Teaching Nexus. In: I. Kinchin and N. Winstone (Eds) *Pedagogic Frailty and Resilience in the University*. Rotterdam: Sense Publishers, pp. 135–149.

Hosein, A. (2019) Girls' Video Gaming Behaviour and Undergraduate Degree Selection: A Secondary Data Analysis Approach. *Computers in Human Behavior*, 91(1), pp. 226–235.

Hosein, A. and Harle, J. (2017) The Vulnerability of a Small Discipline and Its Search for Appropriate Pedagogy: The Case of Medical Physics. In: E. Medland, R. Watermeyer, A. Hosein, I. Kinchin and S. Lygo-Baker (Eds) *Pedagogical Peculiarities – Conversation at the Edge of University Teaching and Learning*. Leiden, Netherlands: Brill (Sense) Publishers, pp. 69–85.

Jenkins, A. and Healey, M. (2005) Institutional Strategies to Link Teaching and Research. Available at: http://www.heacademy.ac.uk/assets/documents/research/Institutional_strategies.pdf (accessed 9 March 2020).

Josephson, P., Karlsohn, T. and Östling, J. (2014) *Scientific and Learned Cultures and Their Institutions: The Humboldtian Tradition, Origins and Legacies*. Leiden: Brill.

Kinchin, I., Rao, N., Hosein, A. and Mace, W. (2018) Migrant Academics and Professional Learning Gains: Perspectives of the Native Academic. Available at: https://www.srhe.ac.uk/downloads/reports-2016/Kinchin-Rao-Hosein-Research-Report.pdf (accessed 9 March 2020).

Le Grange, L. (2016) Decolonising the University Curriculum: Leading Article. *South African Journal of Higher Education*, 30(2), pp. 1–12.

Leask, B. (2005) Internationalisation of the Curriculum. In: J. Caroll and J. Ryan (Eds) *Teaching International Students: Improving Learning for All*. Abingdon: Routledge, pp. 119–129.

Maynard, D. and Joseph, T. (2006) Are All Part-Time Faculty Underemployed? The Influence of Faculty Status Preference on Satisfaction and Commitment. *Higher Education*, 55(2), p. 139.

Muzaka, V. (2009) The Niche of Graduate Teaching Assistants (GTAs): Perceptions and Reflections. *Teaching in Higher Education*, 14(1), pp. 1–12.

Peters, M. (2015) Why is My Curriculum White? *Educational Philosophy and Theory*, 47(7), pp. 641–646.

Weinkle, L., Stratford, J. and Lee, L. (2020) Voice in Digital Education: The Impact of Instructor's Perceived Age and Gender on Student Learning and Evaluation. *Anatomical Sciences Education*, 13(1), pp. 59–70.

WHO (2018) Disability and Health. Available at: https://www.who.int/news-room/fact-sheets/detail/disability-and-health (accessed 9 March 2020).

8 Let's keep it casual?

Rising precarity and acts of resistance in UK universities

Esther Muddiman, Rowan Campbell and Grace Krause

Introduction

This chapter explores competing narratives of precarity (insecure employment/income), flexibility and efficiency in higher education (HE). Although discussions of casualisation and precarity have become increasingly prominent in HE, with 54 per cent of UK academic staff on insecure contracts, the way this impacts on working conditions and learning environments in universities is contested. Casualised working is often presented as a flexible and mutually beneficial arrangement for staff and students, or an unavoidable reality in austere times. However, there are concerns that this flexibility is asymmetrical, as workers often find themselves vulnerable, financially insecure and unable to make long-term plans. The material, psychological and social impacts on both staff and students in relation to teaching, research activities and wellbeing are outlined.

The chapter examines how unions and grassroots movements have engaged with these issues through collective bargaining and creative outputs (e.g. #ZinesAgainstPrecarity), emphasising the importance of both online and physical spaces. This will be embedded in critiques of wider societal trends of the gig economy and zero-hours contracts. It concludes by exploring what is next for HE and precarity, setting out alternate visions of university life for staff and students.

What is casualised work, and how prevalent is it in HE?

The word *casual* is often used to refer to work that is temporary or sporadic and/or informally arranged. Some contemporary examples include bicycle couriers (e.g. Deliveroo) and seasonal workers (e.g. fruit pickers or extra shop staff over the Christmas period). The supposed benefits of casualised work are that workers have the flexibility to choose when and how they work, and employers are able to respond to changes in demand for their products and services. The flipside of this 'flexibility', however, is that workers are not guaranteed a certain income or job stability. In some arrangements, it is also unclear how much flexibility workers really have, as their working patterns are often determined by the employer at very short notice. They may not be guaranteed a set number of hours but are penalised for turning work down. This unpredictability may not be an issue for certain groups of workers, including, for example, students wanting to earn some extra money alongside their studies, but is likely to be problematic for those relying on casual work as their main or only source of income, for those needing to take time off for mental or physical ill-health and for those with caring responsibilities. In the UK, relying on a casualised workforce has been a key mechanism for companies to reduce employee costs and increase profits. Concerns have been raised by organisations and charities about the impact of casualisation on workers – including calls from *Better Than Zero* to abolish zero-hours contracts, and legal challenges levelled against ride-sharing apps attempting to secure workers' rights for drivers.

In addition to these well-known examples, casualisation has quietly been taking hold in the UK higher education sector as cash-squeezed departments try to plug gaps in research or teaching provision by employing PhD students or early-career academics (ECAs) either as hourly-paid tutors or on short-term teaching-only or research-only contracts. Increasing numbers of university staff are employed on temporary or zero-hours contracts, meaning that they have fewer employment rights compared to staff on permanent or open-ended contracts. One prevalent example is 'teaching' roles that last for ten months of the year and do not cover the summer months, in which permanently employed staff carry out research and prepare their teaching materials. In addition to losing two months of pay per year and having to re-apply for their role every summer, these university workers are not entitled to statutory benefits such as maternity pay.

Individual/group task

What do you think makes a good job in terms of working conditions? How might that change over the life course of an employee?

The number of insecure academic jobs has exploded over recent years (Lopes and Dewan 2014:28). Higher Education Statistics Agency (HESA) data indicates that 156,295 academic staff were employed with some kind of teaching function in 2016–17. Over a third of this teaching workforce were employed on teaching-only contracts during this period, and within this group, almost three-quarters worked part-time and over half were on fixed-term contracts (HESA, 2017). A 2019 HESA bulletin reports 28,450 hourly-paid teaching-only staff, with 61 per cent of those in this group employed on fixed-term contracts (HESA 2019). According to the University and College Union (UCU), there are a further 71,000 teachers on 'atypical' contracts not included in official HESA statistics – these are predominantly the most casually employed workers with the fewest employment rights. In terms of research staff, UCU estimates that 70 per cent of the 49,000 researchers working in UK universities are on fixed-term contracts, with many more on nominally 'open-ended' contracts which nevertheless have a built-in expiry date (UCU, 2019). UCU estimates that casualised and precariously employed staff are now conducting 25–30 per cent of teaching in many universities (UCU, 2019). Interestingly, casualised working practices seem to be particularly prevalent in the elite Russell Group of universities; in these institutions, up to 70 per cent of those doing 'front-line teaching' are employed on 'atypical' precarious contracts (Bowsher, 2018:2).

A UCU survey of 3,800 casualised university staff undertaken in 2019 paints a worrying picture in terms of staff wellbeing:

- 97 per cent of those on a fixed-term contract said that they would rather be on a permanent contract, while 80 per cent of hourly-paid staff said that they would rather be on a contract that guaranteed them hours, even if it meant less flexibility.

- Almost two-thirds of participants had held two or more jobs over the last 12 months.
- Over half of participants said they had struggled to make ends meet, and 40 per cent experienced problems paying bills.
- Over two-thirds of participants reported that working on insecure contracts had damaged their mental health.
- Over 80 per cent of participants said that it was difficult to make long-term financial commitments or family plans.
- Lack of job security was the key reason that participants cited as a reason to leave academia.
- 78 per cent of participants reported regularly working more hours than they are paid for in order to do their jobs properly, and hourly-paid teachers reported that they do, on average, 45 per cent of their work without pay.

A qualitative study exploring the experiences and pedagogical practices of casualised staff at universities in England and Wales draws similarly bleak conclusions:

> Precarious work is associated with and characterises the effects of neoliberal policy – the transference of economic risk onto workers, and the erosion of workers' rights, the flexibilisation and casualisation of work contracts, self-responsibility, financial insecurity, and emotional stress.
>
> (Lopes and Dewan, 2014:28)

In addition to the human cost of casualisation in terms of chronic financial insecurity, overwork, stress and the inability to plan for the future, figures also suggest that precarious working conditions have a detrimental effect on the quality of teaching and research. Of those casualised staff surveyed by the UCU in 2019, 71 per cent said that they 'did not have enough paid time to give their students the feedback they deserved', and 73 per cent said that the research that they were involved with had been 'negatively affected by employment on short term contracts' (2019:5). Further, 96 per cent of respondents agreed that 'more secure employment would help to foster genuinely innovative research activity' (UCU, 2019:5).

Understanding shifts towards casualisation and 'agility' in HE

However, while UCU describes casualisation as a massive problem for the HE sector (2019), university managers tend to talk more favourably about agility and market performance. To understand the increasing prevalence of such narratives and casual work in UK universities, we need to consider wider trends of neoliberal marketisation and financialisation in HE. As other authors in this volume have described, there have been some significant changes to the way that universities are managed over the last two decades, with the sector becoming 'larger, more financially oriented and less publically funded than before' (Budd, 2016:1). As a consequence, universities are pitted against one another, jostling for students, research grants and national and international rankings (McGettigan, 2013). Indeed, in September 2015, Jo Johnson (then Minister of State for Universities, Science, Research and Innovation) stated that HE providers 'entering and leaving the market is a sign of healthy competition, and it is something of which we should expect to see more'. Shifting risk from the institution to the individual, therefore, is one method of trying to shore up institutional survival. University managers therefore position casualisation as an unfortunate but unavoidable consequence of global forces.

Precarious research, precarious teaching

Here we map out the key interlocking factors contributing to casualisation and outline some of the implications for staff and students in relation to both research and teaching. It has been over 10 years since the university sector (including Universities UK, Guild HE and Research Councils UK) first signed a Concordat (Vitae, 2008) – pledging to improve career structures for research staff with seven key principles. An updated version (Vitae, 2019) acknowledges that there is 'still much to do' in terms of employment and career progression, to 'ensure our researchers are 'given every opportunity to thrive' (p. ii).

Increasing numbers of 'early career' researchers and changes to the ways that research is funded and conducted have dramatically shifted the landscape of research in UK universities. Just as the proportion of young people studying for undergraduate degrees has risen, so too has the number of postgraduate and doctoral (PhD) students. This makes for an incredibly competitive postdoctoral labour market, with many more PhD students passing their viva voce than there are spaces in UK academia (Bowsher, 2018). A surplus of talented and hardworking scholars means that employers can demand ever more from junior academics, and the bar for secure work is set dizzyingly high. In Bowsher's words, 'the boom in insecure teaching contracts is now a way of "getting by" for large numbers of ECAs in the absence of more secure employment' (2018:3).

Intensified competition for research funding has led to a shift away from individual research fellowships towards interdisciplinary and large-scale collaborative projects. This poses another challenge for early career academics: 'as the number of permanent jobs has decreased, the traditional route from postdoctoral researcher to permanent lecturer has been replaced by a new landscape of alternative short-term, part-time 'post-docs' that are attached to large research projects' (Bowsher, 2018:3–4). In this market for 'jobbing' researchers, it becomes harder for junior academics to exercise autonomy or develop a coherent career narrative. These conditions can make it difficult for 'early-career' academics to progress into a permanent post:

> It can be difficult to generate the necessary publications if your research autonomy is restricted by your position in a large project, or if moving from post to post creates a backlog of unfinished publications.
>
> (Bowsher, 2018:4)

Indeed, many casualised staff are no longer 'early-career' and have spent over a decade 'ping-ponging' between various short-term contracts.

The Research Excellence Framework (REF) can also be viewed as a mechanism through which scarce resources can be divided up between universities, according to their research 'performance'. The REF encourages universities to ignore riskier, less proven researchers as institutions scramble to maximise their score and secure their standing as five-star centres of excellence (Bowsher, 2018). There are currently no rules to stop universities including work undertaken by research staff who are no longer employed by them. This means that institutions can benefit from the labour of casualised staff even after their contract has been terminated or they have been made redundant.

Traditionally, academics have been employed both to undertake research and to teach and supervise students, with one practice informing the other. Indeed, the elite Russell Group of universities puts much stock in its cutting-edge 'research-led teaching'. Casualisation in the sector now means that these two roles are often separated – with senior academic staff being 'bought out' of their teaching responsibilities in order to pursue research, and junior staff being drafted in to teach, or to labour under senior staff on research projects. The widespread practice of 'outsourcing' teaching to less experienced early-career academics often entails the allocation of heavy teaching loads to staff who require more time to prepare, relative to more experienced academics (Bowsher, 2018). This leaves such staff with little time to develop a publications profile that will help them to move into a permanent lectureship. This is significant because junior academics need to acquire both teaching *and* research experience in order to progress in their careers. Furthermore, as Ivancheva (2020) points out, students are attracted to institutions because of big-name researchers but will have the most direct contact with precarious faculty – reinforcing the fact that casualisation is a relevant issue for students to engage with.

Individual/group task

How do you think that teaching might be impacted by increases in casualised working at universities?

Issues of equality

In addition to the separation of teaching from research, a two-tier system exists with regards to who is able to participate in the pursuit of post-PhD academic jobs (often referred to as 'post-docs'). Geographic mobility is an expectation of the academic labour market (see Cohen *et al.*, 2020), but the ability to move one's life for a short, fixed-term post-doc/early-career contract is a privileged one that disadvantages people in a variety of ways. Not only is the financial cost of moving considerable, but also the practical and emotional costs can be severe, especially for those who are embedded in a local community or kinship network of care and support. With cuts to welfare and to child- and elderly-care services, more people with caring responsibilities rely on family in order to work – and are subsequently tied to one geographical location. Their resultant immobility in the labour market can lead to the 'trap' of hourly-paid and other precarious teaching and research situations in their locality or affordable commuting distance (Ivancheva, 2020). Similarly, people with specific physical or mental-health needs may not be able to easily move and leave their support network.

The proliferation of short-term contracts or opportunities for early career academics means that people who are able to absorb financial, 'contractual' and locational insecurity, namely those with families which can support them long into adulthood, will be more able to take such jobs. There is an additional gendered aspect to the inequalities mentioned thus far, in that women are disproportionately represented in part-time and fixed-term roles in HE (see O'Keeffe and Courtois, 2019) and are discriminated against in recruitment processes (González *et al.*, 2019) and funding applications. For example, since introducing gender-blinded assessment for funding applications in 2014, the Irish Research Council reports 'a significant improvement in the representation of female researchers across disciplines' (2018:2). The shift was particularly striking in STEM (science, technology, engineering and mathematics) postdoctoral programmes: before gender-blinding, in 2013, women represented 43 per cent of applicants but only 35 per cent of awardees. Post-gender-blinding, this rose to 44 per cent of awardees in 2014 and 57 per cent of awardees in 2017. Gender inequality within university workspaces (as elsewhere) can also be prompted by the 'caring imperative' that still exists for women to be primary caregivers, but as Ivancheva et al.'s (2019) qualitative study shows, women with no children or caring responsibilities are also at a disadvantage as there is often an expectation on them to do more in the workplace, 'free' as they are from the requirement to (for example) pick children up from school.

Structural racism is another barrier to equality of employment opportunities in universities. Using fixed-term contracts as a proxy for insecure work, Black and minority ethnic (BAME) people make up 22 per cent of academics on fixed-term contracts and only 14 per cent of those on open-ended/permanent contracts (HESA, 2020 – these figures do not include 'atypical' contracts, which are often used for short-term teaching). It is also worth noting that including all ethnic minority backgrounds together can mask further levels of discrimination and racism, as 'model minorities' such as people from Indian or East Asian backgrounds may face less employment discrimination than their black or Middle Eastern counterparts (Di Stasio and Heath, 2019). Indeed, statistics are particularly stark when looking at the highest levels of promotion in universities: there are only 25 black female professors in the UK, making up less than 0.1 per cent of all professors, while white men make up 68 per cent of professors (Rollock, 2019; see also Hosein and Rao in this volume). This highlights the need to take an intersectional approach when considering the inequalities faced by casualised staff in HE (see e.g. Joseph, 2019: 527, who describes an 'unexplained variance' between empirical data and labour market theories which 'do not adequately centre race and its complexities').

University employee responses to casualisation

Casualised staff often have few opportunities to interact with one another or with the wider body of more securely employed HE staff. While some institutions do invest in staff on fixed-term contracts, the logic of casualised staff as 'disposable assets' means that they are not normally included in training and capacity-building activities. Research staff, in particular, who may be working on a project that includes five or six people, may struggle to make connections with anyone beyond their immediate colleagues. The temporary nature of many of these appointments can also make it hard for individuals to make meaningful connections with colleagues. This is compounded by the fact that the early-career experiences of senior academic staff are almost certainly very different to the circumstances facing postdoctoral job-seekers now. A lack of awareness about the mounting crisis of casualisation amongst large swathes of tenured university staff has been a huge barrier to tackling it. As a result, the burdens facing casualised staff have largely been individualised and articulated in terms of personal shortcomings or 'bad luck' rather than as symptomatic of structural issues in the HE sector.

A key turning point in transforming issues of casualisation into a cause for collective action was the industrial action undertaken by members of UCU in 2018 in response to a dispute about pensions provision. This hitherto unprecedented action acted as a catalyst for discussions about workload, staff wellbeing, equality, pay and conditions – and, we argue, moved the issues of precarity and casualisation up the agenda and brought about new ways of community-building in HE. Gail Davies (2018) gathered UCU member testimonies following the 2018 industrial action to describe a sense of 'snapping' or breaking down of trust between employees and employers, suggestive of a strong desire for change. Online communities and hashtags such as *USS Briefs* (originally conceived to fact-check claims made by the university pensions provider USS during the first phase of industrial action) and #WeAreTheUniversity proved to be a vital means of connecting striking workers across institutions, sharing information and building solidarity. Informal offline communities also formed, most of which would be impossible to account or detail here due to their ephemeral nature – communities of strikers formed around the daily picket of particular university buildings. One such community that coalesced and formalised at Cardiff University was the Common Room, a lunchtime meeting grounded in self-care and mutual support during the emotionally difficult USS strike. It continued after the strike as a chance for workers and students in HE to build solidarity and reclaim and democratise the university. Although the initial dispute centred on pension provisions, the connections forged during the industrial action provided space for 'a set of more utopian discussions about transforming the university' (Bowsher, 2018:1).

'Zines' as resistance to casualised work in HE

The practice of creating 'zines' emerged during the 2018 industrial action as a surprising and powerful way for casualised staff to build solidarity and raise awareness about precarity. An important trigger was a British Sociological Association Early Career Forum in May 2018 centred around resistance to the neoliberal university. This event included a zine-making workshop, and the resulting 'Precariosaurus' zine about fighting precarity was released under the collective name *Co-authoring Resistance*. In addition to the pdf link, meaning that anyone could read it online and print it out, individual pages took on a life of their own as they were shared as stand-alone images and used in formal presentations. In this way, they had the power to become 'viral', or at least (in the more niche online community of academia) to be shared as #relatable content by precarious academics who recognised their situation in the collaged, handwritten or meme-like pages. This example is titled 'Individualising discourses are pretty useless':

MINDFULNESS
GRIT
PERFORMANCE MANAGEMENT
RESILIENCE

SERIOUSLY?

Keep your courses I want REAL structural CHANGE

The zine was shared and widely commented upon on Twitter by academics and UCU branches. Zines have a long history as tools and materials of resistance. Originally deriving from 'fanzines', they are DIY booklets typically created by and for niche subcultures – starting off as outlets for those involved in particular pop-culture fandoms to create and share their own theories and interpretations 'often in ways that resist[ed] the dominant messages of mass culture' (McLaughlin, 1996:52). The punk and riot grrrl scenes provided a segue into political and feminist zine-making (e.g. Creasap, 2014). The low production costs and technical requirements of zine-making (no more is needed than pen, paper, scissors and glue – and access to a photocopier to create multiple copies) meant that they became associated with the radical act of giving anyone a voice, particularly those rejected by mainstream or 'official' ideologies (Kempson, 2014). One of the ways zines do this is by making heavy use of intertextuality – indeed, what McLoughlin calls 'unauthorised textual pleasures' (1996:54), using de Certeau's term 'poaching' to describe how zine-makers repurpose and manipulate the source text to make it mean 'what [they] need [it] to mean' (ibid.). This can be seen in the Precariosaurus zine and Anti-Precarity Cymru zines which cut up headlines from HE magazines and prospectuses to transform them into messages that mock or parody the language of neoliberalism in education. As McLoughlin notes, zine-makers 'tend to approach texts with a sceptical and rebellious attitude' (1996:53), which is in this case embodied through the physical act of cutting up source texts to subvert their message.

In this way, zines could be said to be made more for insiders in a community or subculture than for outsiders looking in. Zines 'live in the culture they describe' (McLaughlin, 1996:54), and this personal, involved (as opposed to 'objective' or academically detached) stance allows them to help create and sustain these communities. Diversity of voice and experience is accepted in zine communities, which are characterised by heterogeneity and 'social differentiation without exclusion' (Piepmeier, 2008:214–215). As mentioned above, these communities are typically outside of the mainstream and marginalised in some way – it is thus fitting that the casually employed (and often female) 'non-citizens' of academia (O'Keefe and Courtois, 2019) have started to use zines to express their reality, resist the power structures of the neoliberal university and build solidarity as a class of workers. Additionally, the vulnerability expressed in the hand-made, imperfect aesthetic of zines (Piepmeier, 2008:230) reflects the vulnerable working situation of casual employees.

This DIY aesthetic of a zine – unpolished, messy – makes them compelling material objects that invite a personal connection between reader and maker. The 'roughened' art forms they utilise subvert the commercialisation of art, craft and culture that positions the reader as a consumer; the zine instead positions them as friends and equals (Piepmeier, 2008). To extend this even further, communities of resistance favour roughened art forms because these can only be processed outside of the mindset and values of the dominant culture, while easily processed, polished art 'doesn't draw attention to itself as a strategy of cultural power' (McLaughlin, 1996:75). Thus we can see zines as a theoretical practice that questions and resists the means of production in corporate economies, from collectives like Tiny Tech Zines opening up space for creativity and critique in the tech industry (Sum, 2020), to zines that explicitly challenge the consumerist university and the emotional costs of emergent labour demands (c.f. Academics Against Networking; On Being Used).

This subversion of and resistance to commodification is present in many aspects of zine-making, from the cheeky nods to using your employer's photocopying facilities to produce zines (Behrooz, 2020), to the gift culture and free distribution (or charging a minimal cost to break even) that goes hand in hand with zine sharing (Piepmeier, 2008). This takes on a new element in the digital age: while some of the materiality of the zine may be lost when pages are shared online, anyone with access to a printer can print and distribute their own copies, democratising the publishing process in a way that is particularly pertinent to the restricted and expensive academic publishing world. Finally, the collective nature of the academic precarity zines discussed above involves getting together in groups and creating real-life communities around a shared activity that has no monetary reward (Piepmeier, 2008). This can bring pleasure from the act of physical creation, and catharsis from sharing or expressing one's lived experiences.

At our own institution, the collective Anti-Precarity Cymru (APC) was created as a vehicle for sharing the zines that we had begun to make. We organised various zine-making sessions, open to all and attended by casualised staff from within and beyond the university sector, as well as more securely employed university staff hoping to learn more about precarity and to become better allies. Initially, we shared individual images and collages of tongue-in-cheek resistance via Twitter (@CymruPrecarity) and Instagram (@AntiPrecarityCymru) accounts under the hashtags #ZinesAgainstPrecarity #anticas and #antiprecarity. These pieces were then collated into zines and a 2019 calendar, free to download, which includes contributions such as 'ACADEMIA IS A PYRAMID SCHEME' with quotes taken from relevant Twitter accounts under each image. Our zines and calendar have been shared widely and printed out, and they adorn various doors and office spaces. At the time of writing, APC has close to 1,000 Twitter followers.

Individual/group task

Why do you think zine-making emerged as a practice to fight for better working conditions for casualised staff specifically?

On- and offline campaigning

Online platforms also put us in touch with other local anti-precarity groups, including, for example, @NUAntiCas (Newcastle), @UoK_Precariat (Kent) and @WarwickAntiCas (Warwick). A number of anti-casualisation groups from across the UK and beyond worked together on a campaign in 2019 to raise awareness and share personal (but anonymised) stories about precarity with the hashtag #precaritystory. In addition to sharing experiences, providing mutual support and publicly challenging the dominant HE narratives, these virtual networks became important for sharing information on strategies to challenge casualisation at a managerial and institutional level. Our virtual discussions have also stimulated greater involvement in the national UCU Anti-Casualisation Committee.

It is important to note that zine-making as a practice should be seen in the broader context of trade union tactics. At our institution, APC operates semi-independently of the local UCU branch but with key figures in APC holding elected UCU positions and many other (non-casualised) UCU members engaging with the zine-making sessions or the finished zines. While zine-making and creative forms of resistance have had an important function in building solidarity and offering an avenue to criticise the university, they in no way replace traditional trade union organisation. Rather, there seems to be a symbiotic relationship between the creative work being done by activists and the more structured trade union work carried out through negotiations and specific campaigns.

The current general secretary of the UCU – Jo Grady – was elected on a platform that included a sharper focus on casualisation than her predecessor Sally Hunt, and there has been a notable shift towards considering the plight of early-career staff. This was particularly visible in the most recent round of UCU industrial action, structured around four fights – pay, pensions, inequalities and precarity. For example, on Twitter, @iancooketal produced a set of 'top trumps' cards for universities that included information on gender and race pay gaps as well as the proportion of staff on fixed-term contracts to create a 'worker's rights' score. In Newcastle, Lydia Wysocki (@lyd_w) created a series of strike comics illustrating the various issues in the #FourFights campaign, including the insidious impact of casualisation on staff wellbeing and a 'precarity hopscotch' outlining the following steps:

1. Get PhD funding
2. Teach part-time

3. Give papers
4. Get PhD
5. Apply for fellowships
6. Work casual contracts
7. Get an overdraft
8. Write every night
9. Work all weekend
10. Apply for fellowships
11. Mark 100s of essays
12. Publish an article
13. PI takes credit
14. KEEP GOING
15. Join UCU (Wysocki, 2020)

A number of student-led groups also emerged during the 2020 strike action, sharing messages of support that highlight the links between staff conditions and student experiences (e.g. @CardiffStrike, who posted a number of memes with the tagline 'staff working conditions are student learning conditions' on Twitter during the strike). Outside of industrial action, at both local and national levels, there have been various campaigns to improve conditions for casualised staff, including a shift from hourly-paid to fractional contracts for graduate teaching assistants at Exeter University, and the *Fractionals For Fair Play* campaign at SOAS for better wages and conditions for academic staff members on temporary, part-time contracts, supported by all three unions on campus (UCU, UNISON and Unite). Anti-casualisation efforts have also spread beyond the traditionally academic focus of the UCU to work with sister unions and the Independent Workers Union of Great Britain (IWGB) to stop the outsourcing of *all* university workers (see Chakrabortty, 2018). Similar anti-precarity activism can be found internationally, including, for example, the COLA wildcat strikes in California amongst graduate students and faculty members campaigning for a Cost Of Living Adjustment (Agrawal, 2020). Most recently, a #CoronaContract petition instigated by Jordan Osserman (@Ossermania) and colleagues at Birkbeck University has gathered international support in its campaign for a two-year minimum to be added to all casual contracts in HE during the global Covid-19 pandemic to see the most vulnerable university staff through the social and economic turmoil that is likely to follow the current crisis.

Individual/group task

What are the limitations of zine-making in relation to fighting casualisation? What other forms of activism are necessary to get better working conditions?

Conclusion

Thanks to creative campaigning from casualised staff at various universities, issues of precarity have never been so visible. However, notwithstanding the pandemic enveloping all aspects of UK life at the time of writing, there remain huge barriers to the implementation of more secure contracts and better working conditions for university staff, as there are for employees in many sectors across the UK.

One such barrier to change is the dominant framing of the challenges facing the higher education sector – characterised by Nickson (2019) as a 'death by ecology narrative' in which the university sector has been hit by a succession of massive and unpredictable storms, and that:

> to mitigate the consequences … we have to change how we do things. The storms are presented as natural phenomena and the consequences as nobody's fault, making the responses inevitable [and] necessary for survival. The role of professional staff, academics and other workers becomes riding out this storm and just accepting the things which 'have to be done', guided by managers.
>
> (Nickson 2019: online)

University managers tend to frame sector-wide challenges as external, and marketisation as an unstoppable force requiring changes to pensions, restructuring and the shifting of risk away from institutions and onto individuals. This dominant narrative, Nickson (2019) argues, underplays the agency of universities themselves: the HE sector is a powerful economic actor, worth approximately £95 billion per annum to the UK economy (Bothwell, 2017). It thus has the clout to lobby the government. Lybeck (2018), amongst others, champions the idea of 'civic university studies' and makes a strong case for the political defence of civic values in HE and a renegotiation of the balance between critical and managerial interests. We contend here that the activism of casualised university staff, made visible through DIY zines, awareness-raising and solidarity-building, is a key component of this nascent reconceptualisation of the purpose and character of universities. On a more concrete level, UCU makes the following recommendations in their 2019 report on casualisation:

- 'The Office for Students should put a new duty on universities to disclose the amounts of teaching – measured in classroom hours – that are being done by hourly paid staff as a proportion of their total classroom hours' (p.5).
- 'The Concordat Strategy Group's revised Concordat document must include the recommendations that relate to calling for greater action on fixed-term contracts and more support to help researchers develop their own research agenda. Research councils should make it a condition of grant to employ research staff on open-ended contracts and to support greater stability of employment' (p.5).
- Universities 'should invest in de-casualising their workforces and engage in negotiations with UCU locally to negotiate the transition of precariously employed staff onto more secure contracts' (p.5).

Questions remain about how long-term solidarity between precariously employed staff can be sustained. Bowsher, for example, argues that more resources should be directed to this cause in order to move beyond 'the tendency to naturalise the insecurity of ECAs as paying one's dues' (2018:2). Concerns have also been raised about the nature of 'vertical solidarity' – solidarity that connects university staff of differing status and career stage. Importantly, a UCU ballot for industrial action on casualisation failed to reach the required 50 per cent threshold in February 2019, leading many casualised staff to feel left out or left behind by more senior colleagues. We take a strong lead from Burton and Turbine (2018), who talk about 'lively and mobile' solidarity – not necessarily built on 'sameness' but on an ethic of care arrived at through mutual recognition and generosity, recognising the unequal structural positions that we occupy within HE and fostering co-operation across these divides.

Summary points

- Precarious and casualised work benefits the employer more than the employee.
- This has negative implications for equality and diversity of those working in the HE sector.
- Unions such as UCU and IWGB have been challenging precarity in HE, which affects all types of staff, including academic, professional services and outsourced agency workers.
- Creative outputs such as zines have become a way for precarious workers to resist casualisation, draw attention to their situation and build solidarity.
- Universities have agency as economic actors to create widespread change; through a combination of traditional union activities and grassroots movements, pressure for positive change can be applied.

Acknowledgement

We would like to thank our colleague and fellow activist Renata Madeiros Mirra for her comments during the writing process.

Recommended reading

We recommend having a look at some of the zines, comics and online resources created by casualised workers and other HE staff:
Precariousaurus Zine: https://coauthoringresistance.files.wordpress.com/2018/06/precariosaurus.pdf
APC Zines: www.tinyurl.com/APCzines
Lydia Wysocki Strike Comics: https://appliedcomicsetc.com/portfolio/strikecomics/
USS Briefs: https://medium.com/ussbriefs

References

Agrawal, N. (2020) UC Graduate Students Threaten More Strikes as Movement Grows. *Los Angeles Times*, 7 March. Available at: https://www.latimes.com/california/story/2020-03-07/graduate-student-movement-at-uc-gains-momentum-with-faculty-support-demonstrations-and-pledges-to-strike (Accessed 4 April 2020).

Behrooz, A. (2020) Protest Poetry: UCU University Strikes & Creative Solidarity. *The Skinny*. Available at: https://www.theskinny.co.uk/sexuality/deviance/protest-poetry-on-the-university-strikes-and-creative-solidarity (Accessed 30 March 2020).

Bothwell, E. (2017) Universities 'Generate £95 Billion for UK Economy'. *Times Higher Education*. Available at: https://www.timeshighereducation.com/news/universities-generate-ps95-billion-uk-economy (Accessed 20 February 2020).

Bowsher, J. (2018) Precarity in the Neoliberal University: Some Notes on the Plight of Early Career Academics. *USS Briefs 31*. Available at: https://medium.com/ussbriefs/precarity-in-the-neoliberal-university-some-notes-on-the-plight-of-early-career-academics-587adddba620 (Accessed 20 April 2020).

Budd, R. (2016) Undergraduate Orientations Towards Higher Education in Germany and England: Problematizing the notion of 'student as customer.' *Higher Education*, 73, pp.23–37.

Burton, S., and Turbine, V. (2018) Solidarity in the Neoliberal University? Acts of Kindness and the Ethics of Care During the UCU Pensions Dispute. *Discover Sociology*. Available at: https://discoversociety.org/20 18/03/31/solidarity-in-the-neoliberal-university-acts-of-kindness-and-the-ethics-of-care-during-the-ucu-pensio ns-dispute/ (Accessed 4 April 2020).

Chakrabortty, A. (2018) The Cleaners Who Won Fair Wages and a Way to Belong. *The Guardian*, 18 July. Available at: https://www.theguardian.com/commentisfree/2018/jul/18/cleaners-fair-wages-university-in-ho use-working-lives (Accessed 4 April 2020).

Cohen, S., Hannah, P., Higham, J., Hopkins, D., and Orchiston, C. (2020) Gender Discourses in Academic Mobility. *Gender, Work and Organization*, 27(2), pp. 149–165.

Creasap, K. (2014) Zine-Making as Feminist Pedagogy. *Feminist Teacher*, 24(3), pp. 155–168.

Davies, G. (2018) Goodwill Hunting After the USS Strike. *USS Briefs 66*. Available at: https://medium.com/u ssbriefs/goodwill-hunting-after-the-uss-strike-3b2e302d0dc7 (Accessed 20 February 2020).

Di Stasio, V., and Heath, A. (2019) Are Employers in Britain Discriminating Against Ethnic Minorities? *GEMM Project*. Available at: http://csi.nuff.ox.ac.uk/wp-content/uploads/2019/01/Are-employers-in-Britain-discrimi nating-against-ethnic-minorities_final.pdf (Accessed 13 April 2020).

González, M., Cortina, C., and Rodríguez, J. (2019) The Role of Gender Stereotypes in Hiring: A Field Experiment. *European Sociological Review*, 35(2), pp. 187–204.

HESA (2017) Higher Education Staff Statistics. Available at: https://www.hesa.ac.uk/news/24-01-2019/sb253-higher-education-staff-statistics (Accessed 11 July 2020).

HESA (2019) Higher Education Staff Statistics. Available at: https://www.hesa.ac.uk/news/23-01-2020/sb256-higher-education-staff-statistics (Accessed 11 July 2020).

HESA (2020) HE Academic Staff by Ethnicity and Academic Employment Function. Available at: https://www.hes a.ac.uk/data-and-analysis/staff/table-4 (Accessed 13 April 2020).

Irish Research Council (2018) Gender Strategy and Actions. Available at: http://research.ie/assets/uploads/2 018/08/04108-IRC-Gender-flyer-proof03-single.pdf?fbclid=IwAR2EF-HrFiVnyVLW6dub7SeAOwKJ-O6D1LuHa UV9tjlGmBRIM7nEQgQ0-Wc (Accessed 25 February 2020).

Ivancheva, M. (2020) The Casualization, Digitalization and Outsourcing of Academic Labour: A Wake-Up Call for Trade Unions. *Focaal Blog*. Available at: http://www.focaalblog.com/2020/03/20/mariya-ivancheva-t he-casualization-digitalization-and-outsourcing-of-academic-labour-a-wake-up-call-for-trade-unions/ (Accessed 9 April, 2020).

Ivancheva, M., Lynch, K. and Keating, K. (2019) Precarity, Gender and Care in the Neoliberal Academy. *Gender, Work and Organization*, 26(4), pp. 448–462.

Joseph, E. (2019) Discrimination Against Credentials in Black Bodies: Counterstories of the Characteristic Labour Market Experiences of Migrants in Ireland. *British Journal of Guidance and Counselling*, 24(1), pp. 1–19.

Kempson, M. (2014) 'My Version of Feminism': Subjectivity, DIY and the Feminist Zine. *Social Movement Studies*, 14(4), pp. 1–14.

Lopes, A. and Dewan, I. (2014) Precarious Pedagogies? The Impact of Casual and Zero-Hour Contracts in Higher Education. *Journal of Feminist Scholarship*, 7(8), pp. 28–42.

Lybeck, E. (2018) The Coming Crisis of Academic Authority. In: T. Geelan, H. González Hernando, and P. Walsh (Eds), *From Financial Crisis to Social Change*. London: Palgrave Macmillan.

McGettigan, A. (2013) The Great University Gamble: Money, markets and the future of higher education. London: Pluto Press.

McLaughlin, T. (1996) *Street Smarts and Critical Theory: Listening to the Vernacular*. Madison: University of Wisconsin Press.

Nickson, M. (2019) All Change: The Rise of 'Agility' in University Management. *USS Briefs 85*. Available at: https ://medium.com/ussbriefs/all-change-the-rise-of-agility-in-university-management-f601b78828f4 (Accessed 4 April 2020).

O'Keefe, T., and Courtois, A. (2019) 'Not One of the Family': Gender and Precarious Work in the Neoliberal University. *Gender, Work and Organization*, pp. 463-479. Available at: https://doi.org/10.1111/gwao.12346 (Accessed 20 April 2020).

Piepmeier, A. (2008) Why Zines Matter: Materiality and the Creation of Embodied Community. *American Periodicals: a Journal of History, Criticism and Bibliography*, 18(2), pp. 213–238.

Rollock, N. (2019) Staying Power: The Career Experiences and Strategies of UK Black Female Professors. *UCU [pdf]*. Available at: https://www.ucu.org.uk/media/10075/Staying-Power/pdf/UCU_Rollock_February_2 019.pdf (Accessed 13 April 2020).

Sum, C. (2020) Tiny Tech Zines Builds a Community Around Art, Critical Theory and Tech. Available at: https://blog.bigcartel.com/tiny-tech-zines-builds-a-community-around-art-critical-theory-and-tech (Accessed 30 March 2020).

UCU (2019) *Counting the Costs of Casualisation in Higher Education: Key Findings of a Survey Conducted by the University and College Union.* London: University and College Union.

Union, S.O.A.S. (2020) Fair Pay for Fractionals. Available at: https://soasunion.org/activities/society/8760/ (Accessed 4 April 2020).

Vitae (2008). The Concordat to Support the Career Development of Researchers. Available at: https://www.vitae.ac.uk/policy/vitae-concordat-vitae-2011.pdf (Accessed 4 April 2020).

Vitae (2019). The Concordat to Support the Career Development of Researchers. Available at: https://www.vitae.ac.uk/policy/concordat/Download_Concordat_PDF (Accessed 4 April 2020).

Wysocki, L. (2020) Strike Comics. *Applied Comics etc.* Available at: https://appliedcomicsetc.com/portfolio/strikecomics/ (Accessed 4 April 2020).

9 Meanings, models and muddles
Two tales of the pursuit of teaching excellence

Tanya Hathaway and Namrata Rao

Introduction

Contemporary models of higher education (HE) focus on developing various aspects of institutional excellence, including teaching excellence. The Teaching Excellence Framework (TEF), a metrics-based teaching quality and assessment mechanism (Forstenzer, 2016), was operationalised in universities in the UK in 2016–17 'to enable diverse forms of teaching and learning excellence' (DfE, 2017: 23). The TEF assessment was proposed as a way of developing a foundation for teaching and learning leading to 'a high-quality student academic experience' (DfE, 2017: 9). The knowledge base pertaining to teaching excellence is derived from wide-ranging empirical research into the teaching and learning process, contributing to the definition of measures of educational quality. In common with the TEF's definition of teaching quality, research reveals that one aspect of a high-quality experience for students is teaching which encourages student engagement and effort (Gibbs, 2010). Effectiveness of course design, assessment and feedback are also considered essential aspects of the teaching quality that affords rigour and stretch to learners, and so are part of teaching excellence (DfE, 2017; Gibbs, 2010).

Whilst the TEF framework offers a structure for assessing the quality of teaching, it has ignited a debate about what constitutes quality teaching and learning in higher education. One consequence of this is that both new and established university lecturers are increasingly being bombarded with advice on how to achieve teaching which is of a high quality. Paradoxically, there is currently no mandatory requirement, apart from institutional requirements, for university lecturers to have a formal teaching qualification to teach in HE. Currently, only a set of teaching standards referred to as the revised UK Professional Standards Framework (PSF) exist (Advance HE, 2011). The PSF is nationally recognised as a framework for effective HE teaching. Demonstrating understanding of how students learn and evidence-informed approaches to teaching which are based on research and scholarship in the discipline constitute essential parts of the PSF standards. Indeed, Evans *et al.* (2015: 62) conclude that 'greater evidence on research-informed practice is required along with more sophisticated notions of pedagogy'. Existing in concert with the PSF is Advance HE's teaching fellowship programme, which offers holders national and international recognition as HE teachers.

Nevertheless, when recruiting for academic positions, many institutions state as desirable that lecturers hold a qualification to teach such as a Postgraduate Certificate (PG Cert) in Higher Education. In some cases, they also desire that lecturers hold a Fellowship or even Senior Fellowship of Advance HE. If not, then appointments are often obliged to successfully gain a PG Cert and/or complete a successful application for fellowship during their probationary period. This may explain the rise in the number of university lecturers between the academic years 2014–15 and 2017–18 holding a teaching qualification (Table 9.1) either through individuals obtaining a qualification or registering with their employer that they hold a qualification to avoid having to undertake a PG Cert. In many cases, institutions offer academic development to support new and experienced lecturers in applying for a form of Advance HE fellowship (Fellow, Senior Fellow, etc.) depending on their level of lecturing experience and expertise as identified by the PSF framework. The various forms of guidance associated with these memberships and frameworks detail the scholarly approaches, qualities and aspirations that those teaching in HE should adhere and aspire to (Gov.UK, 2020; Advance HE, 2011; Advance HE, 2019).

Unsurprisingly, new entrants to lecturing in HE are often submerged in a day-to-day teaching and learning discourse that is awash with a broad range of constructs related to student engagement in learning that are associated with quality teaching, such as student involvement, level of intellectual challenge and student–faculty interaction (Evans *et al.*, 2015). These constructs are now ingrained in common parlance at the institutional level, and are influential to the discourse portraying university teaching and student learning. Åkerlind (2008) demonstrates that considerable variation exists in university teachers' understanding of the nature of teaching and learning, meaning that different facets or perspectives of student engagement at the individual lecturer level can be variously interpreted. This can lead to variation in university teachers' understandings of classroom practice. She argues for conceptual development through postgraduate courses and other developmental programmes for university teachers.

Notwithstanding, for individual constructs, considerable detail and meaning is lost during their representation and translation into teaching guidance and practice, raising questions about the accuracy of their portrayals, meanings and implications for the quality of student engagement and learning in contemporary HE. Guidance is often generic, failing to consider discipline-specific approaches to pedagogy and distinctive forms of teaching (Evans *et al.*, 2015). Moreover, the detailed evidence base beyond such official guidance on quality teaching is often unexplored; detail is missing about what research demonstrates is pivotal to successful learning designs which many new and established lecturers may be in need of and do not realise or do not necessarily have the

Table 9.1 Comparison of academics holding and not holding a teaching qualification, between the academic years 2014–15 and 2017–18 (Source: HESA Open data license: CC-BY-4.0)

Academic year 2017–18 *Academic employment function*	*Teaching qualification held*	*No teaching qualification held*	*Not known*	*Total*
Both teaching and research	57,115 (63%)	23,520 (26%)	10,185 (11%)	90,820
Teaching only	25,050 (45%)	19,810 (36%)	10,525 (19%)	55,380
Academic year 2014–15 *Academic employment function*	*Teaching qualification held*	*No teaching qualification held*	*Not known*	*Total*
Both teaching and research	46,455 (53%)	21,775 (25%)	19,220 (22%)	87,455
Teaching only	17,505 (35%)	14,385 (29%)	17,565 (36%)	49,450

time to look for. Negotiating the demands of the teacher-researcher role at the research and teaching nexus, set within the context of performance management and promotion policies, means that university teachers are often conflicted about where to focus their efforts when navigating their early career pathways. Further, the push for measurable indicators evidencing quality teaching as per the TEF has promoted a mechanistic model of teaching (Forstenzer, 2016).

This chapter considers the prevailing discourse on teaching and learning in HE which both lecturers and students partake in and starts with an analysis of a selection of terms which often inform the design intentions for quality teaching and learning. In the process, it explores contemporary notions of quality teaching in the sector that are defined by ways of talking and the terms and phrases which they incorporate. Drawing on the authors' lived experiences, it examines the common use of each term or construct in matters related to teaching and learning. It then offers a literature-based definition for each term, and finally draws out the elements that are most critical to successful practice. Next, two authentic case studies are offered which illustrate how, within the prevailing HE discourse, new university teachers approach their practice with the intention of enhancing the quality of their teaching. Through examining the learning structures (e.g. group work) and the intentions behind their learning designs, we reveal the dissonance between the research on teaching and the actual implementation of the research evidence in practice. Finally, the conclusion and summary make recommendations for minimising this dissonance between theory and research-based evidence, and teaching practice.

Individual/group task

What are your expectations of teaching excellence – do they align with the TEF framework?
Should we measure excellent teaching?
If so, how would you measure excellent teaching?

The prevailing discourse on teaching and learning in higher education

The pervasiveness of the teaching and learning discourse in HE has been deepened by the introduction, in the UK, of the TEF in 2016–17. New and established academics react and contribute to the TEF discourse in a way that mediates their professional identities and ambitions and fulfils competing expectations (Bartram *et al.*, 2018). This influences the learning designs teachers attempt, how these are enacted, their effectiveness, the assessment regimes adopted and university teachers' engagement with pedagogical research. Trowler (2001) defines *discourse* to mean the language of HE as a social practice, shaped by social structures. The language of HE exists in different forms, including written and spoken formats alongside images used to communicate messages. When academics talk about quality teaching and learning in their professional encounters, it is often in very simple terms and descriptions such as 'intellectual challenge' or 'group work'. Whilst the aim of teaching and learning may be simple, what is involved in successfully enacting its constituents such as 'group work' is a lot more complex than can be relayed or explored conversationally (Case, 2015).

In terms of academic interpretations of teaching and learning designs, these understandings are influenced by what is made available in the discourse, that is, the content that is highlighted and discussed, and what is discerned or noted by the individual as important to the quality and effectiveness of any given practice. Experience of teaching and, importantly, variety of experience (Marton *et al.*, 2004) enhances the teacher's learning and awareness of the process; thus, awareness can be more or less sophisticated, impacting on an individual's ability to develop as a teacher and make improvements in practice. University teachers who have a variety of teaching experience, perhaps gained in several institutions where they have been exposed to the full range of the teaching and learning practices, may develop a more sophisticated awareness of what is pivotal to effective practice. For the new lecturer with limited or no teaching experience, learning about teaching becomes a process of listening to others' tales, stepping in at the deep end and reading the available guidance for teaching. Thus, the new lecturers' interpretation of teaching is arguably influenced by what is made available through the prevailing discourse.

In the beginning, their first focus is often on the content – 'Do I know my stuff?' (Gibbs, 2014) – rather than delivery, as they may be allocated a wide variety of topics to teach which may be beyond the bounds of their disciplinary and subject knowledge. Teaching may then become very content-driven with a focus on information transfer – a teacher-focused approach which increases the pressure to perform, but in a very instrumental way (Prosser and Trigwell, 1999). In response to this approach, students may adopt a surface approach to learning, focusing on memorising facts and figures and failing to integrate subject content and engage in new meaning-making. In today's climate with the focus on teaching quality, the transmission approach to teaching is severely under threat (Jones, 2007; Omelivheva and Avdeyeva, 2008), although evidence for the effectiveness of the transmissionist lecturer method does exist (Charlton, 2006; Jones, 2007). Arguably, lecturers need to evolve to include the interactive and innovative forms of teaching which engage students in deep, rather than surface, approaches to learning (Jones, 2007). Specifically, pedagogical practices which foster students' intrinsic engagement with the content they are studying are considered critical for a quality learning experience (Gibbs, 2010).

Gibbs (2010) suggests that there are specific pedagogic practices which impact on student learning. These include the level of intellectual challenge, irrespective of the learning spaces (i.e. lecture, workshop) they are enacted in, alongside the curriculum level studied, the study approach adopted by students and students' level of engagement with study (Gibbs, 2010). At the disciplinary level, Evans *et al.* (2015) demonstrate that such practices are nuanced and are what account for variations in meaningful learning across disciplines. These practices do not act in isolation but are embedded in the strategies – the structures, systems, methods, techniques, procedures and processes – that a teacher uses during instruction that influence what and how students learn in the teaching environment (Evans *et al.*, 2015). Students experience intellectual challenge when they perceive the demands of the learning context to be high through certain course features (Ramsden, 1979). Intellectual challenge is a feature of the level of difficulty or complexity that the curriculum offers students, that is, what students are expected to do with the content (Gibbs, 2010). During teaching, intellectual challenge is provided by presenting ideas, tasks and concepts/content that are hard to grasp. The aim is to engage students in thinking at the higher levels of Bloom's Taxonomy – analysis, synthesis and evaluation (Krathwohl *et al.* 1964). Alongside appropriate academic challenge, student engagement is linked to sufficient active and collaborative learning and the level of student–faculty interaction (Gibbs, 2010).

With experience, a teacher's attention may shift towards a focus on what is effective and on quality teaching in the context of the prevailing teaching and learning debates. Academic development can play a significant role in influencing the translation of teaching guidance into quality teaching practice through several connected ways: (1) encouraging the analysis and unpacking of teaching and learning phenomena using educational theory and frames of reference; (2) influencing the discourse surrounding teaching and learning phenomena by contributing to and disseminating existing pedagogical research; and (3) through guiding academics in critiquing the available guidance on teaching and learning in a way that helps teachers to identify what is critical to the effective learning design and enactment of learning structures that will significantly influence student learning in their respective contexts. Table 9.2 outlines a selection of constructs and practices that are commonly associated with contemporary learning designs and are used as indicators of teaching quality and engaged student learning, and sometimes as innovation implemented at an institutional level (Gibbs, 2010; Drugova, 2019): student-centred learning, active learning, group-work and blended learning (using a mix of online learning and face-to-face learning with students). Each of these is illustrated through common interpretations and enactments during teaching, compared to the more complex definitions available in the literature. Finally, identification of what is essential to the effective enactment of the learning design is included as an indicator of meaningful learning and quality teaching practice. Together, these practices illustrate that there are a variety of ways to foster meaningful student learning. However, operationalising these strategies in a way that demonstrates high-quality teaching is of course influenced by the context of practice, including the structural complexities which are linked to the discourses within an institution and the individual's sense of agency that is the individual's engaged response to the structural conditions in which they operate (Fanghanel, 2007).

Case study analysis: Dissonance between evidence and action in the HE classroom

In the following section we present two case studies, each based on the practice of a new university lecturer, someone who is considered as having up to seven years' experience (parallels with ESRC's definition of new researchers) or an individual who is unfamiliar with an activity or teaching context which creates the same kind of instability. Both lecturers had three to four years' experience of teaching in HE and have a similar disciplinary focus (Education) at the time. In both cases, we examine the learning design adopted by the lecturer which aims to improve student engagement by offering intellectual challenge. Each case study can be analysed through the TEF Assessment criteria Aspect of Quality and highlights Student Engagement (TQ1), Rigour and Stretch (TQ3) and Feedback (TQ4).

Case study 1: Active learning and group work

This case study sought to capture the process of active learning of six groups of students studying on a first-year Education-based course. Learning took place over a six-week period as they engaged in a collaborative inquiry through workshop activities and a group-based assignment with the expectation to work together to support each other's learning and achievement. Evidence-informed collaborative inquiry (Sinnema et al., 2011) underlaid the lecturer's teaching strategy and was directly connected to authentic assessment requiring students, in groups, to think about complex issues. The learning design focused on increasing the level of intellectual challenge and collaborative learning element of the task through an active learning and group-work approach.

Table 9.2 Essential features of effective learning design

Term	Common understanding	Literature definitions	Essential elements
Student-centred learning	Students are the focus of learning in the learning activity – lecture, workshop or practical session – and are engaged in responding to tasks and activities. The role of the lecturer is more as a facilitator in the learning process.	Student-centred/learning oriented conceptions as an orientation to teaching (Kember, 1997). Students are active in discovery and directing their independent learning through choice of topic/content relating to their evaluation of the available subject matter (Burnard, 1999). Similarly, a student-focused teaching strategy aimed at student activity which changes students' subject-matter conceptions, restructuring their views of the world (Prosser and Trigwell, 1999)	As a cognitivist notion, student-centred learning takes place within the student's mind. Constructivist view is focused on activity and performance, e.g. the workshop task or the project. Student-centred learning represents a change in the student–teacher relationship, with power shifting from the teacher to the student (O'Neill and McMahon, 2005). Consulting students about teaching and learning; creation of powerful learning environments (Elen, Clarebout, Leonard and Lowyck, 2007)
Active learning	Engaging students in tasks during lectures and workshops, practicals etc., can involve group-work and physical tasks, e.g. construction, often leading to presentation of work and discussion.	Active participation in learning as opposed to transmission and passive recipient of knowledge and externalising cognitive processes (Mizokami, 2014); engaging higher-order thinking (Bonwell and Eison, 1991). Cognitive processes are externalised through learning structures/formats including heuristic learning, problem-based learning, experiential learning, investigative learning and group work (Mizokami, 2014).	Move towards engaging students in deep active learning; learning leading to depth of understanding and internal change in the learner signified by competency (Matsushita, 2018). Active learning cannot simply be the fostering of generic skills, attitudes and dispositions – it needs to be content based, connecting knowledge and activities.

| Group work | Organising students into groups to work on short tasks during lectures and workshops, fieldwork, etc., or longer group tasks and assignments. | A goal-based structure for cooperative and collaborative learning, often involving learning through discussion (Yasunaga, 2018). Cooperative learning leads to student enjoyment and satisfaction with learning, and academic growth (Yasunaga, 2018). Through social interaction, collaborative learning designs elicits student engagement including knowledge building (Gibbs, 2010; Paz Dennen, 2000). | Spirit of cooperation underpins cooperative learning (Yasunaga, 2018); to achieve this, students must be aware of the basic elements of cooperative learning: positive interdependence, promoting interaction, individual accountability, interpersonal and small group skills and group processing (Johnson et al. 1994). Collaborative learning with a high level of discussion of learning content (Summers and Volet, 2010). |
| Blended learning | Using a mix of online learning and face-to-face learning with students. | 'The thoughtful integration of classroom face-to-face learning experiences with online learning experiences' (Garrison and Kanuka 2004: 96) Learning that happens in an instructional context which is characterised by a deliberate combination of online and classroom-based interventions to instigate and support learning (Boelens, Van Laer, De Wever, and Elen, 2015:5) | Facilitates critical, creative and complex thinking skills (Garrison and Kanuka, 2004:99). Allows flexibility of learning spaces and leads to learner autonomy emphasising the need for self-directed learning (Smith and Hill, 2019) |

Task methodology

The task involved small groups of students (five or six) collaborating to present a 30-minute workshop considering the nature of learner diversity and demonstrating specific teaching strategies and techniques that would meet the diverse needs of learners. Students were randomly allocated (by the lecturer pulling names out of a hat) to a group being divided into six workshop presentation groups for assessment purposes. The lecturer, as well as two peer assessors, would assess each presentation using a rubric created and discussed with students at the start of the workshops so that they were aware of the assessment criteria and how to meet them. A single grade was awarded to the group. This was thus the grade each individual would receive as part of their total module score. Two concluding workshops were dedicated to the presentations over a two-week period.

Group work offers a learning structure for engaging students in active learning, rather than passive receipt of knowledge; it offers an intellectual challenge and stimulus for students. The lecturer's instruction and rubric made it clear that all learners were expected to actively participate in each group's session when requested. In the assignment preparation and presentation, each group was not only expected to draw on each other as a resource, but also encouraged to use their peers as actors in the workshop, thus engaging them in inquiry into the teaching and learning process. The students were expected to meet outside of the workshop and lecture hours to plan and develop their response to the assignment. There was an assumption that students already had the motivation and possessed the knowledge, skills and understanding to engage in group work.

The evidence–action dissonance – the teacher's perspective

In this case, the random process of selecting learners and assigning them to a group proved to be problematic for a variety of reasons. For five out of the six groups, the groupings proved to be generative, leading to individual and collaborative learning gains and enhanced learning outcomes for the students. However, the remaining group of students experienced an unhelpful group dynamic; the make-up of the group proved to be unproductive and diminished the learning gains for students. Rather than experiencing enjoyment, satisfaction with learning and academic growth, the students in the least successful group experienced challenges as tensions arose between group members. These were brought to the attention of the lecturer, who attempted to mediate and steer the group towards cooperation. The learners were diminished, and it became clear that the grouping lacked leadership and at least one student who was academically strong. This impacted on the quality of their assignment. Furthermore, when two members of the group were asked to be assessors, the tensions resurfaced, requiring the lecturer to mediate and to determine the grading of the group. In contrast, in the most successful grouping, the students thrived and flourished under a strong leader and strong academic characteristics within the group.

During the activity, the lecturer became aware that the design and enactment of the task were both flawed. Much later, the lecturer decided to investigate the research and evidence base related to group work to inform her analysis of the problem.

Analysis of the problem

In hindsight, the lecturer's thinking appeared to be shaped by the broader objective of improving students' learning through offering intellectual challenge. Improving teaching was a subsidiary objective with regards to quality. The approach was rather to enact a common learning structure considered to enhance students' learning, without sufficient consideration having been given to the substantive evidence base and educational theory related to designing an effective approach to group work that would foster genuine cooperative and collaborative learning. The random selection of groups was a critical error in the learning structure, resulting in some groups being homogenous in terms of academic attainment and others heterogeneous. For some, an unhelpful group dynamic diverted their energy and attention away from the object of learning to focus on their differences. Discussion did not reach the higher levels required for knowledge building; rather they focused on the students' personal disagreements and, for some, dissatisfaction with the activity. Whilst all the students completed the activity, for some their motivations were arguably driven by the external demands of the task.

Possible solutions

To be successful in shifting from passivity, successful group work which enhances learning through peer–peer instruction (Brame and Biel, 2015) needs to be based around cooperative learning, with students taking ownership of a set of shared goals (Johnson and Johnson, 2008). In this task, students formed formal cooperative learning groups, the goal being to generate knowledge through collaborative learning to complete a joint assignment (Johnston *et al.*, 2014). The design and enactment of the tasks lacked the following critical elements that are required for effective collaborative learning:

1. An assessment process for allocating marks to individuals within a group, rather than allowing all group members to receive the same mark. Habeshaw *et al.* (1992) suggest assigning the groups points equating to their percentage and asking the students to divide the points amongst themselves, acknowledging their contributions. Brame and Biel (2015:1) indicate that group assessment should 'promote positive group interdependence as well as individual accountability'.
2. A strategy for ensuring groups contain a heterogenous mix of students that ensures coverage of the particular skills and abilities relevant to the task (Johnson *et al.*, 2014). This could involve, for example, conducting a diagnostic of students' attainment levels prior to group forming, or using student achievement data to inform the make-up of the groups.
3. Ensuring that groups have sufficient command of problem solving. Brame and Biel (2015) suggest that at least three members of the group exhibit competent performance in some problem-solving tasks (Johnson *et al.*, 2006; Heller and Hollabaugh, 1992).
4. A range of strategies to develop students' abilities at group work, that is, in the preparatory phase prior to the assessment task, using diagnostic tasks to inform the assigning of group roles; and, at the enactment phase, increasing group-work opportunities with students taking part in regular problem-solving tasks where participation is required and assessed to gain credit (Heller and Hollabaugh, 1992).

Individual/group task

The previous case study discusses the analysis of the group-work task from the teacher's perspective. Analyse the task objective from the students' perspective.
What would be your expectations of learning in a group-work task?
How would you react to being placed in a group rather than being allowed to choose a group?
As a student, what do you think is essential for the success of the task and what is the aspect you would attribute as being chiefly responsible for the group-work task?

Case study 2: Active learning and blended learning

This case study seeks to capture the processes of asynchronous online forums which first-year students undertaking a combined undergraduate degree in the broad disciplinary area of Education were engaged in at an English university. The learning design focused on engaging students in independent learning by offering them intellectual challenge and by encouraging them to actively engage in an online dialogue following a face-to-face session. The online forum was 'characterised by a deliberate combination of online and classroom-based interventions to instigate and support learning' (Boelens *et al.*, 2015: 5). There was an attempt via the online forum to achieve 'the thoughtful integration of classroom face-to-face learning experiences with online learning experiences' (Garrison and Kanuka, 2004: 96). The concept of collaborative learning by active engagement in the forum discussion with peers underpinned the lecturer's teaching strategy.

Task methodology

The forums were part of a blended learning degree programme wherein the students were engaged in a weekly face-to-face evening session at a satellite site some distance from the main university campus. The evening face-to-face session would provide students with a general overview of the topic, and typically would last three hours. Lecture-style teaching was interspersed with some group discussions and tasks. Following the face-to-face session, which would be delivered by a university-based tutor travelling to teach at the satellite centre, students would be invited to contribute at least one forum post in response to the question posed by the tutor. The tutor would respond to the posts from the students during the week and pose further questions or encourage them to pose questions to each other in response to the forum posts. This would then typically be followed by a brief discussion in the face-to-face session in the subsequent week. The students were encouraged to summarise their learning from participation in the forum and reading other posts in addition to drawing on any further readings set for the week. The forums were a means of ensuring that the students actively engaged with self-directed study on the topic discussed each week by engaging in the independent study tasks and responding to a related forum question posed by the tutor, which they were to then discuss in each subsequent session. At the end of the year, students were assessed on the basis of their contributions to the online forums. The purpose of the activity was to:

- reinforce learning that happened in class by framing a forum question that required students to apply their knowledge and understanding on the topic;
- develop students' critical thinking and analytical skills and their ability to make judgements about what to include in a succinct response, which further reinforced their writing skills;
- build a virtual student community that allowed an opportunity for collaborative peer learning;
- sustain the dialogue beyond the face-to-face session that would allow for tutor-facilitated but student-directed independent learning.

The evidence–action dissonance

In an ideal world, online discussion forums such as the one outlined here should help facilitate 'critical, creative and complex thinking skills' (Garrison and Kanuka, 2004: 99) if appropriately designed (i.e. forum question carefully thought through, and the forum carefully scaffolded by tutor facilitation). The forum should offer a flexible learning space which should lead to self-directed learning characterised by significant levels of learner autonomy (Smith and Hill, 2019). However, Table 9.3 indicates some of the key challenges the lecturer faced in operationalising the online discussion

Table 9.3 Asynchronous online discussion forums: Bridging the dissonance between evidence and action

The Problem	The Proposed Solution
1. Time-intensive activity for tutor. It required the tutor to set up the forum each week, monitor contributions and post responses to student forum posts. This is to acknowledge their contributions and to engage them to reflect and engage more critically by asking further questions.	• Time needs to be built in for the tutor to scaffold student discussions and hence their learning on the online discussion forums. • Graduate teaching assistants (GTAs) could be employed to promote a student-centred learning approach which supports a more indvidualised learning whereby GTAs contribute prompts to engage students in deep active learning through online peer dialogue.
2. Challenge of trying to maintain a safe space where no student feels intimated by their peers in sharing their ideas on a forum. This was often coupled with the challenge students (often mature learners) faced in using the technology involved and lack of confidence in their academic writing skills.	• Pre-forum preparatory face-to-face tasks could be organised to build in individual accountability where students are encouraged to contribute to forums in class. This thoughtful integration of face-to face learning to enable learner autonomy by creating opportunities for students to get comfortable with the technology and to set expectations of the do's and don'ts of engaging in online forums. • Basic rules on who and how often individuals contribute to the forum can be set up to facilitate self-directed cooperative and collaborative learning with peers. • GTAs could be employed to reinforce some of the expectations of online dialogue and monitor contributions.
3. Decrease in levels of participation/ forum contributions over time.	• Introduction of a series of formative assessments of forum contributions will allow for a scaffolded goal-based structure to the forums whereby feedback for each formative assessment will lead to greater learner autonomy whilst also allowing for a more personalised learning as opposed to that facilitated by a single a summative end-of-year assessment of the forum posts. • Positive reinforcement for students via monthly recognition of best forum posts and formative feedback on features of good post to encourage student participation and sustain motivation to participate for academic growth.
4. Plagiarism of forum contributions in written assessments.	End-of-year students should be asked to compile their forum posts and upload via Turnitin as a final submission to avoid plagiarism issues.
5. Lack of social dimension where meaning-making is based on written/verbal cues and not on the basis of non-verbal cues, along with domination of the forum by some more articulate and confident student; often counterproductive for the very purpose these forums were established, as these might often dissuade the relatively less confident from contributing.	• As above for point 2. • In addition, students can also be asked to form groups and discuss the forum questions by arranging informal group meetings which would facilitate collaborative learning with a high level of discussion of learning before the response is posted online. Initial posts can be presented as a group response by a group leader nominated by the tutor/ peers, followed by contributions from individual group members, moving from cooperative to more self-directed individualised learning.

forums and poses some possible solutions to bridge the theory/research evidence and practice/action divide.

There is indeed dissonance between the ideal blended learning practice as described in the literature and the results often achieved in such an online/blended learning provision in practice during its real-world implementation. We should acknowledge from the outset that many of these issues could be resolved by offering tutors time and space to develop and enact these activities.

Conclusion

Bridging the evidence–action divide in university teaching is fundamental to developing quality teaching and engendering meaningful student learning. Lecturers' intentions and approaches to teaching are influenced by both internal and external guidance for teaching and pressure to engage students' intrinsic motivation in learning. The discourse of contemporary HE and the lived experience of teaching are both influential to an academic's response and attempts to develop novel teaching activities. Students vary in their abilities and motivations to adapt to new teaching and learning designs and activities. This is central to their academic success, individual learning gains and achievement of learning outcomes. Overcoming the mismatch created by inexperience, a lack of evidence-informed planning and the challenges of student engagement requires more technically detailed guidance for teaching and integration of research evidence during the planning and enactment of teaching (Evans *et al.*, 2015).

Summary points

- The gap between research-based evidence of effective practice in teaching and learning and teaching action needs to be narrowed to support quality teaching.
- University teachers, at all levels, need to be immersed in a teaching discourse which is substantive, supportive and critical of new approaches and which recognises the academic pressures in universities.
- Student-centred teaching approaches and designs require research-based evidence and resource-rich approaches, that is, time to support the development of effective teaching.
- Institutions need to support a variety of measures of teaching performance which afford evidence and research-based teaching enhancements to be developed, generative spaces for collegial discussion and realistic expectations for university teachers to hone their teaching delivery.

Recommended reading

DfE (2019) Teaching excellence and student outcomes framework. Available at: https://www.gov.uk/government/collections/teaching-excellence-framework (accessed 2 March 2020).

Evans, C., Muijs, D., and Tomlinson, M. (2015) *Engaged Student Learning: High-Impact Strategies to Enhance Student Achievement*. York: Higher Education Academy.

Gibbs, G. (2010) *Dimensions of Quality*. York: Higher Education Academy.

Marton, F., and Booth, F. (1997) *Learning and Awareness*. Mahwah, NJ: Lawrence Erlbaum Associates.

References

Advance, H.E. (2011) *The UK Professional Standards Framework for Teaching and Supporting Learning in Higher Education*. York: Advance HE.

Advance, H.E. (2019) Advance HE. Available at: https://www.advance-he.ac.uk/ (accessed 2 March 2020).

Åkerlind, G. (2008) A phenomenographic approach to developing academics' understanding of the nature of teaching and learning. *Teaching in Higher Education*, 13(6), pp. 633–644.

Bartram, B., Hathaway, T., and Rao, N. (2018) 'Teaching excellence' in Higher Education: A comparative study of English and Australian academics' perspectives. *Journal of Further and Higher Education*, 43(9), pp. 1284–1298.

Boelens, R., Van Laer, S., De Wever, B., and Elen, J. (2015) Blended learning in adult education: Towards a definition of blended learning. Available at: http://hdl.handle.net/1854/LU-6905076 (accessed 2 March 2020).

Bonwell, C., and Eison, J. (1991) Active learning: Creating excitement in the classroom. *ASHE-ERIC Higher Education Report*, No.1, George Washington University: Washington, DC

Brame, C., and Biel, R. (2015) Setting up and facilitating group work: Using cooperative learning groups effectively. Available at: http://cft.vanderbilt.edu/guides-sub-pages/setting-up-and-facilitating-group-work-using-cooperative-learning-groups-effectively/ (accessed 2 March 2020).

Burnard, P. (1999) Carl Rogers and postmodernism: Challenged in nursing and health sciences. *Nursing and Health Sciences*, 1(4), pp. 241–247.

Case, J. (2015) Emergent interactions: Rethinking the relationship between teaching and learning. *Teaching in Higher Education*, 20(6), pp. 625–635.

Charlton, B. (2006) Lectures are such an effective teaching method because they exploit evolved human psychology to improve learning. *Medical Hypotheses*, 67(6), pp. 1261–1265.

DfE (2017) *Teaching Excellence and Student Outcomes Framework Specification*. Department for Education. Available at: https://www.gov.uk/government/collections/teaching-excellence-framework (accessed 2 March 2020).

Drugova, E. (2019) The key characteristics of Teaching Excellence Programs for academic leaders: A review of high-ranking universities' experiences reflected in international publications. *Educational Studies Moscow*, 4, pp. 8–29.

Elen, J., Clarebout, G., Léonard, R., and Lowyck, J. (2007) Student-centred and Teacher-Centred Learning Environments: What students think. *Teaching in Higher Education*, 12(1), pp. 105–117.

Evans, C., Muijs, D., and Tomlinson, M. (2015) *Engaged Student Learning: High-Impact Strategies to Enhance Student Achievement*. York: Higher Education Academy.

Fanghanel, J. (2007) Teaching Excellence in Context: Drawing from a socio-cultural approach. In: A. Skelton (Ed.), *International Perspectives on Teaching Excellence in Higher Education*. London: Routledge.

Forstenzer, J. (2016) *The Teaching Excellence Framework: What's the Purpose? Report*. The Crick Center - Center for Engaged Philosophy and the University of Sheffield. Available at: http://eprints.whiterose.ac.uk/127959/ (accessed 2 March 2020).

Garrison, D., and Kanuka, H. (2004) Blended learning: Uncovering its transformative potential in higher education. *Internet and Higher Education*, 7(2), pp. 95–105.

Gibbs, G. (2010) *Dimensions of Quality*. York: Higher Education Academy.

Gibbs, G. (2014) Graham Gibbs on teaching lecturers to teach: Could training schemes for teachers help to improve student learning? Ask Graham Gibbs. *Times Higher Education*. Available at: https://www.timeshighereducation.com/news/graham-gibbs-on-teaching-lecturers-to-teach/2016202.article (accessed 2 March 2020).

Gov.UK (2020) Collection: Teaching excellence and student outcomes framework. Available at: https://www.gov.uk/government/collections/teaching-excellence-framework (accessed 2 March 2020).

Habeshaw, S., Habeshaw, T., and Gibbs, G. (1992) *53 Problems with Large Classes: Making the Best of a Bad Job*. Bristol: Technical and Educational Services.

Heller, P., and Hollabaugh, M. (1992) Teaching problem-solving through cooperative grouping. Part 2: Designing problems and structuring groups. *American Journal of Physics*, 60(7), pp. 637–644.

Johnson, D., and Johnson, R. (2008) Active learning: Cooperation in the classroom. *The Annual Report of Educational Psychology in Japan*, 47, pp. 29–30.

Johnson, D., Johnson, R., and Holubec, E. (1994) *The New Circles of Learning: Cooperation in the Classroom and School*. Edina, MN: Interaction Book Company.

Johnson, D., Johnson, R., and Smith, K. (2014) Cooperative learning: Improving university instruction by basing practice on validated theory. *Journal on Excellence in College Teaching*, 25, pp. 85–118.

Johnson, D.W., Johnson, R.T., and Smith, K.A. (2006) *Active Learning: Cooperation in the University Classroom* (3rd edition). Edina, MN: Interaction.

Jones, S. (2007) Reflections on the lecture: Outmoded medium or instrument of inspiration? *Journal of Further and Higher Education*, 31(4), pp. 397–406.

Kember, D. (1997) A reconceptualisation of the research into university academics conceptions of teaching. *Learning and Instruction*, 7(3), pp. 255–275.

Krathwohl, D.R., Bloom, B.S., and Masia, B.B. (1964) *Taxonomy of Educational Objectives: The Classification of Educational Goals. Handbook II: The Affective Domain.* New York: David McKay Company.

Marton, F., Runesson, U., and Tsui, A. (2004) The space of learning. In: F. Marton and A.Tsui (Eds.), *Classroom Discourse and the Space of Learning*. Mahwah, NJ: Lawrence Erlbaum.

Matsushita, K. (2018) *Deep Active Learning: Towards Greater Depth in University Education*. Singapore: Springer.

Mizokami, S. (2014) Deep active learning from a perspective of active learning theory. In K. Matsushita (Ed.) Deep Active Learning: Deepening higher learning, pp. 31–51. Tokyo:Keiso Shobo.

Omelivheva, M., and Avdeyeva, O. (2008) Teaching with lecture or debate? Testing the effectiveness of traditional versus active learning methods of instruction. *Political Science and Politics Online*, 41(3), pp. 603–607.

O'Neill, G., and McMahon, T. (2005) Student-centred learning: What does it mean for students and lecturers? In: G. O'Neill, S. Moore, and B. McMullin (Eds.), *Emerging Issues in the Practice of University Learning and Teaching*. Dublin: AISHE.

Paz Dennen, V. (2000) Task structuring for on-line problem based learning: A case study. *Journal of Educational Technology and Society*, 3(3), pp. 329–336.

Prosser, M., and Trigwell, K. (1999) *Understanding Learning and Teaching: The Experience in Higher Education*. Buckingham: SRHE and the Open University Press.

Ramsden, P. (1979) Student learning and perceptions of the academic environment. *Higher Education*, 8(4), pp. 411–427.

Sinnema, C., Sewell, A., and Milligan, A. (2011) Evidence-informed collaborative inquiry for improving teaching and learning. *Asia-Pacific Journal of Teacher Education*, 39(3), pp. 247–261.

Smith, K., and Hill, J. (2019) Defining the nature of blended learning through its depiction in current research. *Higher Education Research and Development*, 38(2), pp. 383–397.

Summers, M., and Volet, S. (2010) Group work does not necessarily equal collaborative learning: Evidence from observations and self-reports. *European Journal of Psychology of Education*, 25(4), pp. 473–492.

Trowler, P. (2001) Captured by the discourse? The socially constitutive power of new higher education discourse in the UK. *Organization*, 8(2), pp. 183–201.

Yasunaga, S. (2018) Class design based on high student engagement through cooperation: Toward classes that bring about profound development. In: K. Matsushita (Ed.), *Deep Active Learning: Towards Greater Depth in University Education*. Singapore: Springer.

10 Mental health and wellbeing in higher education

Clare Dickens

Introduction

A core aim of this chapter is to create a space for dialogue in which preconceived or rigid ways of seeing, hearing and viewing mental health and wellbeing in higher education (HE) can be challenged. Key questions are about the causes of the alleged mental health crisis, and the interface between HE and the National Health Service (NHS) in improving students' mental health and wellbeing. The reader will be asked to consider whether the dominant bio-medical perspective of mental health truly serves the diverse and complex student body in universities today.

The intention is not to force us into a paradigm war, or to suggest that anything that exists is wrong or in error. Instead it is proposed that, to establish a truly inclusive environment where students can flourish and grow, our understanding of human distress needs adjustment. The chapter will focus on inclusivity and wellbeing to show how this can offer supportive and enabling HE environments in which all students can develop healthy relationships with learning, with critical reflection and with themselves. The chapter proposes the reconfiguring of models that are seen to be no longer fit for purpose and discusses how we need to revisit our assumptions and practice in the HE sector. The focus is primarily on student mental health, but it also considers the needs of staff; the underpinning principles and considerations can apply to us all as fellow human beings and community members.

The mental health 'crisis' in higher education

The scale of the mental health crisis in UK universities is allegedly revealed in a study by the Institute for Public Policy Research (IPPR) think-tank (Thorley, 2017). It shows that, over a decade, the number of students who disclosed a mental health problem in their first year rose fivefold to reach 15,395. We might question the narrative of 'crisis' if it is derived from increased disclosure from students. Campaigns such as 'Time to Change' are intended to reduce the stigma associated with mental health issues, and to call for social action to talk and break the silence. There were also calls from the Equality Challenge Unit and University Mental Health Advisors' Network for students to disclose their difficulties. Such campaigns may be the cause of increased disclosures, rather than an actual increase in students' mental health problems. Reflecting on the trend of increased disclosures, there may be no crisis at all, but rather an indication of success in campaigns for disclosure. The 'crisis' perhaps derives from how well equipped HE institutions (HEIs) are to actually respond to the needs these disclosures reveal, and the extent to which this increasing demand has exposed the defects of the model we currently use.

Thorley (2017:1) notes

> Poor mental health and wellbeing can affect students' academic performance and desire to remain in HE. In the most severe and tragic circumstances, it can contribute to death by suicide – levels of which have also increased among students in recent years. The Higher Education sector and government, both have an interest in helping to improve the mental health and wellbeing of students.

He goes on to advise that universities should make the issue a strategic priority, as there is currently too much variation in how well equipped universities are to meet this challenge. This has led to a call for action called *Step Change* chaired by Professor Steve West (2017). The campaign acknowledges the increasing number of students dying by suicide and the duty of care that universities owe their students. It also highlights the need to adopt a whole-population approach to student mental health, and asks universities to reconfigure themselves as health-promoting and supportive environments. It recommends that universities should provide a compassionate environment aided by mental health literacy training to staff and students and early intervention.

Questions for discussion

- In your university, how is mental health support currently set up?
- What does it look like?
- What is your impression/experience of university mental health support?
- Do you feel students are given enough information about support services?
- What might HEIs do to improve support services, as far as you are aware?

A brief history of HE's relationship with mental health

Universities have almost a 1,000-year history, which has seen a strong regard for their role in developing the characters of the students studying with them. It is only in the last five decades or so that this sense of mission has allegedly declined. The origins of a more explicit emotional support offer can be traced back to the University of Leicester's counselling provision over 70 years ago. In the years since, many others have followed, and mental health advisors are commonly employed at universities and are the primary signpost for student support. There has been a growing unease for over a decade now about whether it is the role of the counselling services to compensate for what seem to be shortfalls in NHS provision (Cowley, 2007). Given increasing demand and complexities, counsellors and mental health advisors also have to support students to access, and in many cases wait for, NHS provision. In the timeline of a student's academic year, a large proportion of it can be spent on a waiting list for NHS support. Indeed, Gask *et al.* (2017) articulate a concern that HE staff trained and identified as 'gate-keepers' experience a high degree of frustration in that mental health services are often not receptive to the referrals they make. Here we risk losing skilled and highly committed individuals, who may find themselves exhausted and distressed by a mismatch of provision and need. It possibly becomes more difficult to nurture kindness and a sense that behind the next referral is a human being who has both need and capabilities. A student might lose their sense of self when they have been assessed and referred and now sit in a void.

The interface between higher education and health professionals

The Improving Access to Psychological Therapies (IAPT) services were introduced during the financial crisis in an attempt to meet the challenge of high levels of unmet needs. It was the NHS's answer to improve outcomes in the 'treatment' of common and 'low-level' mental health difficulties. In 2018–19, the IAPTS received 1.6 million GP and self-referrals. No doubt many people found the intervention and support both enlightening and useful; however, despite evidence to support the efficacy of the model and the truly committed professionals behind it, it would be fair to suggest that many of these referrals possibly did not improve availability of treatment. Many HE mental health professionals have negotiated direct referral routes with external provision to aid the triage and referral process for students. This may pose an ethical dilemma if an HEI's desire to have their students supported sooner conflicts with the demands external services face, and especially so when triage decisions should be based on clinical need alone.

In their 2003 publication *Mental Health of Students in Higher Education*, the Royal College of Psychiatrists (RCPsych, 2003) presents varying notions of student mental health difficulties and how they may present on a continuum from severe (bipolar disorder and schizophrenia) to lower-level mental ill health (distress, anxiety and low mood). The authors point out that more severe onset of mental ill health symptomatology in the general population more commonly occurs within the 18–25-year-old age category, and they link this to the entry point at which students join HE. However, this age group is not necessarily typical in many university courses. More and more we see mature, part-time and first-generation students who have entered HE from backgrounds that have limited engagement with HE until later on in their lives. This relates to MacIntyre's (1985) suggestion that a student's life should not be seen as separate from the specific roles they assume throughout the time prior to, during and beyond their studies. Furthermore, we should be mindful of the challenges and opportunities that exist within these roles; indeed, we need to ask if the 'typical' student even exists anymore.

More pressingly, this suggestion by the RCPsych implies that universities are opening their doors to those who already have, or who are developing, a 'mental illness'. This may be true, but it does little to help students 'coming with', or who 'later develop', mental health difficulties to gain a positive sense of mental wellbeing, beyond a notion that their experiences are 'due to their illness'. Through the experience of actually engaging in higher education, they can rewrite their story. Or those living with supposed mental illness can, and do, live mentally healthy and well lives. The university can be a place where individual recovery capital can be built and finessed, based on a student's individual view of what recovery principles actually matter to them; this may not necessarily include an absence of symptoms associated with and aligned to a deficit model.

The medical model of student wellbeing

There is a well-established debate about the role of the medical model in human wellbeing. Laing (2016) offers further insight referring to 'the gentrification of cities' and also of emotions. She alludes to the notion that emotional distress is becoming a socially constructed medicalised term typified by labels referring to anxiety, depression, rage and loneliness; they have become a standard part of our vocabulary and binary understanding. All of these labels are presented as the result of 'unsettled-brain chemistry' which needs to be healed. It is, therefore, worth considering whether this psychiatric meta-narrative deprives us of the ability to consider other valid analyses which, in Springer's terms, view the emotional distress of a student as a personal rational response to trauma and structural injustices in the university context. It focuses attention on the student or groups of students and diverts attention from the structural inequalities and systemic stressors that higher education creates and in turn need to be improved (Springer, 2016).

One of the most powerful models of disability, which still dominates professional policy and institutional practices, as well as existing at a popular level, has been the 'bio-medical model': 'diagnosable' mental ill health as defined and protected by the 2010 Equality Act. Characteristically, as part of a conservative tradition of political thought, this emphasises individual loss or incapacities, implying that the impairment limits, and thus defines, the whole person (Evans, 1999). The category 'disabled student' is also seen as problematic in the literature. The 'administratively useful' catch-all term 'disabled' has been argued to be powerful and empowering in some circumstances, yet negative and stigmatising in others (Jacklin *et al.*, 2007: 46). Who is considered disabled, by whom and for what purposes lies at the heart of this problem. Ever aware that we can be tribally drawn to take a position regarding our perceptions of how things really are and how things really work, it is worth us considering whether there is a need to create a truly inclusive HE environment that first embraces a variety of paradigms instead of, in Marsh's terms, being drawn into a 'compulsory ontology of pathology' (Marsh, 2010: 31).

Questions for discussion

- Is there a risk that national policy on student mental health and wellbeing is set by people based firmly on what their student experience was like?
- What are the barriers that students may experience in coming forward and telling someone they are struggling?
- What roles do capability, motivation and opportunity play in seeking support in an HE context?
- What makes help helpful?

How can we avoid leaving students behind?

We need to consider how we can concede that any mental health difficulty, whatever its name or construct, relates to how someone feels, thinks and acts, and how they then connect and interact with their sense of self and, indeed, with others. Woven into these apparently simple questions are layers of complexity, choice in how one perceives the origins of these changes and the fact that actions can often serve as communications. Origins, stories, experiences and meaning-making are all richly diverse and unique to each individual and their own cultural context. In the vein of the social model of disability (Oliver, 1990) and with application to the HE mental health context, Mertens (2005) warns that academic and scientific communities which validate and legitimise knowledge claims and dominant ways of understanding unwittingly contribute to systems of oppression. Ceci *et al.* (2002) argue that the social and psychological theory which underpins the scientific paradigm, and our perception of mental ill health and disability, was developed by white, able-bodied men, and, as knowledge claims are always embedded in sequences of truth, we should be particularly mindful of domination, exclusion, privilege and marginalisation.

In an HE context, we may inadvertently be failing to consider the diversity of the student population; we need to consider the further distress this may invite, and how this, in Meyer's (1995) terms, may add to minority stress. For many cultures, the Western construct of mental illness does not exist or resonate well. Other beliefs in turn influence attitudes and perceptions of self and of wellbeing to include remedies for distress. However, in a Western HE context, some students may have no choice but to adopt, absorb and possibly become the narrative that they are measured against, and to be assimilated into the society and institutions of a dominant culture, with its understanding and contextualisation of human distress. This is a problem and a challenge we must accept, with a commitment to remedying it.

Proactive inclusion and wellbeing by design

Inclusive pedagogy emerged from the civil rights movement as an approach to promote respect and equity for a wide range of cultural groups. Healey *et al.* (2006) argue that it is invidious to treat disabled students as a separate category; rather they fall along a continuum of learner differences and share similar challenges and difficulties that all students face in higher education. Other literature draws attention to international students' experiences of difficulties and adjustment to their host institutions (Currie, 2007; Ledwith and Seymour, 2001; Volet and Ang, 1998). We need to consider Hocking's stark point that students do not want to stand out as different but do want to be recognised as individuals (Hockings, 2010). Epidemiological perspectives that seek to generalise characteristics and features in order to predict likely need in relation to mental health cannot be used as a basis for planning the provision for mental health support in HE contexts.

There is also a sentiment within current mental health practice that almost waits for the proverbial horse to bolt: waiting for students to hit breaking point and being more effectively supportive once this breaking point is reached. A key principle of the 'Positive University' approach put forward by Sir Anthony Seldon and Alan Martin in 2016 is to avoid this pitfall by considering all students against a threshold of needs and strengths, capabilities and opportunities. They concede that many stresses are inevitable and that the approach will not remove workload and exam stress for students, but will equip them with the ability to cope with them better (Seldon and Martin, 2017). To a large degree, this may be a legitimate argument and aim, but there is an invitation to consider the possible lines of tension further. What makes for a stressful assessment? Does this lie in the fact that to students, the outcome matters? Does it lie in a practical or imagined fear or trauma related to failure? Where is the dignity and autonomy for students within this process? Are all students able to 'connect' with the module content? Does it excite and challenge them? Does it include people like them? Do they 'look up' to HE academics as beacons of success, having never heard their stories of failure, and more importantly, how they overcame them? Are there enough formative opportunities within the module to fail and navigate improvement before it really counts?

Taking this exploration a step further, there is a challenge in embracing principles that consider the pedagogical and andragogic design of those stress points that are perceived as inevitable, as part of the HE mental health and wellbeing offer. We should consider how an educational system creates equity in teaching and learning, and which acknowledges students' cultural, social and educational backgrounds in combination with the presence of physical and sensory impairments and mental wellbeing issues (Morgan and Houghton, 2011). May and Bridger assert, in respect of developing an inclusive culture, 'making a shift of such magnitude requires cultural and systemic change at both policy and practice levels' (2010:1).

It may be advantageous to consider a baseline that commences with a belief that no one will be disadvantaged by an inclusive curriculum design, delivery and assessment measure and that in our everyday practice, academics must embrace the challenge, accepting personal responsibility to create a more inclusive environment and design that doesn't necessarily depend on strategic instruction, enhancement plans and expectation alone. Regarding students as partners and embedding principles of wellbeing into teaching are not universally popular ideas. Ecclestone and Hayes (2009) express concern about the increasing emphasis on wellbeing, termed the 'therapeutic turn in education', arguing that it can act as a distraction from academic scholarship and promote a 'diminished subject' (p.3). This doesn't necessarily have to be the case, and one could argue for principles of constructivist learning and andragogy, which firmly place the responsibility for learning with the learner (Glasersfeld, 1989), as well as embracing students as adult learners with experiences and knowledge in their own right. However, varying demands, stresses and needs exist that could be ameliorated at the academic stressor's source, not invited as an arrogant measure of resilience as to whether students are fortunate or tough enough to overcome them. Nor should HE simply be a production line of absorbing knowledge that students can regurgitate through assessment at the end of each module.

Yates (2005) draws a distinction between 'the effective teacher', as demonstrated by an analysis of student outcomes, and 'the good teacher', who arouses positive affective reactions in students, and it could be argued that if we do not consider inclusive pedagogy at the design stage, we serve to exclude some of our own students from their education by disenabling their full and equitable participation in HE (Morgan and Houghton, 2011). Biggs and Tang (2007) provide a rich source of prompts for us to consider in how we should aim to improve inclusivity in education from design and delivery to assessment and feedback. Utilising constructive alignment theory (Biggs, 2003), and considering the work of Neary (2011) on students as producers within a process of active collaboration, we should place students at the heart of the system, working alongside academics.

Consult, reconfigure, roll out and repeat

Etherington (2004) refers to the 'reflexivity' which develops in our responses to the world around us: other people and events, knowledge we use to inform our actions, our communications and understandings. It is something we should seek to nurture in students within and beyond their HE journey and within their professional, familial and community roles. The challenge lies in how we can offer this for as many as possible, if not all, of the students studying in HE, but is possibly more limited with the model we find ourselves navigating. Cottam (2018) offers some rich insights into our HE context. Her observations over 30 years focused on the failure of the welfare state, once boasted of as one of the greatest social innovations. She suggests it is no longer fit for purpose and that we are *all* limited if we live and grow in a society riddled with inequality. She posits that neither money nor management alone can solve these problems, and that simply trying to find new solutions to fit an old system is destined to repeat the same problems. In an HE context, we need to move from the margins of what works and what we are here to provide, right to the centre of what we do and what we stand for. We need to avoid getting lost in the wrong kind of debates that distract us from the drivers of distress in our HEIs. Scaling up mental health provision and streamlining processes with thresholds that are unable to adapt, driven by a commitment and aim that we can offer something for everything, is possibly the wrong approach.

Cottam sets us a challenge in how we transition to newer collaborative ways of thinking and working, whereby we grow capabilities, with scaling-up seen as a limited approach. She posits that we need to consider how we embrace and design for the needs of our own communities, to lead and commit to shared values where time and space are offered so that we can grow through our networks. It could be argued that this can present itself in facilitative teaching styles, dialogic-based feedback and feed-forward in assessments. In considering our own student body, in getting to know who they really are and what drives both their need and their capabilities, we may find that what actually defines them is their differences; in fact, they will at an individual level never be repeated again. Here the crux lies in not trying to fit students into a box but in how we enable personal growth for each and every student navigating HE. All of its complex systems, processes, demands and transitions can be the equivalent of landing any one of us on the surface of the moon. Even if we manage to adapt and assimilate, we can still find ourselves as disconnected strangers and struggling in what is a more familiar landscape.

It would be naive not to concede that some ideas stick, but we must avoid the pitfall of being stuck in them. Their sticking factor can be due to any number of reasons, including dominant ways of seeing, hearing and doing. But the more we focus on reconfiguring and polishing services and systems born of an impatience for change to occur, we risk focusing on the wrong thing. We miss an opportunity to create a culture where everyone is enabled to flourish and to grow their own capabilities. If we want students to survive and thrive in HE and to bring about change in students' lives, our focus shouldn't be merely on how we can fix these services and in-roads to access them. We also need to consider how we can support students to create change and how we can help to create and build on their capabilities with a strong regard for societal and structural barriers. In doing so, we can never allow ourselves as a sector to settle for compliance with potentially questionable targets. Our students and their needs and capabilities will change, as will the society in which they live and navigate their sense of self, and we need to be switched on to embrace this challenge.

So do we need to revisit our roots as a sector? Do we again need to place ourselves not just as HE providers, but also as character developers? Do we need to embrace the core challenge set out in the step-change model to shift the vision from the simplicity of service provision to the environment of HE as somewhere that proactive and anticipatory need should be considered? We can take this a step further by bringing the design of 'things' that all students are exposed to in this environment: teaching and learning (T&L). We need to invest in mental health, yes, but pouring money into a system that is struggling already may continue the malady already playing out, and one in which our students are forced to perform to its tune as it sings the loudest and is familiar to everyone's ears. Cottam provides the model of a twentieth-century welfare management system versus a twenty-first-century radical-help model. Augmented with the considerations explored above, within our HE context, Table 10.1 considers these as contradictions, complexities and indeed opportunities.

Conclusion

What hasn't been presented in this chapter is any explicit definition of what mental health and emotional wellbeing actually are, and if we considered a notion of developing a definitive happy and healthy human being, we may find this a more difficult task than it initially appears. If we move attention to the World Health Organisation definition, avoid the pull to critique and simply take it at face value in the first instance, it argues that it is when someone feels good, can reach their full potential and work productively, contributing to their communities. This does pose a challenge to consider whether we can foster some of the capability and connection that this definition requires in order for it to be achieved for each

Table 10.1 A flexing paradigm for student support and wellbeing

20th-Century Student Support	21st-Century Student Health Capital
Individual Level	**Individual Level**
• View the student as the root of the problem, and seek to fix the problems with sticking plasters that are in some cases destined to fall off. • Individuals forced to view themselves as the sole source of focus, without any due regard for the structural or political stressors they navigate. • Students and HE staff spend long periods of time navigating thresholds that will not flex. • Focus in and manage acute need, then repeat, which can nurture co-dependence, learnt helplessness, hopelessness and unmet demand; at the exit strategy, can risk pushing students off the edge of a cliff with nothing there to catch them.	• View the student as an array of needs and strengths, resilient in their own right, but possibly less so in a new environment; introduce new thinking, self-awareness, compassion and worth, pride, grow the good life and opportunity. • Develop capability, problem- solving skills, emotional intelligence, psycho-education, resilience and resourcefulness. • Health promoting vs. need enhancing.
Provision Level	**Provision Level**
• Closed; targeted on particular groups which risks leaving people behind, no consideration of intersectionality or dominance of narrative within models and who conceived them; which can oppress, force assimilation and risk students falling between the gaps.	• Open; no high-risk low-risk narrative, reduced bolt-on adjustments and provision, take care of each other. • If we treasure them, we should measure them; 'how do we measure student success?' Aside from external mandatory measure of *our* success as an HEI, what do we value as successful for students? • More importantly, students as partners – what do they value as success? Should we dominate this measure or co-produce with students?
• Manage and contain risk, create medicalised thresholds, restrict capability and capacity of staff and students, objectify students, increase wait and demand and invite crisis.	• Mitigate risk, increase capability and capacity of staff at an appropriate community and compassion-based level, ensure safety and wellbeing planning for all, carry out smart triage supported by common and inclusive language, remove barriers and gate-keeping and create possibility and hope.
Strategic Level	**Strategic Level**
• Focus on financial audit; look within command resource, which risks duplication, props up a model that can never be adequately funded, and distracts from our main focus of T & L.	• Look out to the community in which we sit and serve. Connect multiple forms of resource who are already commissioned to deliver and have them aware of student specific needs and work with them. • Consider wellbeing at curriculum design by people who want to see students do well and grow, knead in self-help and motivation, sign-posting and social support; promote this to students as part of our offer, making it easy to navigate and access if needed.

- Transactional culture; strategic thinking that believes it knows the problems that require attention and sets out change to fix them; lacks indigenous awareness, creating distance where good intentions get lost.

- Above all a proud community of practice enhanced by relationships, internal consultation and co-production. Impact-assessed quick wins.
- Establish longer-term hopes and goals, celebrate success and turn up the volume, make a commitment to review, learn lessons and adapt; nurture local pride and loyalty.

Social Level

- External relation of HE evolving to be a place that nurtures ill health and stress, and survival of the fittest; entrenched by those who demand more MH provision, a provision attached to a model that has seen little progress since the 1950s.
- Students say 'never again' as staff are seen as the source of stress; this risks corporatising distress without having a firm definition of what mental health/wellbeing is.
- Deliberate Destiny of Failure?

Social Level

- HE the place to be ... a relationship with life-long learning and critical engagement, where reinvestment in self can be achieved, where challenges are opportunities, where HE is seen as a mainstay in people's lives, somewhere safe, where 'bouncing back' can be finessed.
- Community focused but also values the individual, their success and their journey to include where they come from and where they want to be. Aiming high and looking beyond pre-determined limits of success.

of the students entering HE. We also need to acknowledge that some may not know what good feels like if they have never felt good, and that in the notion of 'full potential', we should concede that perhaps this can never be realised unless we are challenged, and that our failures may not be due to our capability but more to barriers and blockers to opportunity. Our ability, therefore, to work productively and contribute to our communities depends on our relationships with others and indeed ourselves.

One of the main aims of this chapter has been to unsettle and expand possibly rigid understandings so that we do not become complicit in continuing to add to the long line of hopeful students who do have personal responsibility for their own mental health, but who are also not the sole source of any mental health issue. Students may find themselves within arm's length of so much opportunity, but that can mean very little if its design hasn't been considered. None of what has been discussed may prove to be particularly enlightening to readers who understand and agree with some of the points put forward. Yet, we need to ensure we do not fall into the trap of default ways of thinking that are nurtured through dominant ways of understanding, possibly chasing a desire to increase what is on offer without really considering what is actually needed.

The chapter has considered whether as a sector we need to deconstruct and view the differing components, to consider how our current curriculum design meets the requirements for inclusivity and the wellbeing of students. A strategic analysis of the mental health crisis in HE requires us to critically explore where this crisis really lies. In considering potential solutions, the first tenet to consider is that the crisis doesn't lie in the fact that fewer than 20,000 HE students disclosed a mental health issue, but that at around the same time, we had 2.34 million students studying in UK HE, each and every one of them entering with varying degrees of need and capabilities. Furthermore, if each of them did disclose a mental health difficulty, no amount of finessing a bolt-on provision model would accommodate them all.

Therefore, we should consider the need to disrupt and expose imbalances of power and partial understandings of the origins of distress so we can design the support we provide and fully consider the role HE has in supporting the mental health of its students. Inviting critique within our cultures and practices does not begin with the assumption that what exists is wrong. Rather, it is a critique that seeks to examine the assumptions that those structures rest upon, and which can proliferate the need born of an assumption that this way of knowing distress is the correct framing, or that we can ever achieve a solution for everything. If we don't consider an inclusive threshold and continue to enforce assimilation and binary understandings, we may always be destined to let some students down and leave them behind.

Summary points

- The narrative of crisis that surrounds student mental health is eminently questionable; in reality, it is more likely an indication of the success of campaigns aimed at encouraging disclosure.
- We need to challenge rigid understandings of mental health that are rooted in a medicalised model.
- It is important for HE to reconsider and reconfigure curriculum design and assessment to better accommodate the wellbeing of all students.

Questions for discussion

- Can we move to an inclusive and democratised vision of student support and wellbeing, wherein we all play our own role based on our function within HE?
- How would we avoid the pitfall of singular ways of viewing and offering provision for mental health and distress in HE?
- What does mental health mean to you and what would you need to lead a happy and healthy life? Are the ingredients the same for us all, and who owns that definition anyway?

Recommended reading

Barden, N. and Caleb, R. (2019) *Student Mental Health and Wellbeing in Higher Education: A Practical Guide.* London: Sage.
Houghton, A. and Anderson, J. (2017) *Embedding Mental Wellbeing in the Curriculum: Maximising Success in Higher Education.* York: Higher Education Academy.
Hughes, G., Panjwani, M., Tulcidas, P. and Byrom, N. (2018) *Student Mental Health: The Role and Responsibilities of Academics.* Oxford: Student Minds.
Hughes, G. and Spanner, L. (2019) *The University Mental Health Charter.* Leeds: Student Minds.

References

Biggs, J. (2003) *Teaching for Quality Learning at University.* Buckingham: SRHE and Open University Press.
Biggs, J. and Tang, C. (2007) *Teaching for Quality Learning at University.* Buckingham: SRHE and Open University Press.
Ceci, C., Limacher, L. and McLeod, D. (2002) Language and Power: Ascribing Legitimacy to Interpretive Research. *Qualitative Health Research,* 12(5), pp. 713–720.
Cottam, H. (2018) *Radical Help: How We Can Remake the Relationships Between Us and Revolutionise the Welfare State.* London: Virago.

Cowley, J. (2007) Stepped Care: The Cardiff Model. *AUCC Journal*, December, pp. 2–5.

Currie, G. (2007) Beyond Our Imagination: The Voice of International Students on the MBA. *Management Learning*, 38(5), pp. 539–556.

Ecclestone, K. and Hayes, D. (2009) Changing the Subject: The Educational Implications of Developing Emotional Wellbeing. *Oxford Review of Education*, 35(3),pp. 371–389.

Equality Act (2010) *(c.15)*. London: The Stationery Office.

Etherington, K. (2004) *Becoming a Reflexive Researcher: Using Ourselves in Research*. London: Jessica Kingsley Publishers.

Evans, J. (1999) Feeble Monsters Making Up Disabled People. In: J. Evans and S. Hall (Eds.), *Visual Culture: A Reader*. London: Sage.

Gask, L., Coupe, N., Green, G. and McElvenny, D. (2017) Pilot Study Evaluation of Suicide Prevention Gatekeeper Training Utilising STORM in a British University Setting. *British Journal of Guidance and Counselling*, 45(5), pp. 593–605.

Glasersfeld, E. (1989) Cognition, Construction of Knowledge and Teaching. *Synthese*, 80(1), pp. 121–140.

Healey, M., Bradley, A., Fuller, M. and Hall, T. (2006) Listening to Students: The Experiences of Disabled Student of Learning at University. In: M. Adams and S. Brown (Eds.), *Towards Inclusive Learning in Higher Education: Developing Curricula for Disabled Students*. Abingdon: Routledge.

Hockings, C. (2010) *Towards Inclusive Learning and Teaching: Principles into Practice*. The Higher Education Academy – 2010 workshop presentation, Promoting Equity in Higher Education, 27–28 January 2010, Eastwood Hall, Nottingham.

Jacklin, A., Robinson, C., O' Meara, L. and Harris, A. (2007) *Improving the Experiences of Disabled Students in Higher Education*. York: The Higher Education Academy.

Laing, O. (2016) *The Lonely City: The Art of Being Alone*. London: Cannongate Books.

Ledwith, S. and Seymour, D. (2001) Home and Away: Preparing Students for Multicultural Management. *International Journal of Human Resource Management*, 12(8), pp. 1292–1312.

MacIntyre, A. (1985) *After Virtue: A Study in Moral Theory*, 2nd ed. London: Duckworth.

Marsh, I. (2010) *Suicide: Foucault, History and Truth*. Cambridge: Cambridge University Press.

May, H. and Bridger, K. (2010) *Developing and Embedding Inclusive Policy and Practice Within Higher Education*. York: The Higher Education Academy.

Mertens, D. M. (2005) *Research Methods in Education and Psychology: Integrating Diversity with Quantitative and Qualitative Approaches*, 2nd ed. Thousand Oaks: Sage.

Meyer, I. (1995) Minority Stress and Mental Health in Gay Men. *Journal of Health and Social Behavior*, 36(1), pp. 38–56.

Morgan, H. and Houghton, A. (2011) *Inclusive Curriculum Design in Higher Education: Considerations for Effective Practice Across and Within Subject Areas*. York: Higher Education Academy.

Neary, M. (2011) Student as Producer: Reinventing HE Through Undergraduate Research. Available at: https://www.theguardian.com/higher-education-network/blog/2011/sep/22/student-as-producer-university-lincoln (accessed 28 February 2020).

Oliver, M. (1990) *The Politics of Disablement*. London: Macmillan.

RCPsych (2003) *The Mental Health of Students in Higher Education: Report CR112*. London: RCPsych.

Seldon, A. and Martin, A. (2017) *The Positive and Mindful University*. Oxford: HEPI.

Springer, S. (2016) Fuck Neoliberalism. *ACME: An International Journal for Critical Geographies*, 15(2), pp. 285–292.

Thorley, C. (2017) *Not by Degrees: Improving Student Mental Health in the UK's Universities*. London: IPPR.

Volet, S. and Ang, G. (1998) Culturally Mixed Groups on International Campuses: An Opportunity for Inter-Cultural Learning. *Higher Education Research and Development*, 17(1), pp. 5–23.

West, S. (2017) *New Framework for Universities to Help Improve Student Mental Health*. London: Universities UK. Available at https://www.universitiesuk.ac.uk/news/Pages/New-framework-for-universities-to-help-improve-student-mental-health.aspx (accessed 9 March 2020).

Yates, G. (2005) 'How Obvious': Personal Reflections on the Database of Educational Psychological and Effective Teaching Research. *Educational Psychology*, 26(6), pp. 681–700.

11 The development of knowledge in the modern and postmodern universities

Stephen Ward

Introduction

This chapter examines the development of the university and university knowledge. The first section traces the growth of knowledge from its religious origins in the medieval universities to the principle of reason as the basis for knowledge in the modern university. The second considers the postmodern university in the context of mass higher education (HE) and the effects of academic freedom and the role of the state and the market in defining university knowledge.

Medieval origins of the university

Originating in Bologna and Paris in the twelfth century, the European university has a history of nearly a millennium and has left some traces in today's universities. They like to recall their medieval and liturgical origins with chancellors, vice chancellors, professors, deans, masters and honours degrees. They indulge in graduation ceremonies with processions decked out with the academic regalia of hoods, gowns, bedel and mace. Other features have lasted: students live away from home in accommodation overseen by university staff and there is a separation from society and the state. Toswell (2017: 15) notes that 'the governance and physical structure of a university campus remains highly medieval', with an infrastructure that 'replicates the push-pull of wanting to be part of the community and wanting to maintain full autonomy as an independent institution'. This 'push-pull' will permeate our discussion of knowledge and governance of the university through the ages.

The term *university* derives from the Latin *universitas*, meaning 'a community'; the notion of a universal kinship of scholars underlies the original concept of higher education (HE). The medieval European universities were internationally linked, borderless institutions sharing knowledge across Europe. This was made possible by two characteristics of the time: the relative weakness of national frontiers, which allowed academics to interact freely across geographical areas; and the use of Latin as a *lingua franca*, which enabled easy communication. There appears to have been a form of cross-European quality assurance in the recognition of diplomas between institutions. A third factor enabling unity of scholarship across the medieval universities was a singular commitment to the theological teachings of the Roman Catholic Church.

MacCulloch (2004:12) argues that a purpose of the medieval university was to explain the miracle of the corporeal presence of Christ in the bread and wine of the Eucharist. The twelfth and thirteenth-century concept of university knowledge was adapted from Aristotle: 'a logical system of questioning and listing data from the authorities ... called scholasticism' (p. 25) This reached its highest level with Thomas Aquinas, who tried to show that human reason was a gift of God designed to give human beings as much understanding of divine mysteries as they needed.

The Renaissance began to free universities from the Church to allow tutors to be recruited from civil society; less doctrinal teaching allowed the fermentation of new ideas and the development of knowledge. This was driven by the invention of the printing press, the proliferation of texts and the development of Humanism. The power of words could be used actively to change human society for the better. This saw the emergence of what now would be known as 'critique': the analysis of texts and the questioning of their assumptions. As well as a change of curriculum in the universities, the Renaissance brought the formation of nation states, border controls and the use of national languages in education. Universities lost their universal, borderless quality and became a function of national systems. The modern university became a national institution, and attempts to develop a common university curriculum across Europe have been frustrated by government resistance and closed national systems. It is ironical that the European Union now struggles to reinstate the convergence in HE which existed in the thirteenth century.

It would be a mistake, though, to see the medieval university as representing a golden age of academic freedom in HE. While an elite of academics was free to engage as a scholarly community, the knowledge they were allowed to share was largely determined by the Roman Catholic Church. For example, the Sorbonne in Paris was based upon a contract between the college and the crown to teach theology. The control of the Church over university knowledge persisted throughout the Renaissance. Universities developed the idea of 'nation' through scholarship, defining the culture of their area of origin, but there was no original research, and privileges were guaranteed only so long as the tenets of the Church remained unquestioned. The development of Humanism within the universities was slow, and many humanists chose to stay outside the university system, working on scholarly editions in cooperation with printers in large commercial centres from where there were good distribution systems for their books. The restraint on scientific enquiry in the universities is demonstrated by the fact that in 1633 they supported the Church in Galileo's trial for heresy, with the sentence against him read publicly in every university. The role of the university at this time was restricted to preserving and deepening the officially recognised knowledge of the Church: 'revealed', rather than verifiable, knowledge. The disciplines in the medieval university reflected the seven liberal arts, grouped according to the nature of matter to be studied in the *trivium* of grammar, rhetoric and knowledge and the *quadrivium* of arithmetic, geometry, astronomy and music. The unifying principle of knowledge was 'theodicy': its confirmation of the goodness of God.

The development of the modern university

The modern university began with the Enlightenment and the industrial revolution. Whereas the Church sought only the reinforcement of the traditional, the entrepreneurial society of the late eighteenth and early nineteenth centuries turned to the university for scientific knowledge and a trained professional elite. Instigated by Wilhelm von Humboldt in 1809, the University of Berlin introduced research and innovation: 'The university became a privileged place where the future of society is forged through research' (Haddad, 2000: 32). Humboldt's was the first university to provide the highly educated professionals required by industry and civil administration in exchange for freedom from the state and autonomy in the knowledge it produces.

The underlying philosophy of the modern university derives from nineteenth-century German ideal-ism, notably the work of Immanuel Kant. For Kant (1992), the basis of the university is 'reason', in contrast to superstition and tradition. Readings (1996: 57) summarises Kant's thinking, suggesting that 'the life of the Kantian university is … a perpetual conflict between established tradition and rational enquiry'. While theodicy was the only unifying principle of the medieval university, 'Kant ushers in the modernity of the university by naming this principle reason … And reason has its own discipline, that of philosophy, the lower faculty' (p. 56). In contrast, the higher faculties of theology, law and medicine draw on the 'unquestionable authority' of the Bible, law on the civil code and the decrees of the medical profession. For Kant, the authority of the lower faculty of Philosophy is autonomous. It depends on nothing outside itself; 'it legitimates itself by reason alone, by its own practice' (p. 56).

The higher faculties draw upon external authority and are accused of promulgating acceptance of tradition and of controlling the people by making them accept established authority. The 'conflict of the faculties', then, reflects the tension between superstition and reason. Kant does not see the university as divorced from culture and society, but he strikes a balance between the autonomy of reason and the power of the state. Kant also argues that the role of the university is to produce technicians for the state – 'men of affairs'. However, knowledge should be used in the service of the state, and philosophy must protect the University from the abuse of power by the state, in limit-ing the establishment's interests in the higher faculties. The modern university, as conceived by Humboldt, is a means of the realisation of state nationalism, culture and identity. Humboldt's genius was to create a system in which the state finances the university but allows it autonomy and ensures academic freedom for its teachers.

The university contributes to a definition of the nation state itself in the form of the transmission of national culture and knowledge traditions. It also prepares for citizenship and the highest admin-istrative responsibilities. The Humboldt University of Berlin was the pattern for European universities in the nineteenth and twentieth centuries.

Academic freedom in the modern university

One way of examining the role of the university in relation to the state is to analyse the notion of 'academic freedom'. Tight (1988) points out that, in human rights terms, all have academic freedom in the sense that both university staff and students have the freedom to learn what they wish: there is no legal or political restriction on learning. What is problematical is the freedom within the context of employment as an academic or as a student on a course. It is a matter of freedom *from* the con-straints on intellectual activity as well as the freedom *to* engage in intellectual activity – academic freedom which is provided by the provision of time and resources to carry it out. Neave makes an important distinction between 'university autonomy' – the freedom of the institution – and 'academic freedom' – the freedom of individual academics within the institution.

The extent to which HE can separate itself from the wider society is limited by the power of the professional associations. For example, the British Medical Association (BMA), the Royal Institute of British Architects (RIBA) and the British Psychological Society (BPS) all have a varying interest in, and influence on, the curriculum for their relative subjects in universities. The question which emerges here is the extent to which society has influence and to which the state has direct control. In contrast with medicine, architecture and psychology, where the professional associations exert influence, in

England and Wales, HE in teacher training is now directly controlled by the state through specified standards which define the curriculum in its entirety through the *Standards for Teaching* (DfE, 2013).

O'Hear (1988) sees the nature of the university itself in terms of academic freedom. Academic freedom and freedom of speech are two inter-related concepts which he attempts to distinguish. He suggests that, while freedom of speech might be accorded to anyone, academic freedom is a particular form of freedom peculiar to the university and thereby defines the nature of the university – making, again, the distinction between freedom *from* interference, which can be enjoyed by all, and the freedom *to*, which can be offered by a university's resources: 'It implies a long-term commitment on the part of the institution concerned to provide conditions in which the academic can study and teach' (p. 7). But O'Hear goes on to dismiss the justification for academic freedom as the freedom to be creatively productive through research and the creation of new knowledge. He suggests that what is newly produced by universities is 'miniscule for all the work and resources that go into universities' (p. 7). Instead, he cites Newman's (1852) concept of a university, which is less to do with extending the boundaries of knowledge than the cultural one of playing a role in the life of society. He offers F.R. Leavis's definition of the educational and cultural task of the universities:

> to explore the means of bringing the various essential kinds of specialist knowledge and training into effective relation with informed general intelligence, human culture, social conscience and political will. Here in this work we have the function that is pre-eminently the university's; if the work is not done there it will not be done anywhere.
>
> (Leavis, 1979: 24)

This provides a reason for the existence of the university in which the cultivation of the intellect is valued for its own sake, with staff free of the pressure to publish, attract students and fulfil the needs of industry. O'Hear (1988) argues against the whole concept of the university, suggesting that we need simply to have a cost-effective means of carrying out scientific research on the one hand and specialist teaching on the other 'without being shackled by the belief that there is some virtue in having a lot of different subjects grouped together in the same institution' (p. 12).

Universities and the state in England and Wales

In Britain, the relationship between the university and the state has been ambiguous. Kogan and Hanney (2000) stress the relative autonomy of UK universities under governments. Direct control by the state over university knowledge was limited for much of the twentieth century. On a list of criteria for autonomy by Frazer (1997), British universities score highly: legal status, academic authority, self-determined mission, governance, financial independence, freedom to employ staff, control of student admissions and freedom to determine the content of courses.

Neave (2000) suggests that the universities of Continental Europe were firmly embedded into national bureaucracies, whereas in Britain 'the status of universities as a property-owning corporation of scholars ... was preserved' (p. 109). The liberal argument for the strength of the university is given by John Stuart Mill, who argued that government intervention in universities should be limited simply to avoid the evil of adding to government power. Mill's formulation leads to the notion of a 'facilitatory state which provides resources to universities whose freedom would be enjoyed within an area of negotiation largely controlled by the universities themselves' (Kogan and Hanney: 30). Their central point, though, is that the ambivalence towards universities is shared by successive governments and is reflected in the actions of the government agencies, the University Grants Commission (UGC) and the National Advisory Body (NAB), which tended to bolster the power of universities. Universities, then, became used to enjoying the benefits of high levels of government funding, together with freedom from state control: universities were the guardians and codifiers of knowledge.

A feature of twentieth-century HE in England and Wales was the so-called 'binary divide' between those universities with a royal charter, and polytechnics and colleges whose degrees were awarded by other bodies. There was a duality of thinking behind this. On the one hand, there was a commitment to the virtue of the academic independence of the traditional universities. On the other was the notion that there should be both public accountability and connection with the rest of the education system. Anthony Crosland, Labour Secretary of State for Education, set up the system in the mid-1960s with the ambition of creating separate but equal branches of HE to serve different purposes. There would be the twin virtues of academic independence for the existing universities and, for the new polytechnics, local accountability and an emphasis on applied knowledge for industry. The context for the new system was the future expansion of HE, as recommended by the Robbins Commission (Committee on HE, 1963). The binary system was to keep some public control over what was to be an expanding system, and this was to be achieved through local education authority (LEA) control.

Although the binary system permitted some financial independence for the polytechnics and colleges, it saw distinctly different forms of academic control between the two types of institution. The 'old' universities with royal charters were largely self-governing in terms of their curriculum, while knowledge in the polytechnics and colleges was rigorously controlled by the Council for National Academic Awards (CNAA). CNAA was a government-funded organisation which operated to ensure the implementation of strict guidelines for curriculum structure, content and methods. Degree courses to be taught in the polytechnics were to be approved by the Council and were required to meet all its criteria. Although it employed HE 'peers' to implement its directives, it exercised a high level of control over HE knowledge with rigorous scrutiny (Silver, 1990). The existence of this body signifies the relationship of the institutions to the state. While the chartered universities enjoyed the trust of the state to define and codify knowledge, the polytechnics and colleges were not to enjoy the Humboldt model of relationship to the state. Instead, every curriculum item of knowledge was rigorously audited and approved or rejected.

The contradictions in the binary system meant that it probably could not last. The polytechnics had been created through the merger of small institutions and often became large and powerful bureaucracies. LEA control tended to be weak, and the polytechnics succeeded in managing their funding. But it was freedom from LEA control that the Committee of Directors of Polytechnics (CDP) sought. This was granted by Secretary of State for Education, Kenneth Baker, in 1989 with the incorporation of polytechnics as independent financial institutions, but the request for the university title of 'Polytechnic Universities' was refused. However, things were to change rapidly with the new Secretary of State, Kenneth Clarke, in 1991, who was reported to have said, "'Let's take the great plunge and make them all universities, let's get rid of all the arguments'" (Kogan and Hannay: 139). With that the binary system was abolished at a stroke, with no analysis of the issue or consultation.

While this might appear to foreshadow an increase in independence for the HE institutions, the outcomes were not so simple. The end of the twentieth century brought the New Right in British politics with a different view of the management of public organisations and the professions. These are characterised by New Public Management (NPM) in 'the evaluative state' (Henkel, 1991). NPM is intended on the one hand to devolve power to institutions, but on the other to retain central control in order to reduce the power of professional bodies, which is depicted as 'professional hegemony'. Margaret Thatcher's 1980s Conservative government reforms were supposedly intended to roll back the state in a shift from academic control towards both the market and the incorporation of universities in the generality of state control.

Differing from continental Europe, in Britain, 'the university was neither incorporated as part of the national bureaucracy, nor was it subject to any one coherent constitutional or administrative theory of the relationship between state and university' (Kogan and Hannay: 37). Universities were property-owning corporations of independent scholars. They enjoyed an exceptionally high level of autonomy, not because governments considered that the state would benefit from such an arrangement, but simply because there was no concept of the state as 'a distributive or regulative entity' and because of the more general view that the state had no role in education. So the Humboldt model of the state as buffer to ensure commitment to scholarship did not exist; it was simply guaranteed by a self-regulating academe. The feature common to Humboldt was the 'facilitatory' state which provided the resources.

This section has shown how university knowledge has developed from the theodicy of the medieval university to the modern university's critical analysis based on reason. It has reviewed the changing role of the university in relation to the state, the issue of academic freedom and, in Britain, the rise and fall of the binary system. The next section considers the effects of postmodern thinking and the influence of the market on universities and on HE knowledge.

The postmodern university: knowledge, the state and the market

In the latter part of the twentieth century and in the early twenty-first century, government policy in Britain was to create a mass HE system in a market in which students pay tuition fees and universities compete with each other for students who have 'choice'. The neo-liberal rationale for such a policy is based on a simple industrial model of efficiency and productivity: competition creates quality and improvement. As well as the introduction of tuition fees in England and Wales, British governments have implemented a variety of measures to enhance the market: the National Student Survey (NSS, 2020) allows for an evaluation of university 'services' and the formation of league tables of universities to enable student choice. The Office for Students (OfS, 2018) is a regulatory body designed to protect the rights of students as customers. One self-evident feature of knowledge in the postmodern university is the wide range of subject offerings to students; the choice of subject matter is determined by the market as universities offer student-popular subjects such as Media Studies, Sports Science and Dance. And within the subjects, students are offered a range of module choices: the modules which run are the modules students 'like'.

The term 'postmodern university' is commonly used to characterise developments in HE. Coulby and Jones (1995: 10) point out that, despite the temporal suggestion in the prefix 'post', postmodernism itself is not a matter of chronology: 'It is part of a long history of conflict between hegemonising and fissile tendencies within Europe, accentuated by the creation of states and their supportive mass education systems'. It is, then, not a 'postmodern era', but an era in which postmodern thinking has affected the development of universities – the complex changes in the relationship between the university and the state and the ways in which university knowledge has been shaped by the intervention of the market.

Delanty (2001) refers to the 'democratisation of knowledge' with a new role for the university in the context of cultural and epistemological changes in society. He proposes that the university is brought closer to society. It is not that the university is no longer involved in definitions of knowledge, but that the process has become more complex with a variety of interpretations:

> The university cannot re-establish the broken unity of knowledge but it can open up avenues of communication between these different kinds of knowledge, in particular between knowledge as science and knowledge as culture.
>
> (p. 6)

Delanty goes on to cite Bourdieu's (1988) critiques of Habermas's (1971) and Parsons's (1974) views of the university. Parsons sees the university as a shared normative system with a functional link between knowledge and citizenship. For Habermas, the university has an emancipatory function in society, freeing the individual. Bourdieu, on the other hand, depicts the university as a self-preserving institution, an autonomous site in which different orders of power clash and struggle for self-reproduction. Using Foucault's (1972) notion of knowledge as power, in which the academic institution serves the interests of the dominant group, the university reproduces society and legitimates inequalities. Bourdieu sees all culture as symbolic violence and based on 'misrecognition' (*méconnaissance*). Education is reduced to the means that modern society has devised for the transmission of cultural capital – the cognitive structures of the dominant cultural models in society. For Bourdieu, culture is a cognitive system which offers groups the means of imposing and maintaining classifications – cultural capital. But beneath the cultural level is economic power. Delanty suggests that the difference between Parsons and Bourdieu is the concept of power. Parsons's notion of a shared normative system does not include power, whereas Bourdieu's sees culture as a site of contestation, because it is pervaded by power. Where others have seen culture as a means of social integration or of legitimation, Bourdieu sees symbolic systems of difference and exclusion. Kant's conflict of the faculties is between knowledge and rationality; for Bourdieu, the conflicts are between different sorts of capital: cognitive or cultural. Bourdieu's (1988) *homo academicus* is a product of the field of academic power to control and classify knowledge and restrict the academic field. Academic power is associated with the canonical disciplines of literature, classics and philosophy: a social magistracy. It is a cognitive machine that organises cognitive structures, disciplines and social space, creating symbolic boundaries.

Cowen (1996) analyses government policy for university knowledge in terms of global economics and market forces:

> the governmental critique of the university, in several of the OECD countries, delegitimates the traditional assumptions made by universities about their own excellence, proposes a rebalancing of the relationships between the state, the productive economy and universities and outlines the ways in which the contribution of the universities within this new social contract may be encouraged, even enforced.
>
> (p. 3)

The university loses its autonomy from government. The effect of this is a shift from knowledge as truth to knowledge as 'performativity': that which is seen to be useful in employment in the economy. It is a part of the dynamic of epistemological change described by Lyotard (1986) as the postindustrial, postmodern collapse of meta-knowledge and the contestation of the nature of knowledge itself. Cowen explains the change in terms of government warnings of economic crisis. He makes strong claims for Lyotard's analysis of the power relationship between the government and the university, suggesting that universities have become part of the training for business in order to cope with the move from material production to the techno-sciences of the global economy. The university is diverted from its role as a custodian of knowledge and forced to concentrate on its existence as a player in the free-market economy. However, Cowen warns of too strong a reliance on the market notion and stresses the variance between different state systems. Performativity is not a necessary function of the move from elite to mass HE. The German system at the end of the nineteenth century was elite but certainly performative in serving industry and the economy. Conversely, Japan has a mass system which is less strongly dedicated to industry.

Cowen makes the point that performativity is both 'an epistemological condition … and an explicit political project' (p. 8) and that it is socially constructed. Performativity depends on the government's perception of the role of knowledge in a competitive world and on the political decision that the university is the right location for connecting state, industry and business concerns. Cowen's conclusion is that, through the pursuit of performativity, the university is reduced, or *attenuated*, in a variety of ways: spatially, financially and pedagogically. Above all, because its quality is defined externally through the absorption into national research policies and measured by managers, it has become 'quality attenuated'.

Barnett (2000) rejects Cowen's notion of the completely attenuated university, seeing it as having multiple roles.

> The contemporary university is dissolving into the wider world … The postmodern university is a distributed university … It is a multinational concern, stretching out to and accommodating its manifold audiences. It lacks specificity; it is a set of possibilities … no longer a site of knowledge, but, rather a site of knowledge possibilities.
>
> (pp. 20–21)

The postmodern university is like a company with many product lines and activities. It has no centre, no boundaries and no moral order. It is globally located, with its research and activities conducted across the world by the internet: an example of 'glocalisation'. Barnett's concept of 'supercomplexity' is characterised as

- the plastic nature of research;
- the massive growth of knowledge;
- the evaluative society;
- the questioning of professional competence;
- multiple (and conflicting) frames of understanding, action and self-identity. (p. 6)

He criticises the conversion of university knowledge into performative skills through government evaluation procedures, regretting that there are no longer historians, only those who possess a range of transferable skills for society. There is, though, optimism in Barnett's possibilities for the future of the university in that it may be able to retain some of its modern role. Although industry demands skills, and the university responds to the demands, the wider society longs for knowledge, breadth, critical reason and freedom; society is hesitantly intimating that it needs the universities to live up to their rhetoric as guardians of reason. 'The university seems intent on constructing itself in narrower frames of self-understanding. A trick is being missed' (p. 34).

The notion of the university dissolving into society is reflected by Aronovitz (2000), who sees the same picture in terms of intellectual decline. Writing from the American perspective, his analysis of the change in the university derives from its links with industry in which it becomes simply the training site for business. With presidents as full-time fund-raisers, students are no longer required to challenge intellectual authority or criticise. Graduates enter minor administrative positions in the entertainment industries; knowledge is irrelevant. 'They have learned the skills to tolerate boredom' (p. 10). In other ways, universities are sites for technological change, for making things that advance production. The university now mirrors society; it doesn't stand back from it and comment on it.

Green (1997) warns against assuming the end of the nation state in the university picture. He criticises the extremist account of postmodern education by Aronowitz and Giroux (1991), who argue that the search for a common curriculum is futile and advocate choice and diversity in HE. As typical postmodernists, they portray the breakdown of Keynesian economics with governments that are no longer able to deliver services and, with education fragmented and individualised, university education out of state control. But Green argues that this is overstated and that governments will still continue to seek national identity through education, and particularly through the HE curriculum.

He goes on to conclude that postmodernism has little to offer educational theory and criticises free-market notions of education. Successful education systems in Europe and Japan do not have marketisation. Choice in education, he insists, disadvantages the poor and working class. The argument for choice is not that it raises standards, but that it is an inevitable concomitant of the changing cultural configurations of modern societies.

Barnett, Parry and Coate (2001) suggest that in many university subjects, the curriculum has become increasingly 'performative', with emphasis on knowledge for vocational outcomes. They advance a three-domains model of the university curriculum: knowledge, action and reflective critique of self. In an empirical study, they find that the weight of each of the three domains varies across different curricula. For example, science and technology are knowledge-dominated with a high level of action; arts and humanities are knowledge-dominated with little action; and professional subjects – in their example, nursing – are action-dominated and there is a particularly strong self-reflection element as students are asked to reflect on their practice in journals or logs.

For Readings (1996), the university of 'excellence' is a mere simulacrum of the university: 'culture' is no longer the watchword of the university:

> The university is no longer Humboldt's, and that means it is no longer *The* university. The Germans not only founded a University and gave it a mission; they also made the University into the decisive instance of intellectual activity. All of this is in the process of changing: intellectual activity and the culture it revived are being replaced by the pursuit of excellence and performance indicators.
>
> (p. 55)

The last decades have seen attempts to link university research and teaching to the world of work with new teaching methods and by widening access. Haddad (2000), for example, argues that universities have moved from elitist groups in ivory towers and have become closer to society, and he suggests that they need to go further in developing openness and producing research for peace, human rights and a sustainable future. He points to the mixture of respect and distrust there has always been about universities and suggests that, with the revision of missions, society now has a better idea of university roles and responsibilities. Democratisation of education and increased access remove the old elitism, but bring with them challenges of pertinence and quality. The expansion of HE dilutes the original role of the university in that it can no longer be seen to deal exclusively with an elite; it must engage with a broader range of the population (50 per cent of the 18–30 cohort).

The university in the marketplace

Kogan and Hannay present the abolition of the binary system (see p. xx) as whimsical: a cavalier action by Kenneth Clarke following a period of horse-trading and pressure from the directors of the polytechnics. Readings (1996), however, sees the move as part of a larger process of converting the whole British university system into the 'excellence' model, with performance indicators to reflect the United States model of HE. The conversion of polytechnics into universities, he argues, was not an ideological commitment to expanding HE as such, but is a mechanism to bring all institutions into the same competitive market in which the successful – as measured by the performance indicators – are rewarded. He describes the action as 'a classic free-market manoeuvre ... analogous to the repeal of sumptuary laws that permitted the capitalization of the textile trade in Early Modern England' (p. 39).

This marks the move towards government control through market forces or, more particularly, the use of government controls to enable a free market: not a magnanimous egalitarian gesture towards the polytechnics, but an example of pure Thatcherism. Gray (1998) helps to explain this apparent contradiction in Conservative government policy where 'rolling back the state' appears to mean the removal of government controls, but actually involves controls on institutions through nationally prescribed curricula and criteria. Strong government intervention is always required to permit a free market; encumbered markets are the norm in every society, whereas free markets are a product of artifice, design and political coercion. *Laissez-faire* must be centrally planned; regulated markets just happen (p. 17).

The removal of the British binary system should be seen as a move to the American free market in HE and the mixture of freedoms and controls which that has brought. Readings (1996) argues that the very foundations of the traditional Western university are crumbling into postmodern chaos.

The commodification of knowledge as information and the proletarianisation of the student population means that the university ceases to be a function of the state's realisation of itself and becomes an economic instrument, like a privatised national airline. There is a distinction between American and European universities here. The European model of the university is about realising the existing cultural content. For the American university, there is no cultural content, but a contract, a promise to deliver on the future. Readings argues that, while the European university was a continuation of culture and the nation state, the American university should be seen as a private institution working in the public service. American-style globalisation Readings describes as 'culturally vacuous' (p. 40).

UK universities and the state in the twenty-first century

In legislative terms, the UK government is still restrained from direct influence on the curriculum of its universities. The 1988 Education Act (HMSO, 1988) shifted government control into the state school system and included a major reconfiguration of the funding for HE. However, it contained no changes to the relationship between government and universities in terms of the curriculum, assessment and HE awards. Changes to funding in the 2004 Education Bill and the controversy which surrounded it saw no suggestion of intervention in university knowledge. Decisions by some universities to close certain subject departments which created controversy in the popular media saw the government maintaining its considered distance from decisions about university knowledge. The Augar Report (DfE, 2019: 9–10) makes only limited recommendations in respect of knowledge or the curriculum. Its main thrust is to press university education closer to industry and the economy by 'strengthening technical education' and by 'bearing down on low-value HE' which does not ensure preparation for the workplace.

The studied remoteness of the UK government from the university curriculum might be seen to be a continuation of the 'post-war political consensus' in education (Lawton, 1992), in which the government kept back from interference in the school curriculum because of fears of the replication of totalitarian governments in which the education system became a state propaganda machine. Ironically, it was Humboldt's University of Berlin which fell into the Soviet sector of the city in 1945 and lost its autonomy from government. However, Neave (2000) argues that the traditional relationship between university and society is now being challenged with increasing and 'unforgiving scrutiny' by the state. Furedi (2004) argues that the government role has become stronger through academic auditing and that it is made powerful by enlisting the service of academics themselves in policing the audit process through government agencies. This makes it appear that the universities retain autonomy, but Furedi argues that the removal of university autonomy through audit leads to the denigration of intellectual life. Intellectuals are turned into professionals who act on behalf of the institution, rather than academics in the search for objective truth. It is, then, a case of a shifting balance between Neave's three factors: increasing state control and increasing control by the institution, resulting in the diminishing of the third, academic freedom. Furedi's argument is that the government is controlling university knowledge through the agencies and mechanisms for audit, employing the university itself as a means of controlling intellectuals and knowledge. The Quality Assurance Agency (QAA) is a large bureaucracy designed to police HE in Britain. Its mission is

> to safeguard the public interest in sound standards of HE qualifications and to inform and encourage continuous improvement in the management of the quality of HE. (House of Commons Business Innovation and Skills Committee
>
> (2012)

It is concerned, then, with standards and quality, but not with knowledge in the sense of curriculum or content.

Neave sees the developments as inevitable, although his term, 'the supermarketed university' expresses his criticism of the direction which Britain is taking. He argues that the HE system in Britain is even more stratified than it was before, defined by state evaluative methods of 'the conjoined workings of audit, assessment, public statements of quality, performance evinced by the services provided, by output achieved' (p. 18). Stratification, then, is an explicit instrument of state policy in creating a HE market, the variables being the knowledge available, teaching or research and differentiated length of courses (honours degrees and foundation degrees). Neave regrets the loss of Britain to the American model, leaving its commitment to European collaboration in the

Bologna process 'on the back burner' (p. 19). More recently, Collini (2018: 1) protested that, while the UK signed up to the treaties in the Bologna Process, universities in Britain do not have the independence from political and economic interference enjoyed by others in Europe: "'An autonomous institution"? Barely a month goes by without a new diktat issuing from Whitehall and its satellite agencies. Governance is as constrained as policy'.

There are criticisms of the very notion of a market in HE in England. For example, Frank *et al.* (2019) argue that, because there is no cap on student numbers and the demand for university places is so high, there is no real competition; universities simply accept more students with lower entry qualifications. However, at the time of writing (March 2020), the Coronavirus crisis was threatening recruitment to universities for the September 2020 entry. Apart from home students' fears of moving away from home, and the possibility of universities still being closed under government regulations, it was recognised that all universities would lose the financially rewarding overseas students, particularly from China. The universities that would lose most severely would be the post-92 institutions, while the older Russell Group universities would sweep up the majority of applications, leaving the rest to be financially unviable. For that reason, for the 2020 entry, capping of numbers was to be reintroduced in order that the recruitment of the lower total number could be spread more evenly across the sector.

Conclusion

The move from the modern to the postmodern university can be seen either as a loss or as an opportunity. It sees the loss of the university control of knowledge and possibly a loss in anti-intellectualism, as the market becomes the arbiter of ideas and academics are concerned only with industry's demands and their students' skills. However, the postmodern university can also be a site of hope and optimism in which the university emerges from its elite shell and draws closer to society - there is the opportunity for society to be recreated and transformed intellectually.

University knowledge can be seen to have metamorphosed over the years in relation to the relative roles of the university and the state, from its origins as Church theodicy through its service of Enlightenment industrialism and to its recent rapid changes with the geo-political effects of global markets. There have been historical distinctions between American and European universities, and we have seen the UK between the two, but latterly inclining to the American fee-paying model.

A continuing theme has been the question of academic freedom and national definitions of culture. The trust invested in university academics in the modern university is now evaporating with the new public management. There is a paradox, though, in that, while the state has gained in strength relative to the powers of the modern university, globalisation has simultaneously reduced the power of the state. What we see is the state using its powers not to define knowledge or to dictate to universities, but to impose accountability measures to set up free-market conditions in which knowledge will be defined. The third factor in the equation, the demands of the mass market, now appears to define the nature of knowledge and even threaten the very existence of the university.

Collini (2012) asks in the title of his book, *What Are Universities For?* The question is being answered: the provision for skills for industry and employment. But while university fees and employment prospects dominate the discourse today, it is up to those of us in universities to argue for a higher order answer to the question: HE as a public good.

Questions for discussion

- Was Kant right to insist that reason should be the foundation of university knowledge?
- Is the modern university with state funding and full academic freedom of knowledge and research the ideal model of HE?
- Should students have choice of subject and modules, or should the curriculum be determined by the university?
- Is Bourdieu right in claiming that the university is a self-preserving institution?
- Student fees are a good idea because they give students the role of customers of HE, which gives them power over the university. Do you agree?
- Stefan Collini (2012) titles his book *What Are Universities For?* How would you answer his question?

Summary points

- Universities have a millennium-long history in which the nature of knowledge has changed and developed.
- The medieval European universities were well networked with Latin as a *lingua franca* before national boundaries were in place. At the behest of the Church, their main function was theodicy.
- The Humboldt University in Berlin (1809) was the first modern university with reason rather than belief as the basis for knowledge in the search for truth.
- The modern university held control over knowledge and enjoyed academic freedom while being funded by the state.
- In the late twentieth and early twenty-first centuries, universities lost control of knowledge and are now subject to the preferences of the market with degrees in popular subjects.

Recommended reading

Barnett, R. (2000) *Realizing the University in an Age of Supercomplexity*. Buckingham: Society for Research into HE and Open University Press.
Collini, S. (2012) *What Are Universities For?* London: Penguin.
Giroux, H.A. (2014)*Neoliberalism's War on Higher Education*. London: Haymarket Books.
Readings, B. (1996) *The University in Ruins*. Cambridge, MA: Harvard University Press.
Ward, S. (2020) The Economics of the University: Knowledge, the market and the state. In: J.A. Bustillos Morales and S. Abegglen (Eds.), *Understanding Education and Economics*. Abingdon: Routledge.

References

Aronovitz, S. (2000) *The Knowledge Factory: Dismantling the Corporate University and Creating the Higher Learning*. Boston, MA: Beacon Press.
Aronowitz, S. and Giroux, H. (1991) *Modern Education: Politics, Culture and Social Criticism*. Boston, MA: Beacon Press.
Barnett, R. (2000) *Realizing the University in an Age of Supercomplexity*. Buckingham: Society for Research into HE and Open University Press.
Barnett, R., Parry, G. and Coate, K. (2001) Conceptualising curriculum change. *Teaching in HE*, 6(4), 435–29.
Bourdieu, P. (1988) *Homo Academicus*. Cambridge: Polity Press.
Collini, S. (2012) *What Are Universities For?* London: Penguin.
Collini, S. (2018) In UK Universities there is a daily erosion of integrity. *The Guardian*, 24 April 2018.

Committee on Higher Education (Robbins) (1963) *Report*. London: HMSO.

Coulby, D. and Jones, C. (1995) *Postmodernity and European Education Systems*. Stoke on Trent: Trentham.

Cowen, R. (1996) *World Year-Book of Education: The Evaluation of HE Systems*. London: Kogan Page.

Delanty, G. (2001) *Challenging Knowledge: The University in the Knowledge Society*. Buckingham: HE/Open University.

DfE (2013) *Teachers' Standards Guidance for School Leaders, School Staff and Governing Bodies*. London: DfE.

DfE (2019) *Post-18 Review of Education and Funding: Independent Panel Report*. London: DfE.

Foucault, M. (1972) *The Archaeology of Knowledge*. London: Routledge.

Frank, J., Gower, N. and Naef, M. (2019) *English Universities in Crisis: Markets Without Competition*. Bristol: Bristol University Press.

Frazer, M. (1997) Report on the modalities of external evaluation of HE in Europe: 1995–1997. *HE in Europe*, XXII(3), 349–401.

Furedi, F. (2004) *Where Have All the Intellectuals Gone? Confronting 21st Century Philistinism*. London: Continuum.

Gray, J. (1998) False Dawn: The delusions of global capitalism. London: Granta.

Green, A. (1997) *Education, Globalisation and the Nation State*. London: Macmillan.

Habermas, J. (1971) The university in a democracy: Democratisation of the university. In: *Towards a Rational Society*. London: Heinemann.

Haddad, G. (2000) University and society: Responsibilities, contracts, partnerships. In: G. Neave (Ed.), *The Universities' Responsibilities to Society: International Perspectives Series*. Oxford: Pergamon.

Henkel, M. (1991) *Government, Evaluation and Change*. London: Jessica Kingsley Publishers.

House of Commons business innovation and Skills Committee (2012) *Government Reform of HE*. London: The Stationery Office.

HMSO (1988) Education Reform Act. London: Her Majesty's Stationary Office.

Kant, I. (1992) *The Conflict of the Faculties*, Trans. Mary J. McGregor. Nebraska: University of Nebraska.

Kogan, M. and Hanney, S. (2000) *Reforming HE*. London: Jessica Kingsley.

Lawton, D. (1992) *Education and Politics in the 1990s*. Lewes: Falmer Press.

Leavis, F.R. (1979) *Education and the University*. Cambridge: Cambridge University Press.

Lyotard, J.F. (1986) *The Postmodern Condition: A Report on Knowledge*. Manchester: Manchester University Press.

MacCulloch, D. (2004) *Reformation: Europe's House Divided*. London: Penguin.

Neave, G. (2000) Universities' responsibilities to society: An historical exploration of an enduring issue. In: G. Neave (Ed.), *The Universities' Responsibilities to Society: International Perspectives*. Oxford: Pergamon.

Newman, J. (1852) *The Idea of a University*. 1976 edition, edited by I. Kerr. Oxford: Clarendon Press.

NSS (2020) National student survey. Available at: http://www.thestudentsurvey.com/ (accessed 17 January 2020).

O'Hear, A. (1988) Academic freedom and the university. In: M. Tight, (Ed.), *Academic Freedom and Responsibility*. Buckingham: Society for Research into HE/Open University Press.

OfS (2018) The regulatory framework for HE in England. Available at: https://www.officeforstudents.org.uk/advice-and-guidance/regulation/the-regulatory-framework-for-higher-education-in-england/ (accessed 4 December 2019).

Parsons, T. (1974) The university 'bundle': A study of the balance between differentiation and integration. In: N. Smelser and G. Almond (Eds.), *Public HE in California: Growth, Structural Change and Conflict*. Berkeley, CA: University of California Press.

Readings, B. (1996) *The University in Ruins*. Cambridge, MA: Harvard University Press.

Silver, H. (1990) *A HE: The Council for National Academic Awards and British HE 1964–8*. Lewes: Falmer Press.

Tight, M. (1988) So what is academic freedom? In: M. Tight, (Ed.), *Academic Freedom and Responsibility*. Buckingham: Society for Research into HE/Open University Press.

Toswell, M.J. (2017) *Today's Medieval University*. Kalamazoo/Bradford: ARC Humanities Press.

12 Disability, diversity and inclusive placement learning

Stephanie Brewster and David Thompson

Introduction

In the United Kingdom, government reports (Wilson, 2012) have recommended that work experience be made a key part of university education to furnish students with relevant skills that will enhance employment prospects. It is our experience that students see the importance of practical experience sought by potential employers who participate willingly in the employability agenda currently dominating higher education. For many students, going on placement or work experience forms a significant part of their degree studies and one that helps either cement or inform their career aspirations.

Within an increasingly diverse university population, it is pertinent to ask whether the benefits of placement learning – namely the enhancement of employability and subsequent access to the labour market – are equally accessible to all. Disabled students, for example, may experience barriers not only when undertaking a placement but also when later seeking employment, although many such challenges can be shared by other students, such as those who commute to university, have paid employment already or have caring responsibilities.

In this chapter, the authors draw on the findings of their own research and use the 'Capability Approach' to consider this broad range of student circumstances and their experiences of going on placement. The Capability Approach was developed by economist and philosopher Amartya Sen in the 1980s, to analyse issues related to standards of living and welfare; it offers a consideration of social justice, quality of life and wellbeing. Sen and other authors have discussed what the Capability Approach might offer to our understanding of education, employment, diversity and disability, amongst many other social concerns. The Capability Approach provides a theoretical perspective that recognises the assets and limitations that all students possess; it takes account of diversity and lends itself to consideration of issues such as disability, gender and race and other groups who may be marginalised. Through this lens, the chapter takes a critical stance towards traditional conceptions of employability and proposes a wider conceptualisation of placement that takes account of students' capacity for meaningful engagement with and contribution to society. We argue that personal experiences of, for example, disability or juggling multiple demands on one's time, while challenging for a student embarking on a placement, can also enhance their own learning and that of the placement setting itself.

Employability and placement learning in higher education

Employability can be defined as 'having the capability to gain initial employment, maintain employment, and gain new employment if required' (Hillage and Pollard, 1998: 1). There has been a growing discourse on the value and appropriateness of employability and work-based learning (WBL) at the levels of both policy and practice (Moreau and Leathwood, 2007). There are different models of work-based learning: at one end of the spectrum, students become learners at work, and the placement 'services' the academic course; at the other end, the focus is on the needs of employers and employees.

However, it should be acknowledged that employability is a contested concept that can be manipulated according to different ideologies; for example, it is mostly determined by the labour market, rather than by individuals based on their skills and experiences (Brown *et al.*, 2003). One critique of WBL is that it represents a simplistic utilitarianism, leading to an education system that merely services the employment market and is subservient to a purely vocational argument where everything is defined only in relation to work (Hyland, 2001; also Boden and Nedeva, 2010). Policies are driven by governments' neo-liberal agendas, with universities having to respond with a greater emphasis on acknowledging and accrediting WBL and monitoring trends in employment destinations for graduates, resulting in universities losing their autonomy. A further caveat is that WBL 'is potentially limiting if the opportunities provided by the workplace do not form a good match to learners' aspirations … trapping the learner into an employer-driven or instrumental agenda' (Lester and Costley, 2010: 569). Furthermore, some students may be encouraged to work uncritically and to other people's agendas, rather than on the basis of their own lived experiences as individuals with particular needs and aspirations. Too often WBL is still viewed in terms of honing specific skill-sets and achieving competencies, rather than the development of meta-cognition that enables people to become independent learners and workers.

Contrary to the disadvantages, 'there is significant anecdotal evidence about the efficacy of work experience in general and of embedded work placements in particular' (Blackwell *et al.*, 2001: 270). It is argued that placements bestow significant benefits on both the students and the organisation. Advantages include easier transition into employment, a stronger vocational identity and increasing self-confidence. Similarly, 'authentic work experience contextualises learning, has a strong influence on graduate employment, and should be integrated into course curricula wherever possible' (Pegg *et al.*, 2012: 45).

The value of WBL can be significant and 'a catalyst for personal growth' (Lester and Costley, 2010). Further benefits include improved academic performance and better employment outcomes such as higher starting salaries. The conclusion is that universities should provide undergraduates with more than academic qualifications, to allow them to compete for employment appropriate for their level of skills and abilities; work placements play an important role in achieving this (Brooks and Youngson, 2016). Others (Rae, 2007) see employability as a priority for higher education which needs to be embedded within the curriculum (Yorke, 2004). Going further than this, Cranmer (2006:183) argues 'it would surely make sense for universities to redirect some of their resources from classroom-based initiatives seeking to develop employability skills to increasing employment-based training and/or employer involvement in courses, which were found to positively affect immediate graduate prospects'.

Question for discussion

- How important is embedding employability in higher education, and what should it look like? Consider what skills are likely to be expected of graduates by employers both now and in the future.

Disability and diversity

The UK higher education system was designed originally for the privileged minority of white, male middle/upper-class non-disabled students, but is now expected to engage with a much more diverse student population. This diversity encompasses many 'non-traditional' students such as those who are the first in their family to attend university, part-time students, mature students and those who are disabled. The underpinnings of equality and diversity are ethical, the case for inclusion of a diverse population being a matter of social justice. A commitment to fairness and social justice would suggest that universities have a responsibility not only to allow access to this newly diverse population but also to meet their complex and differing needs rather than merely assimilating them into the existing system. This is the basis for the development of inclusive practice in higher education. While disability can be viewed simply as but one dimension of this diversity, this neglects the lived experience of impairment of disabled individuals, and inclusive practice alone is not going to meet the often very specific needs of students with certain impairments.

Officially, the term 'disability' includes physical, mental and sensory impairments and health conditions which adversely affect day-to-day living in the long term (Equality Act 2010), but it is widely recognised that many students, for example, those with specific learning difficulties, or who are deaf or who have mental health problems, do not relate to the label 'disabled'. It is currently regarded, nevertheless, as a useful term in establishing the legal entitlement of certain individuals to certain 'reasonable adjustments', such as provision of funding for assistive software or sign language interpreters.

Figures released in 2019 (HESA, 2019) show that there are record numbers of students disclosing disabilities to their university in the United Kingdom. While 13 per cent of entrants are disabled, this is thought to be an underestimate, and there are concerns that this is still below the proportion of working-age adults with a disability. There are therefore calls for universities to increase their intake of disabled applicants and to improve support for disabled students (Skidmore, 2019). Interestingly, significant change has occurred in the proportion of students reporting a mental health condition, which in England has increased from 1.4 per cent in 2012–13 to 3.5 per cent in 2017–18. Thorley (2017) confirms this trend: nearly five times as many students as 10 years ago disclosed a mental health condition to their university.

Disabled people experience disadvantage in the labour market: they are more likely to be unemployed than non-disabled people, are more likely to experience barriers to training opportunities and to employment and, once in work, are likely to be paid less than non-disabled people (Smith, 2016). The proportion of disabled people with no qualifications was nearly three times that of non-disabled people in 2015–16 (Papworth Trust, 2018). Although successfully graduating from university does confer some advantage in subsequent employment, similar disparities persist to some extent when we consider disabled people with a degree. Smith (2016) states bluntly that a *graduate* with a work-limiting disability is more likely not to have a job compared to an *unqualified* person with no disability.

For these reasons, universities clearly need to improve the employability of disabled graduates. But as already indicated, the student population is diverse, and there are other groups that are potentially disadvantaged in employability and employment. Moores *et al.* (2017:9) found that Black and Asian students derived greater positive effects than white students from work experience during their degree programme: 'placements are important for both career and degree outcomes, particularly for students with certain demographic characteristics and prior performance profiles […]. Higher Education Institutions need to invest in resources to motivate hard-to-reach groups and in particular students who enter university with weaker prior achievement'.

Clearly there is a moral and legal imperative to make reasonable adjustments for disabled students and to make provision for all students more inclusive, and there is evidence to suggest that HE continues to make progress towards closing gaps between the experiences of disabled and non-disabled student populations. But this may not be the case for the settings students find themselves in while on placement. Furthermore, many issues faced by a diverse range of students are not matters of legal compliance; for example, commuting long distances or having dependent family members. The research carried out by the authors goes beyond matters of what the equality legislation requires and considers the complexity of many students' lives and how this affects their placement learning experiences.

Questions for discussion

- To what extent are individual students able to make the most of their university experience given their personal circumstances?
- How should universities take such circumstances into account?

Background to the authors' research on placement experiences

The principles of inclusive practice involve anticipating the needs of a diverse student population, such that a more level playing field regarding opportunity for success is created. A placement differs inherently from typical, classroom/campus-based study, in which almost all parameters of the physical and social learning environment are carefully controlled by tutors to maximise student learning; the core element of placement learning is inevitably not within the control of module tutors.

As academic tutors and researchers specialising in disability support, inclusive practice, employability and placement learning, the authors had become increasingly concerned by the challenges being reported by some of our students. Our understanding of their circumstances and the kind of support they would benefit from felt limited, and much of the existing research literature seemed incomplete. We therefore set out to research our own students' experiences and perspectives, underpinned by an understanding of student diversity encompassing disability as but one aspect of the student experience.

Based in our subject area of academic studies in Education, our research investigated the perceptions of students before and after going on a placement of their own choosing in their second year. Although we were interested in disabled students, we also wanted to hear from those with other circumstances that could create potential barriers to successful placement. We also considered the opinions of a range of university staff involved in supporting placement learning, employability, disability support and inclusion more generally. Our data were drawn from 98 survey responses and seven interviews with students, and four interviews and two focus groups with a total of 15 staff.

Analysis of our data showed that although a number of concerns were shared by many students, those who revealed disability or health-related issues were often more worried about their placement situation than those who had no such issues. It appeared that for disabled students, there was a more complex process of interaction between factors (whether personal, environmental or to do with resources) affecting how opportunities could result in desired outcomes. This perspective is explored in more detail below, using the Capability Approach.

Framing the student placement experience: the Capability Approach (CA)

CA makes a distinction between two key concepts, which are illustrated with examples related to placement learning:

- **Achievements or outcomes** (called 'functionings' in the CA) which are valued, for example, being in paid employment, being employable, being literate and educated, participating in community, attending placements, caring for children, going to university. While many are ends in themselves, some may also be instrumental to other outcomes; for example, employability is valuable mainly if you actually want to get a job.
- **Freedoms or opportunities** (called 'capabilities' in the CA) to achieve those outcomes from which an individual can choose, for example, job opportunities, travel, work experience, family life. The concept of opportunity refers to the individual having the personal ability, resources, practical means and knowledge required to achieve outcomes *and* the social/economic/physical environment being such that they could do so, not just the absence of something preventing the individual from doing something. For example, the placement module is only a real opportunity if a student is in a position to take it up – if they have sufficient health, means of transport, access to appropriate settings and so on.

Opportunity is a multi-level concept; opportunities can lead to outcomes, which in turn support the development of further opportunities. For example, placement opportunities lead to employability, which can result in a greater number of job opportunities. The majority of students who completed our survey before going on placement wanted the opportunity to gain experience, knowledge, skills and confidence in relation to working in a professional setting relevant to their career aspirations. Reflecting on what they achieved afterwards, interviewees commented on increased self-knowledge and confidence in their abilities; they clarified or refined their career choices and were able to connect their academic learning to real-world settings.

There is great diversity in the potential of different individuals to convert opportunities into outcomes. Sen's classic example is the bicycle. Simply owning the resource of a bicycle is not enough to achieve the benefits of getting around by bike; you also need cycling skills, smooth roads and the confidence and motivation to cycle. Likewise, an educational resource such as a placement opportunity will not yield the same outcomes for all students: for some it might result in increased confidence, skills and employment choices; others may, for a variety of reasons, gain little in terms of personal development, employability or options for employment in the future.

Students experience many factors which might affect the likelihood of outcomes connected to a placement being achieved. In considering how disability can result from such factors, Mitra (2006) categorises them into three groups: personal/internal, environmental/external and resources. Here, we illustrate these categories with examples that go beyond the case of disability:

1. **Personal/internal characteristics**. For example, gender, health, sex, dis/ability, intelligence. A student who experiences anxiety attacks may not be able to achieve the same level of employability from placement opportunities because anxiety limits their ability to participate and learn effectively while there. This might also apply to lack of confidence and competing personal commitments.

For disabled students, the very nature of their impairment (e.g. severe visual impairment) may be disabling, but some may be able to choose whether to make others aware of this. Considerable attention has been paid in the literature to the issue of disclosure of disability. Our findings endorse those of Cunnah (2015) regarding the salience for students of disclosure of disability in a placement context; our research showed students taking a range of responses to this choice. Many were aware of the advantages of disclosure since individual adjustments can only be made when a student tells their university or placement setting about their impairment. This positive view of disclosure was expressed by students for whom it is a helpful way to establish that they will receive appropriate support and adjustments. For the placement providers, it enables them to prepare for and make such adjustments. But there are also challenges to be acknowledged. Some disabled students had decided not to disclose a condition prior to placement, and those with 'hidden' conditions would have the option to continue to withhold this information. Before their placement commences, some students may have limited insight into both their own strengths and limitations and into the requirements of the placement environment (Botham and Nicholson, 2014). Like Cunnah's (2015) research participants, some students in our research reported only disclosing those medical conditions they deemed less stigmatising, that is, not mental health or behaviour-related impairments. It is widely recognised that 'a stigma remains around mental ill health and students may feel uncomfortable or worry about being discriminated against if they declare a condition' (OfS, 2019: 4). Thus for some students, a very strategic decision is taken regarding what and whether to disclose and to whom, with official numbers likely to be a considerable underestimate.

Aside from disability, other personal characteristics that may affect a student's ability to engage fully in a placement include interpersonal skills, information-seeking skills, basic health and wellbeing and level of literacy and education. In fact, the most prominent theme arising from our research was encapsulated by one student in their comment, 'It's all about confidence'. Although levels of anxiety were greatly heightened for some students with identified mental health concerns, the theme of confidence was relevant for many students. A willingness to tackle the unfamiliar, and to accept feelings of anxiety in the process, is a key way to develop confidence and learn strategies for managing fears and stress. Although it may create discomfort for some students, removal of all uncertainties is not only impossible but also undesirable in that normative stress levels and coping mechanisms to deal with them could be regarded as a part of students' personal development that ultimately leads to increased confidence and skill levels. However, there is a balance to be struck between giving students the space to take responsibility for their own learning and development and offering an appropriate level of support and intervention in such a way that it does not inadvertently disempower the student. Availability of support from the university, and the different forms this might take, is discussed as a resource here. Students viewed increased confidence as not only a desired outcome from their placement opportunity (and this was in fact achieved by many of the students we interviewed after their placement) but also a potential barrier that might limit their enjoyment of or participation in it.

2. **Environmental/external factors:** these include social conditions such as public policies, social norms, cultural practices, legal entitlements, power relations and discrimination. Students in our research demonstrated some insight into such issues, for example, through their fear of discrimination or of unfavourable attitudes if they shared information about their difficulties. Environment can also pertain to a workplace culture experienced while on placement, which may be to a greater or lesser extent inclusive to students with particular personal characteristics. Legal compliance with equality legislation, and local policies or professional guidelines relating to the workplace, also affect an individual's achievements. This category also includes physical factors, for example, means of transport and communication, and the placement environment (room size, lighting, toilet facilities, outdoor terrain, etc.), which might be significant for a student with a physical or sensory impairment.

The additional burdens disabled students might experience, associated with managing their condition and their disclosure of it, warrants additional consideration of environmental factors for those individuals. Support for students to make an informed decision about how, when and what they disclose to their placement provider would be helpful. This may be complex, for example, where the health and safety of the student or of others may be affected by students' functional limitations associated with their condition. In some cases, the suitability and accessibility of a setting for a student with, for example, mobility or sensory impairments, will need to be considered at an extremely early stage. Pre-placement discussions are likely to benefit some students in this regard.

3. **Resources:** these include any material resources, financial factors or time and so on. Poor public transport and being unable to afford a car will narrow the range of placement opportunities open to a student; indeed, a number of respondents in our student survey were concerned about practical issues such as transport. Many students shoulder significant economic burdens – both as a result of their choice to study at university and doing so alongside other financial responsibilities. This has several repercussions regarding placements, due to the additional costs directly incurred, for example, transport costs and purchasing appropriate clothing. Time away from paid employment might also be a factor. Individual students will be endowed with a range of resources in the form of, for example, a family member providing free childcare, or existing connections with the kinds of workplace they wish to experience and advice from friends and family.

The university also provides resources to all students, such as advice and guidance, and links with professional networks offering good quality and appropriate placements. Staff and students in our research identified many specific interventions within the direct control of the university. They also noted resources offered by the placement settings themselves. And some resources could be regarded as arising from interaction between the three main stakeholders.

Structure and clarity of information regarding the requirements of the placement module were identified as important by both students and university staff. Similarly, many students felt the need for structure in the placement setting itself through a workplace timetable, a schedule or breakdown of tasks and clear information. The timing of information is also important and needs to be ongoing or staggered to avoid overload. Certain needs may arise throughout the student journey that do not always exist at the beginning, when most information is usually given to students. The way information, advice and guidance on placement is provided to students – in terms of format, timing, content and so on – needs to be carefully considered to maximise its effectiveness. For university staff, clarity of systems and processes, and the moral and legal obligations and responsibilities held between the university and the placement provider, were identified as priorities. Somewhat in contrast to this, flexibility is likely to be a particularly valuable resource for any student facing additional challenges.

A strong theme generated by data from both staff and students related to the resource of supportive relationships and effective communication between students, staff and placement settings. The quality of relationships and the need for trusting, empathetic and sensitive staff when it comes to students' concerns were raised. The nature of the organisation providing a placement in our research tended to be education-related, such as schools or children's centres. It was felt that such organisations were well-placed to provide additional flexibility and a positive approach to diversity, being approachable and sympathetic to placement students in all their diversity and facilitating the process of disclosure of disability. However, it is difficult to know to what extent this experience translates into other professions and settings.

In summary, each individual has a unique profile of individual, environmental and resource factors. Clearly there is overlap between them, some of which will be shared by a whole group, for example, students who care for their young children; and factors may interact in complex ways which are unique to each individual. Our research showed that the students were acutely aware of their personal characteristics, compared to their more limited insight into the environment they would be entering on placement, or the resources they had which would have a bearing on their placement.

Question for discussion

- Consider your own profile of capabilities that may support you to achieve your employment goals; what personal, environmental and resource factors may affect this?

The Capability Approach, disability and diversity

In the previous section, illustrative examples from our research data were used to explore how, according to the Capability Approach, students will have varying opportunities to achieve their goals in relation to placement learning while at university. Below, CA is explored in more depth in terms of choice, freedom and agency and how this relates to disability and diversity.

Choice and freedom are central to the Capability Approach (and indeed the various rights movements associated with marginalised groups such as ethnic minorities, disabled people, LGBTQ+). It also places important emphasis on the values held by individuals in terms of the freedom to pursue goals of personal significance. All students will have exercised freedom in their choice to come to university and in their choice of course, but courses often offer limited choice about how an individual could fulfil their goals and aspirations, with placements sometimes being a compulsory component of the programme (currently driven by the employability agenda discussed here). This is potentially discriminatory for certain students who may be unable to do a placement in the conventional manner prescribed by their programme of study. By this logic, alternative opportunities should therefore be available, to enable students to achieve outcomes that they value in life, including those that do not entail conventional notions of graduate employability.

This perspective places a high degree of agency with the individual who chooses their own outcomes (Norwich, 2014), but somewhat in tension with this are the responsibilities of university staff and employers (as placement providers) to ensure that genuine opportunities for achieving their goals are available to all students. Staff in our research expressed uncertainty about how much control they should assume in creating appropriate placement environments. According to Van der Klink *et al.* (2016: 75): 'The environment plays an integral role in determining the achievement of functionings by influencing aspects such as choice, preference and importance. Sen speaks of "constrained choice" when external forces (e.g., social forces like stigma or attitudes) constrain personal choice'.

In fact, provision of resources and appropriate design of the environment are a matter of justice because they contribute to more equal opportunities. In relation to disability, the Capability Approach recognises that an impairment's effects on capability depend on social context and resource availability (Norwich, 2014). CA therefore provides justification for differential resource allocation, for example, providing specific students such as those with impairments with help to find a placement, while expecting others to secure their own.

However, resources cannot on their own always achieve greater fairness; for example, one also needs to consider the stigmatising effects (as mentioned by Van der Klink *et al.* above) of some impairments (e.g. mental health issues) which are not a matter of resource. Also, the functional limitations associated with impairment should be given due recognition; in the workplace, these can have very real consequences for health and safety and fitness to work (especially in contexts governed by professional standards).

As Van der Klink *et al.* (2016) point out, the importance of the environment should not be underestimated, although university tutors are often not equipped with the necessary information to anticipate the implications of environmental factors for individual students. It is quite possible that a student's impairment, for example, is not disabling in a campus environment during more conventional (taught) modules, but becomes so when the additional considerations and demands (such as time, travel, attendance requirements and social interaction in unfamiliar settings) of placement are brought to bear. The sometimes complex interaction between individual impairment and environmental factors is illustrated by one student, who commented that her bowel condition was a concern, but that provided she had easy access to a toilet at all times and that occasional sudden disappearances were acceptable to her placement supervisor, she felt perfectly capable of managing. This illustrates how both impairment and environment are relevant to whether the person is disabled in relation to any specific context.

In another example, a student we interviewed referred to her severe anxiety condition; she had learnt strategies to manage it and had disclosed it to her placement, where she received a supportive and sympathetic response and therefore was offered sufficient flexibility or accommodation of her needs. As a result, she was able to convert her placement opportunities into real outcomes related to her employability. In contrast, a hypothetical student who felt stressed and unable to manage their condition, share this information or seek help would have more limited opportunities to achieve their goals.

Examples like these illustrate how placements undertaken by diverse student populations can stimulate inclusive practice in the workplace; this is supported by a Capability Approach perspective, by focusing attention on the interaction between a person and their environment. Instead of simply focusing on individual deficiencies in employability, employers' attitudes and practices regarding employing disabled people are subject to scrutiny and intervention: 'enhancing disabled people's employment capabilities requires changing the context in which disabled employment seekers operate, not simply trying to alter the jobseekers to fit the existing context' (Burchardt, 2004:748). Not only students but also the employers themselves stand to gain from successful placement provision; employers can develop their practice in supporting the employment of diverse individuals and develop the inclusivity of their own organisational culture. Indeed, the relatively inclusive environment of the university may have a positive influence on perceptions of disability in employment contexts (Cunnah, 2015). Some student participants in Cunnah's research felt that being in paid employment could overturn negative perceptions of their impairment and support a positive self-identity, financial independence and social status.

The relationship between disability and employment could and should be one of synergy rather than conflict or tension; several students and staff in our research noted the additional value some students with impairments have because of their personal experience, for example, problem solving and time management. This could also relate to specific areas of experience, such as working with disabled children; one staff member participant cited a student on the autistic spectrum who 'is now working with children with autism because she has a unique understanding of what that child's needs are'. Another said 'the students with disabilities ... I think it gives them a unique opportunity to show what they can do rather than being written off before they even begin. I think it shows whether it is the job for them, whether it's something they can do, and they get an opportunity to use their unique skills and their understanding'. In other words, according to the Capability Approach, such life experiences can be viewed as resource, not just a (negative) individual characteristic.

Although the discussion above has identified some issues specific to disabled students, the Capability Approach enables a shift away from a deficit model of disability to encompass potentially any student whose personal characteristics, resources or environment limit or enhance the opportunities for learning available to them during placement:

> Impairment is one characteristic among many which interacts with the social, economic and physical environment to produce a profile of advantage or disadvantage for different individuals. ... The interaction between impairment and a discriminatory and competitive labour market produces disability in the form of limited opportunities for paid employment for people with impairments; the interaction between being a lone parent and the same labour market produces limited opportunities for single people with children.
>
> (Burchardt, 2004:746)

Although theoretical, this perhaps subtle shift in perspective could support changes in practice in the way all of the diverse student population are supported towards successful achievement of their goals.

Conclusion

Individual practitioners or even institutions can do little to affect the macro-economic and political environments that continue to disadvantage many potential participants in the workforce. Nevertheless, universities can work to change the more immediate environment on campus and to influence the work settings students visit to move towards more inclusive practice.

The current legislative context of the UK is such that certain individual characteristics (such as disability) are 'protected' by the 2010 Equality Act (Legislation.gov.uk, 2013), while others (such as having caring or financial responsibilities) are not. Those who fall into the first category are legally entitled to a supportive and sympathetic response in the form of 'reasonable adjustments' or anticipatory action; other potential claims for adjustments are not legally legitimate. This tension is especially acute for widening participation institutions that explicitly promote themselves as welcoming under-represented groups of students. These students stand to gain most from placement and yet are disadvantaged by this current policy context. As one staff member in our research put it, placements 'privilege those with privilege'.

The Capability Approach is comprehensive in that one of its basic assumptions is human diversity, and all students exhibit some sort of profile of capabilities. This approach then leads to a more fluid consideration of all students, without the need to split them into one group (those who are diagnosed with impairments) who are entitled to adjustments and another group that are not. It moves us away from tensions about 'what counts' as warranting special treatment and from the need to classify students. And, of course, students have various aspects of their identity; as the Office for Students' bulletin on mental health (OfS, 2019: 6) points out: 'The challenge for universities and colleges is to recognise how identities intersect and overlap, multiplying the difficulties students with mental health conditions face. Universities and colleges need to listen to the affected students and ensure that their unique needs are met'.

In emphasising agency – the freedom to choose – in the expansion of a student's capability, we are led towards a broader and more flexible conceptualisation of employability, which can be achieved in a variety of different ways. For example, online participation in a community could be an alternative to a conventional placement for students whose health or other circumstances means they may be unable to follow expected patterns of attendance at placement, or to participate meaningfully and safely.

The challenge for educators is to foster individual learners' capabilities, while working within current structures which limit individual choice. Current national policy requires economic productivity from its education system; it should produce the future workforce and therefore promote national economic competitiveness. This stands in stark contrast to the importance of choice in the pursuit of personal wellbeing and development – outcomes that may be valued by the individual but which are not readily measured or valued by the state.

Summary points

- The HE student population is increasingly diverse, but there is considerable inequality of outcomes between different groups, including in terms of employment after graduation.
- Graduating from university enhances an individual's employability, and this is an area of considerable emphasis in current HE policy and practice.
- Placements are a key element of employability provision at university, but many students experience considerable challenges in participating in placement learning opportunities.
- The Capability Approach suggests how each student has a unique profile of individual characteristics and resources that interact with environmental factors to affect how placement opportunities are converted into employability outcomes.

- The Capability Approach helps us to view challenges such as experience of disability, caring responsibilities and part-time working as also having the potential to be a valuable resource for supporting placement learning.

Recommended reading

Advance HE (2020) Work-Based Learning. Available at: https://www.heacademy.ac.uk/sub-theme/work-based-learning (accessed 28 February 2020).

DBIS (2014) National Strategy for Access and Student Success in Higher Education. Available at: https://www.gov.uk/government/publications/national-strategy-for-access-and-student-success (accessed 28 February 2020).

Simon, C. (2020) Work-Based Learning. In: C.A. Simon and S. Ward (Eds) *A Student's Guide to Education Studies*. Abingdon: Routledge.

Terzi, L. (2010) *Justice and Equality in Education: A Capability Perspective on Disability and Special Educational Needs*. London: Continuum.

References

Blackwell, A., Bowes, L., Harvey, A., Hesketh, A. and Knight, P. (2001) Transforming Work Experience in Higher Education. *British Educational Research Journal*, 27(3), pp.269–285.

Boden, R. and Nedeva, M. (2010) Employing Discourse: Universities and Graduate 'Employability'. *Journal of Education Policy*, 25(1), pp.37–54.

Botham, K. and Nicholson, J. (2014) Supporting the Transition of Disabled Students from University to Practice Placement. *Disability and Society*, 29(3), pp.460–476.

Brooks, R. and Youngson, P. (2016) Undergraduate Work Placements: An Analysis of the Effects on Career Progression. *Studies in Higher Education*, 41(9), pp.1563–1578.

Brown, P., Hesketh, A. and Williams, S. (2003) Employability in a Knowledge-Driven Economy. *Journal of Education and Work*, 16(2), pp.107–126.

Burchardt, T. (2004) Capabilities and Disability: The Capabilities Framework and the Social Model of Disability. *Disability and Society*, 19(7), pp.735–751.

Cranmer, S. (2006) Enhancing Graduate Employability: Best Intentions and Mixed Outcomes. *Studies in Higher Education*, 31(2), pp.169–184.

Cunnah, W. (2015) Disabled Students: Identity, Inclusion and Work-Based Placements. *Disability and Society*, 30(2), pp.213–226.

HESA (2019) *Higher Education Student Statistics: UK, 2017/18 (January 2019)*. London: HESA. Available at https://www.hesa.ac.uk/news/17-01-2019/sb252-higher-education-student-statistics (accessed 2 March 2019).

Hillage, J. and Pollard, E. (1998) *Employability: Developing a Framework for Policy Analysis*. London: DfEE.

Hyland, T. (2001) Vocationalism, Work and the Future of Higher Education. *Journal of Vocational Education and Training*, 53(4), pp.677–684.

Legislation.gov.uk. (2013) *Equality Act 2010 Guidance*. London: Government Equalities Office and Hunan Rights Commission. Available at: https://www.gov.uk/guidance/equality-act-2010-guidance (accessed 28 February 2020).

Lester, S. and Costley, C. (2010) Work-Based Learning at Higher Education Level: Value, Practice and Critique. *Studies in Higher Education*, 35(5), pp.561–575.

Mitra, S. (2006) The Capability Approach and Disability. *Journal of Disability Policy Studies*, 16(4), pp. 236–247.

Moores, E., Birdi, G. and Higson, H. (2017) Placement Work Experience May Mitigate Lower Achievement Levels of Black and Asian vs. White Students at University. *Frontiers in Psychology*, 8, pp.1–10.

Moreau, P. and Leathwood, C. (2007) Graduates' Employment and the Discourse of Employability: A Critical Analysis. *Journal of Education and Work*, 19(4), pp.305–324.

Norwich, B. (2014) How Does the Capability Approach Address Current Issues in the Special Educational Needs, Disability and Inclusive Education Field? *Journal of Research in Special Educational Needs*, 14(1), pp.16–21.

OfS (2019) *Mental Health: Are All Students Being Properly Supported?* Available at: https://www.officeforstudents.org.uk/publications/mental-health-are-all-students-being-properly-supported/ (Accessed 27 February 2020).

Papworth Trust (2018) Disability in the United Kingdom. Available at: https://www.papworthtrust.org.uk/about-us/publications/ (accessed 25 January 2020).

Pegg, A., Waldock, S., Hendy-Isaac and Lawton, R. (2012) *Pedagogy for Employability*. York: Higher Education Academy.

Rae, D. (2007) Connecting Enterprise and Graduate Employability. *Education and Training*, 49(8/9), pp.605–619.

Skidmore, C. (2019) Call for Universities to Improve Support for Disabled Students. Available at: https://www.gov.uk/government/news/call-for-universities-to-improve-support-for-disabled-students (accessed 28 February 2020).

Smith, D. (2016) *Disability in the United Kingdom 2016. Facts and Figures*. London: The Papworth Trust.

Thorley, C. (2017) *Not by Degrees: Improving Student Mental Health in the UK's Universities*. London: IPPR.

Van der Klink, J., Bültmann, U., Burdorf, A., Schaufeli, W., Zijlstra, F., Abma, F., Brouwer, S. and Van der Wilt, G. (2016) Sustainable Employability – Definition, Conceptualization and Implications: A Perspective Based on the Capability Approach. *Scandinavian Journal of Work and Environmental Health*, 42(1), pp.71–79.

Wilson, T. (2012) *A Review of Business–University Collaboration*. London: DBIS.

Yorke, M. (2004) Employability in the Undergraduate Curriculum: Some Student Perspectives. *European Journal of Education*, 39(4), pp.409–427.

13 How to promote real equality in higher education

Ruth Mieschbuehler

Introduction

Educationalists talk about 'equality' without realising that the meaning of the word has changed. The new meaning of 'equality' is the one that most students and academics will be familiar with from discussions of 'equality and diversity' policies but may not entirely understand. To fully understand this new meaning, it is necessary to look back at the older meaning. The older meaning of the term 'equality' referred to the right to be treated the same, to be treated as an equal. The new meaning has been constructed around demands to be treated differently, to have differences recognised and respected. The clearest way of illustrating how the meaning of 'equality' has changed is through contrasting examples from politics and policy, compulsory schooling and higher education.

Examples: Politics and policy

An example that dramatically illustrates the older meaning of 'equality' comes from the Handsworth riots in Birmingham in September 1985. The riots began when hundreds of demonstrators from Asian, black and white backgrounds gathered to protest against police harassment in the context of local poverty and unemployment. The initial spark for the riots was a police parking ticket slapped on an illegally parked car (*BirminghamLive* [1985] 2011). The demonstration became violent and demonstrators set off fire bombs, looted and smashed property and attacked the police. Many people from the area looked on as fires burned and local firefighters struggled with debris that was scattered across the streets. This is an important example as, although the parking ticket was given to a black motorist, it provoked an angry response that grew out of years of deprivation. Most importantly, the demonstrators in Handsworth fought back as one community.

Pogus Caesar, a Birmingham film maker and photographer who was in the centre of the riots when they broke out and managed to document numerous scenes, wrote as part of the OOM Gallery, an online multimedia arts website:

'At approximately 5pm on Monday 9th September 1985, a black man is arrested near the Acapulco Café, Lozells Road for a traffic offence.

Very soon a crowd consisting of African Caribbean, Asian and British people ask the police to let the man go – the police refuse this request and the situation quickly escalates into a riot'.

(Caesar cited in *BBC Birmingham Community Features* [1985] 2014)

Two decades later, in October 2005, other riots in the Handsworth and Lozells areas of Birmingham began because of ethnic tensions between British Caribbean and British Asian groups. The spark for the riots was an alleged gang rape of a teenage black girl by a group of South Asian men. The rape allegations were never substantiated but the Birmingham newspaper *Voice* reported them as fact. The paper was later censured after a complaint to the press watchdog for inaccurate reporting in the front-page article 'Gang of 19 rape teen' which was thought to have contributed to tensions that sparked the riots. Clashes between the groups meant that acts of serious violence were committed against both communities.

Indymedia UK, a network of individuals and alternative media activists, and organisations, which reported on 'The So-Called Lozells Riots', reported how serious violence was committed against both communities in the Handsworth and Lozells district in Birmingham:

> On Wednesday, 2 Asian shops in the area were firebombed, and several other shops were closed down by mobs of Afro-Caribbean youths, who had reportedly also been bricking Asian cars driving on Heathfield Road.

> On Saturday, 22 October, a late-afternoon public meeting was held at the New Testament Church of God over the alleged rape. ... At around 5.45pm, violence erupted outside the church as a group of Asian youths tried to get into the meeting and began to racially taunt those who attended it, calling them 'niggers' and 'slaves'. The police, who were already there, stood between the two groups, but the youths carried on stoning each other.

(*Indymedia UK*, 2005)

What had changed between the two events was council policies, which 'bound people more closely to particular identities' and led them to 'fear and resent other groups as competitors for power and influence' that entrenched 'divisions between black and Asian communities to such an extent that those divisions broke out in communal violence' (Malik, 2015). The emphasis on difference had disastrously replaced the older binding meaning of equality, of all being equal in one community.

Examples: Compulsory education

Another example from the school sector that illustrates the older meaning of 'equality' is the introduction of the comprehensive school system. At the heart of the comprehensive system was the idea of a 'common syllabus' (Rubinstein and Simon, [1969] 2007). Such a syllabus was considered of 'the utmost importance if the comprehensive idea [was] to succeed', since only by this means were the older barriers to be overcome, and pupils 'to enjoy the same opportunities' (Brown *et al.*, 1957: 159–166, cited in Rubenstein and Simon, [1969] 2007: 77). The idea that everybody should be taught the same curriculum was based on the understanding that 'in practice it was useless to talk of parity in education or equality of opportunity in later life' as long as children were stratified at the age of 11 into different types of schools under the 1944 tripartite system (Rubenstein and Simon, [1969] 2007: 18). It was clear to scholars at the time that a common curriculum of the highest academic standard was what was needed to bring about parity and equality of opportunity in education.

Education today has moved away from the common curriculum through a focus on 'individualised learning'. This was an approach to education that entered England's classrooms in the 1990s, focusing on the individual wants and needs of children. 'Individualised learning' seems a positive pupil-centred approach but, precisely because it focuses on the child, it offers a limited education. This limited education is based on what teachers think is relevant to children and where they think their pupils will be employed when they leave school. Individualised learning does not require that all children are taught the same curriculum. The common curriculum ensured equality in sameness of treatment, whereas individualised learning emphasised difference.

Examples: Higher education

An example from higher education that illustrates the older meaning of equality is the decline of subject-based teaching. This was a consequence of a growing interest in student-centred learning that took hold in British higher education after the publication of the *Report of the National Committee of Inquiry into Higher Education* in 1997 (Dearing Report). This ideological shift away from subject-based education is reflected in *Recommendation eight* of the report, which entreated that 'all institutions of higher education give priority to developing and implementing learning and teaching strategies which focus on the promotion of students' learning' (Dearing, 1997). This shift prompted a growing concern with the 'student experience' leading to an emphasis on this becoming an integral part of university policies and practices. In the policies and in the promotional materials of universities, the rhetoric of 'putting the student at the centre' of the university is everywhere. Putting subjects and knowledge at the centre of the university is now considered old-fashioned. The formation of the Office for Students (OfS) as the regulatory body for higher education on 1 January 2018 confirms and will amplify the shift away from knowledge.

The focus on the 'student experience' prioritises the wants and needs of students over the teaching of subjects. It has further implications for teaching in that it also provides the basis for a pedagogical concern with 'relevant knowledge'. There is a widespread belief in all sectors of education that students can only develop their full academic potential if knowledge is relevant to their social background or future lives. Providing students with 'relevant knowledge' individualises learning in higher education.

This concern with the 'student experience' contrasts with the older subject-based approach to education aimed at teaching students what the Victorian writer and poet Matthew Arnold called 'the best that is known and thought in the world' (Arnold, [1864] 2003: 50). Promoting equality in education in this way means believing that all students have the potential to acquire the heritage of human knowledge. 'Equality' in its older meaning emphasised bringing people together in solidarity as it was founded on the belief that everyone should be treated equally despite their racial, ethnic, religious or cultural differences. 'Equality' in the new meaning divides people because it is founded on the belief that everyone should be treated differently according to their racial, ethnic, religious or cultural backgrounds.

Questions for discussion

- Can you think of an example of 'equality' being discussed in an educational setting when you were present? What did people say that may indicate that they understand 'equality' in the older meaning, 'the right to be the same', or in the newer meaning, 'the right to be different'?

The universal versus the particular meaning of 'equality'

'Equality as difference' is how 'equality' is understood today, and 'treating people as equals' means accepting and respecting differences. However, this is not a change that should be unquestioningly accepted. Identifying a shift in the meaning of 'equality' is indicative of a change in the way politicians and educators think about people. It is a change that can be challenged. Kenan Malik, a well-known British author, columnist and broadcaster, argued over two decades ago that it was time to reclaim the older meaning of equality and defend 'the right to be the same' in a universal meaning rather than defending 'the right to be different' which reduced the notion of equality to the particular (Malik, 1996: 261). That reclamation did not happen and is more urgent today.

The fading Enlightenment

The Enlightenment was an historical period often associated with groups of thinkers from the seventeenth to the nineteenth century. The Enlightenment stood for reason, for science, for the search for truth and for human progress. To the thinkers of the Enlightenment, these were universal values, ones that originally came from Europe but were part of what made us human. Modern writers in this tradition illustrate how the universal can be defended against those who emphasise difference (the particular).

A major thinker writing in the Enlightenment tradition was the West Indian psychiatrist and political philosopher Frantz Fanon. In his book *Black Skin, White Masks*, he made his attitude to the conflict between the universal and particular very clear. He was conscious of being a 'black man' but also a 'man' and of not trying to be one particular 'black' or, more disastrously, trying to be 'white', but to recognise the universal in himself and his thought, something that was a constant struggle (see Malik, 2015: 275–278). Fanon expresses this view, for example, when he writes that 'the negro, however sincere, is the slave of the past. None the less I am a man, and in this sense the Peloponnesian War is as much mine as the invention of the compass' (Fanon, [1952] 1993: 225). Defending the older meaning of 'equality' involves a similar struggle to keep alive the belief in a universal human nature.

Kenan Malik, writing in the Enlightenment tradition, also defends universalism and the 'belief in the unity of humanity and the equality of Man' (Malik, 1996: 49). The belief in a universal human nature, Malik argues, 'led logically to the notion that the divisions among humanity were either artificial or to a large extent irrelevant in comparison to its elements of commonality' (Malik, 1996: 48). But, at the heart of the new meaning of equality and discussions about difference 'lies a hostility to Enlightenment universalism' (Malik, 1996: 145). This is a tragedy. The certainty of the Enlightenment belief in a universal human nature 'led to a greater willingness to accept unfamiliar values and to more tolerant humanistic attitudes to non-European peoples' (Malik, 1996: 49). The emphasis on the particular, although it seems more empathetic to different peoples, actually undermines tolerance.

The rise of relativism and the attack on Enlightenment universalism

The shift towards the celebration of difference is also found in the culture of relativism in education and its expression as a fear of making judgements in wider society (Kennedy 2014). This culture of relativism is part of the decline in belief in Enlightenment values which are based on criticism as the way to seek truth. Fear of making judgements about the value of particular beliefs, customs and practices is an attack on Enlightenment universalism as it is indifferent to truth-seeking. Being 'uncomfortable with making value judgements' (Furedi, 2011: 80) is particularly damaging to the university ethos, which is founded on making critical judgements.

In universities, the changing notion of equality from the universal to the particular persists for different, although related, reasons. The shift towards the particular means that equality in contemporary attainment research in higher education is conceptualised as relational, which means it examines how the education or attainment of one group compares to another. When this research reveals seeming inequalities in attainment between ethnic groups, it generates powerful emotional responses. Students who seem to be under-attaining think that they are victims of racism or that their cultures are ignored or disparaged in the curriculum. They may even denounce the curriculum as a 'Western' one that is either indifferent to, or dismissive of, other cultures and values. Demands are often made by students and students' unions to change the curriculum to reflect different cultures and values. These proposals constitute demands to 'relativise' the curriculum and replace it with a variety of curricula that embody different cultures and values. The relativisation of the higher education curriculum, if successful, would undermine the universal values of the Enlightenment by creating a curriculum based on difference.

The university is the embodiment of Enlightenment values in its commitment to the pursuit of knowledge and understanding. It is vulnerable to moves to adopt the new meaning of 'equality' as difference because of the relativistic consequences of emotional responses to issues such as the supposed attainment gap. However, despite the fact that relativism is rife in higher education, it is easily refutable (see Hayes and Mieschbuehler, 2015).

Implications for higher education of the culture of relativism

The culture of relativism is the philosophical basis for the new meaning of equality in higher education. It creates a false sense of empowerment to groups that are oppressed; it nurtures divisive thinking and, at an institutional level, it undermines the universalist project of the university. This is a bold statement that must be explained.

How does the new meaning of equality create a false sense of empowerment?

'Equality' as the right to be different gives oppressed groups a false sense of empowerment because it prevents the powerful from criticising their views and values, but it also prevents oppressed groups from criticising the powerful. The philosopher Paul Boghossian, in his book *Fear of Knowledge: Against Relativism and Constructivism* (2007), argued that, if all knowledge is relative, then 'any claim to knowledge can be dispatched if we do not happen to share the values on which it allegedly depends', and this appears to 'protect oppressed cultures from the charge of holding false or unjustified views' (Boghossian, 2007: 130). The consequence of this 'cultural relativism' is contradictory.

> If the powerful can't criticise the oppressed, because the central epistemological categories are inexorably tied to particular perspectives, it also follows that the oppressed can't criticise

the powerful. The only remedy, so far as I can see, for what threatens to be a strongly conservative upshot, is to accept an overt double standard: allow a questionable idea to be criticised if it
is held by those in a position of power – Christian creationism, for example – but not if it is held
by those whom the powerful oppress – Zuni creationism, for example.

(Boghossian, 2007: 130)

Relativism gives a 'false sense of empowerment because it appears to "protect oppressed cultures"
as the "powerful can't criticise the oppressed", while in fact it censors "the oppressed" as the
"oppressed can't criticise the powerful" either if the same logic is applied' (Boghossian, 2007: 130).

The 'strongly conservative' outcome would be that the powerful would be beyond criticism, and
the oppressed could do nothing about their views. Of course, there is no need to accommodate to
relativism in this way. It would be far better to allow everyone to criticise everything.

How the new meaning of equality nurtures divisions and divisive thinking

'Equality' understood as the right to be different also nurtures divisions and divisive thinking because
it leads to social and ethnic grouping, the process of allocating people to various predetermined
social and ethnic categories for research and policy purposes and in practice.

One reason why the grouping of people is divisive is because it conflates or ignores intragroup
differences and downplays people's individuality. Grouping overemphasises differences between
groups of people and suggests that the experiences of some groups are fundamentally distinct
from those in other categories (Good, 2013). Once the question of how experiences differ is
asked, it answers itself. Minor particularities gain in significance; groups are then differentiated on
the basis of these particularities and in-group differences; people's individuality is diminished. The
emphasis on differences between groups reached a high point in what is known the theory of 'intersectionality' that highlighted competing claims of discrimination by various groups. Although the aim
of intersectionality was to draw attention to how power affects various disadvantaged groups, the
ultimate effect was to reinforce divisions based on identities (Heartfield, 2017). These views have
rarely been challenged and are now mainstream.

Paul Gilroy, the founding director of the Centre for the Study of Race and Racism at University
College London, is one of the academics who has discussed how a concern with the identities of
those in groups 'looked more seductive where all differences had been banished or erased from the
collective' (Gilroy, 2000: 102). Once individual differences within groups are ignored, differences
between groups gain in significance. In this way, group membership becomes more important than
a person's individuality. Questions about how experiences differ between groups are, therefore,
inherently belittling since they deprive people of the possibility of recognising their individuality.
Part of the seductiveness of grouping is that it appears to address what is common and could be
mistaken for being a universalist concern when it really emphasises what become fixed and divisive
identities.

The practice of grouping people damages both their individuality and their humanity by confining
them to specific categories of identity. Simply put, 'to see a person primarily as a "white person" or
a "black female" is to diminish both their humanity and their individuality' (Good, 2013). The practice
of grouping people does more harm than good. It suggests that the experiences of some groups
are fundamentally distinct from those in other groups. It also reverses the previous inequalities of

respect in that the culprits, for example, 'white middle-class men', become the disrespected victim, which means all that is changing is who is the 'oppressor' and who the 'oppressed' without addressing the underlying issues.

The inevitability of using categories to address inequalities is not as self-evident as suggested in much of the literature on equality, identity and inclusivity. At a time when the older meaning of equality was dominant, Martin Luther King, in his *I have a dream* speech on 28 August 1963, envisaged a world where his children would not be judged by their group identity:

> I have a dream that my four little children will one day live in a nation where they will not be judged by the color of their skin but by the content of their character.
>
> (King, 1963)

Treating people as 'individuals rather than category-members is at least as anti-racist, anti-sexist and anti-homophobic as the group approach', and in the long run, it is 'probably the best guarantee of security against discrimination' (Good, 2001, 2013).

Question for discussion

- If grouping – the practice of allocating people to various predetermined social and ethnic categories – was discontinued, what would be the effect on education?

How the new meaning of equality institutionalises divisive thinking

The new meaning of equality that is everywhere in higher education policies and practice institutionalises divisive thinking. These policies and practices maintain and formalise divisions rather than trying to overcome them. Academics and staff in higher education institutions (HEIs) have recently been asked to attend 'unconscious bias' training. This training aims to identify stereotypes and prejudices that people may not be aware of but are thought to influence behaviour. This training embodies the new meaning of equality, as it is based on teaching the importance of understanding differences based on identity. But this training does not suddenly appear because of an academic interest in 'bias'. It arises from institutional structures. These are the formal committees from the governing body to academic boards and many committees lower down the institutional hierarchy such as equality and diversity committees, student experience teams and even student unions. These committees are supported by an array of equality officers appointed to promote equality as difference.

These committees and the individual employees appointed to equality and diversity posts constitute the institutional structures that promote divisive policies. Often, they are influenced by external bodies such as the OfS but also by research assessment and research funding bodies. An illustration of how promoting division becomes institutionalised can be given through a more detailed discussion of the ubiquitous concern with the supposed 'attainment gap'. This is an obsession that higher education institutions (HEIs) have responded to because of pressure from the media and equality campaigners. From the government to governors, it has become a major issue. The 'attainment gap' is an issue not only for large institutional committees; it is also taken up by student experience teams who make it an issue for every teaching and research programme.

The work of the Equality Challenge Unit (ECU) is a good example of how the obsession with the supposed 'attainment gap' begins. The ECU reports statistics on gender and ethnic gaps in attainment within the British higher education sector. For example, according to the ECU, the gap in attainment between white and black and minority ethnic students amounted to 17.6 per cent in 2013 and 15 per cent in 2016 (ECU, 2013, 2017). This refers to 'UK-domiciled' (students whose normal residence was the UK prior to entry into higher education) undergraduate students graduating with a high degree classification (ECU, 2012: 84). In response to ECU reports which are supported by the OfS, demanding that HEIs address attainment gaps between ethnic groups, they have set up specific working groups and research projects. These are also part of the institutional structures that promote the idea of 'difference' by developing initiatives that encourage all staff to consider how students differ from each other because of their race, culture or beliefs. They are then asked to redesign the curriculum and teaching around these perceived differences.

But the way in which these attainment statistics are reported is misleading. They are used to reinforce the idea that there are 'differences' between student groups. The statistics used to report attainment between student groups generally use one variable only to compare attainment to rather than a whole range of factors which are known to affect student attainment. That means statistics on attainment do not show the whole picture. Attainment figures are distorted when they report, for example, the percentage of black students graduating with a good degree classification as compared to white students. The only variable that is taken into account in this instance, besides attainment, is ethnicity, which in this particular case amounts to the skin colour of students. The ECU and statistics departments in universities are part of the national and institutional structures that reinforce 'differences' and, therefore, divisive thinking.

The reporting of the 'attainment gap' consistently ignores other factors that could impact on attainment, including prior attainment, disability, deprivation, age, term-time working, English as an additional language, motivation for embarking on the degree course and the academic aspiration for graduating with a high degree classification. When these factors are considered, attainment gaps between social and ethnic groups tend to become insignificant or disappear altogether. With regard to the 'ethnic' attainment gap in British higher education, 'the statistical evidence does not confirm ethnicity as a determining factor in educational attainment of higher education students in Britain' when other variables are taken into account (Mieschbuehler, 2018: 17).

This simplistic and misleading reporting of statistics is now a major factor in embodying the new meaning of equality as difference in HEIs. The policies and practices that are then implemented to address supposed inequalities are well-intentioned, but they institutionalise divisive thinking. As we have seen, there are a few critics of this new divisive concept of equality, but why do these institutional practices continue to go unchallenged and gain in strength in HEIs? The blunt answer is that no-one is talking about them. They are too afraid.

Towards real equality in higher education: A defence of discussion and debate

There are two reasons why no-one is talking about these issues. The first is political. Writing about educational debate in 2004, a leading educational thinker, Tyrrell Burgess, declared that 'The spirit of the age is against it' (Burgess, 2004: 217). He believed that debate had gone out of fashion in a time when educationalists believed that there were technocratic solutions to educational issues.

Managerialism and a belief in the market were seemingly unchallengeable. The mantra here is 'let's get things done and not engage in semantic discussions'. The second is cultural. The cultural aspect is what some writers refer to as 'therapy' culture. In therapy culture, people are seen as potential victims, and the mantra of this culture is 'be nice, do not offend anyone' (Ecclestone and Hayes, 2019; Fox, 2018).

Therapy culture is complementary to the managerialism that dominates the higher education sector. The spirit in higher education is 'do not raise questions and do not be offensive'. It is the fear that someone speaking on behalf of those said to be disadvantaged or those who consider themselves disadvantaged will be offended by criticism and debate that stop people talking. If anyone challenges policies and practices based on identity politics and divisive group-based thinking, they may appear to be callous or even racist. The fear of someone taking offence has produced uncritical silence. There is no contestation in higher education. HEIs should be the places for thinking the unthinkable and saying the unsayable. In a culture where you are taught what not to think, or say, ideas exist unchallenged and equality just *is* the equality of difference. The fear that debate and discussion might offend undermines the essence of higher education. Higher education is dedicated to the pursuit of truth, which only 'emerges from the clash of opposites' (Andrews, 2009: 3). This clash can be hard for people to deal with and those who fear offending have a point:

> One's beliefs are close to the centre of 'who one is' and criticism of them can cut deep and meet protective resistance. But it is of the essence of human rationality that beliefs are held as valid, as justified by their correspondence to what is the case. The mind expresses itself and thus exposes itself to change through criticism. Criticism and discussion respect these dimensions of rationality, whereas silencing smashes at them, practically denying the capacity, not only to have reached views through some process of experience and reflection, but to go beyond them through further formative activity.
>
> (Skillen, 1982: 145)

The main point here is misunderstood if it leads to anyone avoiding cutting deep with criticism. As Skillen says, criticism and discussion respect human rationality. Even more than this, criticism and discussion respect people as individuals who can develop, change and reach their potential as human beings. Eliminating discussion and debate on the basis that someone might be offended is to disrespect them as individuals and to deny their humanity. The continued use and application of social and ethnic categories is a well-intentioned attempt to address inequalities in higher education, but it fails to recognise people's individuality and humanity.

To bring about real equality in higher education, students and staff need to be treated as individuals. That means people are judged by their character rather than by characteristics such as being 'white' or 'black'; 'female' or 'male'; 'Christian', 'Muslim' or 'Atheist'; from a 'well-to-do' or from a 'less well-to-do' background. If people are judged for what they are as a person, rather than on the basis of their traits, their individuality is recognised. Treating people as individuals, rather than merely as members of a social or ethnic group, means that every and any issue can be openly discussed without prior assumptions about group differences.

It is only as individuals that people can have real access to the human heritage that is higher education. The older meaning of 'equality' recognised the universal, the truly human in each individual. Restoring that meaning and challenging the 'quality' of difference will require some intellectual toughness to debate and discuss whether or not someone cries 'That's offensive!' The debate has to begin not merely for academic reasons but also to ensure that every individual can be assured that in higher education they will have access to real equality.

Questions for discussion

- If you are a student in higher education, how do you think discussion and debate can be encouraged? Can you think of any concrete initiatives that could come from students?

Conclusion: The true meaning of equality

Anyone who aims to promote real 'equality' in higher education must engage in debate and discussion about the two meanings of 'equality'. Without discussion and debate, it is impossible to understand the implications of either meaning for policies and practices that impact on students and staff. It means breaking down the political and cultural barriers that silence debate. This means not giving in to the charge that what is said may be offensive to someone. The pursuit of knowledge in higher education must be undertaken without fear or favour. This chapter is an attempt to open up a debate about the two meanings of 'equality'. The claim that is made here is that the older meaning of the term 'equality', which defends the right to be the same through the recognition of our common humanity and human heritage, must be restored in higher education. It is the *true* meaning of equality. Many readers will disagree. Let the debate begin.

Summary points

This chapter discussed how

- the meaning of 'equality' in higher education has changed. There has been shift from understanding 'equality' as 'the right to be the same' to 'equality' as 'the right to be different';
- HEIs have become obsessed with difference because of the so-called student 'attainment gap';
- cultural relativism is undermining Enlightenment universalism and the pursuit of truth and, therefore, the university itself;
- restoring discussion and debate in higher education is the only way to re-examine the meaning of 'equality' and restore its *true* meaning.

Recommended reading

Andrews, R. (2009) *The Importance of Argument in Education*. Inaugural Professorial Lecture. London: Institute of Education.

Good, G. (2013) Identity Politics is Killing College Life: Learning Becomes Impossible When We Split Students into Racial and Gender Camps. *Spiked-Online*, 23 September. http://www.spiked-online.com/newsite/article/identity_politics_is_killing_college_life/14066#.U0024fldXY4 (accessed 12 December 2019).

Hayes, D. and Mieschbuehler, R. (2015) The Refuge of Relativism. In: A. O'Grady and V.A. Cottle (Eds), *Exploring Education at Post-Graduate Level*. Abingdon: Routledge.

Malik, K. (2015) The Failure of Multiculturalism. *Pandaemonium*. https://kenanmalik.com/2015/02/17/the-failure-of-multiculturalism/ (accessed 10/01/2020).

References

Andrews, R. (2009) *The Importance of Argument in Education*. Inaugural Professorial Lecture. London: Institute of Education.

Arnold, M. ([1864] 2003) The Function of Criticism at the Present Time. In: S. Collini (Ed.), *Culture and Anarchy and Other Writings*. Cambridge: Cambridge University Press.

BBC Birmingham Community Features ([1985]) 2014) Handsworth Riots – Twenty Years On. *BBC Birmingham*, 28 October. http://www.bbc.co.uk/birmingham/content/articles/2005/09/05/handsworth_riots_20years_feature.shtml. (accessed 28 April 2020).

Birmingham Live ([1985] 2011) From the Archive: Police Parking Ticket Sowed Seeds for Riots. *Birmingham Mail*, 14 July. https://www.birminghammail.co.uk/news/local-news/from-the-archives-police-parking-ticket-sowed-157800 (accessed 20 January 2020).

Boghossian, P. (2007) *Fear of Knowledge: Against Relativism and Constructivism*. Oxford: Oxford University Press.

Burgess, T. (2004) What Are the Key Debates in Education? In: D. Hayes (Ed.), *The Routledge Guide to Key Debates in Education*. London/New York: Routledge.

Dearing, R. (1997) *Report of the National Committee of Inquiry into Higher Education*. London: Department for Education and Employment. http://www.leeds.ac.uk/educol/ncihe/ (accessed 20 January 2020).

Ecclestone, K. and Hayes, D. (2019) *The Dangerous Rise of Therapeutic Education, Classic Edition*. London/New York: Routledge.

ECU (2012) *Equality in Higher Education: Statistical Report 2012, Part 2: Students*. London: Equality Challenge Unit.

ECU (2013) *Equality in Higher Education: Statistical Report 2013, Part 2: Students*. London: Equality Challenge Unit.

ECU (2017) *Equality in Higher Education: Statistical Reporter 2017, Students*. London: Equality Challenge Unit.

Fanon, F. ([1952] 1993) *Black Skin, White Masks*. London: Pluto Press.

Fox, C. (2018) *I Still Find that Offensive!* London: Biteback Publishing.

Furedi, F. (2011) *On Tolerance: A Defence of Moral Independence*. London: Continuum International Publishing Group.

Gilroy, P. (2000) *Against Race: Imagining Political Culture Beyond the Colour Line*. Cambridge, MA: The Belknap Press of Harvard University Press.

Good, G. (2001) *Humanism Betrayed: Theory, Deology and Culture in the Contemporary University*. Montreal, QC: McGill-Queens University Press.

Good, G. (2013) Identity Politics is Killing College Life: Learning Becomes Impossible When We Split Students into Racial and Gender Camps. *Spiked-Online*, 23 September http://www.spiked-online.com/newsite/article/identity_politics_is_killing_college_life/14066#.U0024fldXY4 (accessed 12 December 2019).

Hayes, D. and Mieschbuehler, R. (2015) The Refuge of Relativism. In: A. O'Grady and V.A. Cottle (Eds), *Exploring Education at Post-Graduate Level*. Abingdon: Routledge.

Heartfield, J. (2017) *The Equal Opportunities Revolution*. London: Repeater.

Indymedia UK (2005) *The So-Called Lozells Riots*. 19 November. Birmingham: IMC, https://www.indymedia.org.uk/en/2005/11/328123.html (accessed 28 April 2020).

Kennedy, A. (2014) *Being Cultured: In Defence of Discrimination*. Exeter: Imprint Academic.

King, M.L. Jr. (1963) *I Have a Dream*. Speech by the Rev. Martin Luther King at the 'March on Washington'. Washington D. C: Lincoln Memorial.

Malik, K. (1996) *The Meaning of Race*. New York: New York University Press.

Malik, K. (2015) The Failure of Multiculturalism. *Pandaemonium*, https://kenanmalik.com/2015/02/17/the-failure-of-multiculturalism/ (accessed 10 January 2020).

Mieschbuehler, R. (2018) *The Minoritisation of Higher Education Students*. Abingdon: Routledge.

Rubinstein, D. and Simon, D. ([1969] 2007) *The Evolution of the Comprehensive School, 1926-1972*. London: Routledge and Kegan Paul.

Skillen, A. (1982) Freedom of Speech. In: K. Graham (Ed.), *Contemporary Political Philosophy: Radical Studies*. Cambridge: Cambridge University Press.

14 Higher education

Contemplating the contradictions, complexities and challenges

Brendan Bartram

Introduction

This chapter considers the key themes and issues covered throughout the book in an attempt to highlight the varied and inter-connected nature of the complexities and challenges that are central to contemporary higher education (HE). It concludes with an item of HE-related news that reflects and illustrates some of these elements, and invites readers to discuss their own perspectives on these issues.

Higher education – a fraught and diverse arena

Returning to the title of the book – understanding contemporary issues in higher education – it is worth pondering in this final chapter what can be gleaned from this collection of diverse contributions. One thing that they have perhaps served to underline is the fitting nature of the book's subtitle: contradictions, complexities and challenges. The chapters have all shown in different ways that the broad arena of HE is fraught with diverse pressures and competing understandings. There is very little, if anything, that is uncontested or settled with regard to how it operates at any level: at the macro-level, policies are continually evolving and making their effects felt at institutional level; the translation of these policies at local level then plays out in very different ways for the students and staff involved at the micro-level of day-to-day experiences in the sector.

The chapters have illustrated, for example, how notions of precarity and risk pervade the experiences of staff and students in a variety of ways. Sumner and Muddiman *et al.* show us how decisions on where to study, and indeed, where to work, implicate us in complex webs of risk and potential disadvantage. These ideas are reflected to some extent in the needs academics may experience to secure and protect their positions by flexing their online credentials and achievements, as I show in Chapter 4. Additional challenges may emerge through the extent to which our cultural differences articulate with established curricular preferences, individual understandings and institutional policies (as we see in different ways in both Hosein and Rao's and Hathaway and Rao's chapters). Further complexities arise from the pressures students face in negotiating their employment hopes and aspirations (D'Silva and Pugh) while grappling with new knowledge and new technological means for acquiring it (Bailey *et al.*). Dickens' chapter reveals how some of these challenges may link to the growing concerns and debates on mental health in HE, while Brewster and Thompson, and Mieschbuehler too, reveal both the philosophical and practical challenges and tensions in dealing with aspects of diversity and equality in a massified HE system. All of these aspects may again be further troubled by fundamental changes in how we now think about the very nature and purpose of acquiring university knowledge and its relationship with society, employment markets and the economy (as discussed in both Elliot's and Ward's contributions).

Some might argue that this complex and inter-meshing patchwork of issues is not unique to HE. There are certainly similarities with primary, secondary and indeed further education, where a whole host of workforce issues collide with changing demographics and habits, stakeholder expectations, curricular developments and government policies. Outside of education, parallels might even be drawn with the health service (Woodhouse, 2015) and other fields of employment. Many spheres of life now are in fact characterised by greater competition, increased scrutiny, technological change and ubiquitous precarity. All the same, there is a case for arguing that some of these factors are perhaps experienced more intensely in HE nowadays, as the sector struggles with a multiple identity crisis driven by contradictory pressures. Even when institutions have grappled to position themselves along the binary continua I discussed in Chapter 1, universities must still strive to reconcile the competing identities of public service educator/market-driven corporation/agent of social change/labour market supplier/consumer-oriented business and so on, while balancing the long-held principles of academic freedom and autonomy with government control and consumer demands.

In thinking about writing this concluding chapter, and reflecting on the contribution of Bailey *et al.*, I was curious to see what a simple Google search using the terms 'higher education 2020' would produce. Interestingly, but perhaps unsurprisingly, I was struck by how many of the top-listed results echoed many of the themes and issues mentioned throughout the book. The words and phrases displayed emphasised the notions of competition, rankings, challenge, risk, changing expectations, reputation and, of course, the effects of Brexit. Given the time of writing, numerous additional concerns were expressed about the potential long-term effects of COVID-19. The enforced shift to moving teaching and learning online in March 2020 had understandably become the source of much speculation. O'Toole (2020) reflected on some of the possible consequences of the pandemic for HE. Alongside the obvious budgetary implications of huge income losses driven by dramatic dips in the recruitment of 'financially lucrative' international students from countries such as China and India, O'Toole points to the possibility of an equally devastating crisis of identity: if universities are successful in their responses to the outbreak and demonstrate that online pedagogic operations are an efficient and cost-effective route to gaining a degree, both home and international students may begin to question the need for physical attendance and the importance of communal learning and living spaces. ... Only time will tell, of course.

Among the results was also mention of a less catastrophic but nonetheless interesting item of recent news concerning the University of Sunderland, UK. Though this will no longer be live news by the time of publication, the story in question highlighted a number of features that strongly resonate with issues raised in this volume. The educational press in particular made much of the university's 2020 decision to close its History, Politics and Modern Foreign Language Departments because of dwindling recruitment in these subject areas. The closures were accompanied by staff redundancies and redeployment. Metcalfe (2020:1) commented on the university's rationale for its subjects to be 'educationally and financially sustainable'. He goes on to quote John Mowbray, chair of the university's board of governors:

> While recognising the value of the subjects the university is withdrawing from, the board of governors agreed that they do not fit with the curriculum principles of being career-focused and

professions-facing. Nor are they of a size and scale to be educationally viable in the medium to long term, given the competition from other institutions, both regionally and nationally.

Metcalfe explains that under plans to 'reassert and re-orient the University's identity and purpose', there would be an increased focus on technology and business-related programmes with an emphasis on subjects that are considered 'important to the national economy', including engineering, computer science and business. The decision was greeted with much dismay in many quarters. There was widespread criticism of using economic thinking as a basis for dictating considerations of worthwhile university knowledge, as well as much concern for the livelihoods of teaching staff affected and the reduction in student choice available. Metcalfe notes the reaction on Twitter of one Durham University lecturer, Dr Andre Keil:

> It's always been a small programme which served local students, many of whom were the first in their families to go to university. Colleagues did an exceptional job to create educational opportunities and offered exceptional support for mature and working-class students. Now there will be no opportunities for local students to engage with their past, nor their political present, not to mention to shape their international outlook by learning a foreign language. Sad times, indeed!

Questions for discussion

- Reflecting on the news item discussed here, which of the book's key themes (summarised in the second paragraph above) do you see reflected in this feature?
- What are your own views on this decision?
- To what extent do you agree with the above Twitter response?
- What are the risks of closing down subject areas that struggle to recruit 'sufficient' numbers of students?
- How might universities go about reversing the apparent decline in the popularity of certain subjects?
- Search online for current items of HE-related news – in what ways do you see other key themes from the book echoed in these news stories?

Conclusion

Higher education remains a diverse and expanding field, as the preceding chapters have illustrated. The complexities, contradictions and challenges associated with this educational sector are themselves equally diverse and numerous, and it is hoped that the insights provided throughout the book will have given readers a better understanding of some of these wide-ranging phenomena.

Summary points

- HE is fraught with diverse, dynamic and competing pressures.
- Many of these challenges inter-connect in diverse and complex ways.
- Though not necessarily unique to HE, there is some room to argue that competing and contradictory understandings and priorities intensify some of the issues staff and students experience.

Recommended reading

Rudd, T. and O'Brien, S. (2019) The system crisis 2020: The end of neoliberal higher education in the UK? *Journal for Critical Education Policy Studies*, 17(3), pp. 24–49.

References

Metcalfe, W. (2020) University of Sunderland closes history, politics and language departments. Available at: https://www.chroniclelive.co.uk/news/university-sunderland-closes-history-department-17616249   (accessed 23 January 2020).

O'Toole, F. (2020) Coronavirus has made all familiar things strange. *The Irish Times*, 21 March. Available at: https://www.irishtimes.com/opinion/fintan-o-toole-coronavirus-has-made-all-familiar-things-strange-1.4205129?mode=sample&auth-failed=1&pw-origin=https%3A%2F%2Fwww.irishtimes.com%2Fopinion%2Ffinta n-o-toole-coronavirus-has-made-all-familiar-things-strange-1.4205129 (accessed 2 April 2020).

Woodhouse, K. (2015) Health care and higher education. *Inside Higher Ed*. Available at: https://www.insidehighered.com/news/2015/07/20/health-care-and-higher-education-face-similar-challenges-and-transformations (accessed 4 February 2020).

Index

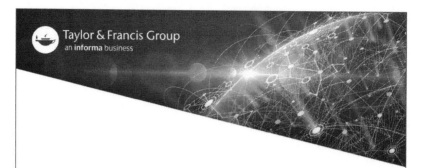

Printed in Great Britain
by Amazon

60815473R00104